"All this time sustainability has been seen by the business c[...] toward future generations – as more of an obligation. This [...] shift in the conventional thinking by showing how sustainability principles can be written into your core business strategies for increased profitability through achieivng a competitive edge, and thus drive progress on the SDGs."

Dr. Thusitha Tennakoon, Consortium of Consultants for Sustainable Development (CCSD; Colombo, Sri Lanka), Lead Consultant

"Bridges and Eubank's book is a new and ultra-accessible exploration of the rapidly evolving intersection of business and sustainability, with a focus on business cases, best practices and practical steps to make progress, and how the subject is shooting up in importance for companies and managers."

Dr. Florian Kohlbacher, Author of "International Marketing in the Network Economy", "Advertising in the Aging Society" and "The Silver Market Phenomenon"

"This book is a great resource and practical guide for senior managers that are responsible for business decisions around sustainability, including around the 'Power of Communication' discussed in Chapter 5 – sometimes, communication is the big differentiator, rather than actions or performance against benchmarks."

Mahadevan (Mack) Ramachandran, Futures Inc., Co-Founder

"Leading Sustainably is an in-depth look at a subject that ought to be paramount in every corporations' business plan. Bridges and Eubank share their extensive expertise on what sustainability in business means and its past and future, while laying out a clear, concise roadmap for corporations to follow."

Maho Uehara-Cavalier, The Humane League, Regional Manager Japan

"'Better Business Better World' published by Business & Sustainable Development Commission notes that the SDGs drive innovations and economic growth, achieving four aspects of economy, including sustainable agricultural production, sustainable cities, energy resources, and health and wellbeing. It is estimated that achieving those aspects will lead to saving cost and further creating USD$12 trillion market value for corporations, and hence are the key to achieving SDGs. Furthermore, a total of 380 million jobs will be created by 2030. The SDGs have a strong influence on economies, society, and environment worldwide in the future. Trista Bridges and Donald Eubank introduced the practical business models and procedures to advance the SDGs in this book, which is highly recommended to all."

Dr. P.C. Wang, Taiwan Institute for Sustainable Energy (TAISE) and Center for Corporate Sustainability (CCS), Deputy Secretary General; and Chung Yuan Christian University (Taiwan), Adjunct Assistant Professor

"Bridges and Eubank have created a useful primer on how business leaders' response to sustainability is evolving today—covering cutting-edge approaches, up-to-date case studies, and effective management practices. More importantly, the writing is fresh and accessible to corporate executives, investment managers, and researches, alike."

William J. Swinton, Temple University, Japan Campus, Director, International Business Studies

"A growing number of entrepreneurs today are building businesses with a social mission, guided by strong sustainability principles. Bridges and Eubank feature five such mission-driven companies and show how traditional businesses can also take meaningful steps to become more like them."

Robin Lewis and Mariko McTier, Social Innovation Japan, Co-founder and Directors

"Businesses must respond to climate change and societal changes. Aiming to address these challenges and improve society is the secret to business success. Reading this book will help you understand the important actions and steps to take."

Kenichi Ishida, Sekisui House, Managing Officer Chief Manager of Environment Improving Department

"'Leading Sustainably' is an engrossing read covering sustainability, why it matters, the role of private enterprise and how profit & purpose can be powerfully combined to develop new ways of doing business in the 21st century. The book is an excellent primer – and even more importantly, a guide – for business leaders who are struggling to grasp the significant complexity of this change but have been charged with re-orienting their businesses and organisations to respond to the new environment. Set against the backdrop of rising public angst around the issues of environmental degradation, climate change, inequality and widening gaps in society, 'Leading Sustainable' is a compelling call to action. The underlying theme – unsurprisingly – is that apathy, inaction and indifference are no longer an option. Not for individuals but even less so for organisations. Without changing and re-examining the underpinning of their business models, their processes and business practices, companies (both large & small) will see their markets shrinking, their customers moving on and their value being destroyed. For those who may find this all a bit overwhelming, Chapter V has ten clearly outlined steps aptly titled, 'Achieving Sustainability: How to get there'. The book is well laid out and sequenced with powerful stories of businesses that have re-aligned themselves to the changing world.

I particularly enjoyed the Vignettes – they are fresh & invigorating examples of amazing change in these uncertain times. Read them all – and the read the book in full. You will not regret it."

Shantanu Bhagwat, Sr Advisor, VC Funds & Impact Investments, Sr Advisor VC Funds, Department for International Trade (DIT), UK Government

"An informative guide for companies seeking to integrate the UN SDGs and sustainability into their business. The book provides valuable insights and practical steps for how to put sustainability at the core of your business."

Jin Montesano, LIXIL Group Corporation, Chief Public Affairs Officer and Chief People Officer

"'Leading Sustainably' provides an in-depth discussion of how to measure and manage impact. It showcases practical ways for businesses to manage their non-financial effects on people and planet, and their contributions towards the SDGs."

Karl Richter, EngagedX, Executive Director and Co-founder

"This book draws a complete scene of sustainability development for business. The authors give concrete steps, practical suggestions, and questions you may face during the process. It's a great reference for business to start sustainability planning, also a helpful checklist for businesses that have been on the road to sustainability."

Sharon Lin, Shin Kong Financial Holding (Taiwan), CSR Project Assistant Manager

Leading Sustainably

The business world is at an important crossroads. The age of the stakeholder is rapidly superseding that of the shareholder as climate change and political and societal shifts upend years of seeming prosperity. To move past this agitated age, business and society must learn to lead sustainably by putting purpose on equal footing with profit. The first step is understanding what's meant by sustainability and how it offers an opportunity for both business and society.

Inspired by the launch of the 2030 United Nations Sustainable Development Goals (SDGs), the book captures the ideas of more than 100 change makers from around the world about how business is putting sustainability at the core of strategy to survive, thrive, and realign its interests with society's. *Leading Sustainably* looks at how sustainability has evolved in a business context, offering powerful insights, key facts, and guidance on building sustainability capability within companies, measuring and managing impact, sustainable finance's transformation, and other topics critical to aligning businesses' central activities with sustainable principles.

The book introduces five vignettes profiling best-in-class companies that were sustainable from the start and international case studies on business sustainability efforts, spanning industries from hospitality to waste management, fashion, finance, and more. Finally, Bridges and Eubank provide frameworks and in-depth advice firms can leverage when accelerating their transition to more sustainable business models.

The book is a perfect guide for mid-level to senior managers seeking to understand this fast-changing business environment, how to factor sustainability into their decision-making, and why the SDGs changed everything.

Trista Bridges is a strategy and marketing expert with extensive experience across various geographies and sectors including consumer products, financial services, technology, and healthcare. As co-founder of Read the Air, she advises organizations on sustainability, providing them with the insights and solutions needed to transition to sustainable business models.

Donald Eubank is an experienced manager who's worked across the IT, finance, and media industries in Asia. As co-founder of Read the Air, he serves as a key advisor to businesses that are integrating sustainability into their core strategy, guiding their teams to lead sustainably and apply critical tools for managing impact.

Leading Sustainably

The Path to Sustainable Business and
How the SDGs Changed *Everything*

**Trista Bridges and
Donald Eubank**

LONDON AND NEW YORK

First published 2021
by Routledge
2 Park Square, Milton Park, Abingdon, Oxon OX14 4RN

and by Routledge
52 Vanderbilt Avenue, New York, NY 10017

Routledge is an imprint of the Taylor & Francis Group, an informa business

© 2021 Trista Bridges and Donald Eubank

British Library Cataloguing-in-Publication Data
A catalogue record for this book is available from the British Library

Library of Congress Cataloging-in-Publication Data
A catalog record has been requested for this book

ISBN: 978-0-367-42836-5 (hbk)
ISBN: 978-0-367-49524-4 (pbk)
ISBN: 978-0-367-85546-8 (ebk)

Typeset in Bembo
by Swales & Willis, Exeter, Devon, UK

Contents

*Mission-driven vignettes: throughout the book there are five vignettes profiling
best-in-class examples of "mission-driven" companies that have been sustainable
from the start.

Contributors

The following contributors helped to collect data, perform analyses, or assist with interviews:

Y. Vivian Huang: analysis of SDGs' interlinkages, analysis of recent trends and developments in the SDGs, Shin Yi interview, TBM Co., Ltd.-LIMEX interview, WBCSD Taiwan interview.

Hsiao-Hsuan Chu: approaches of sustainable market indices, ESG (environmental, social, and governance) market performance analysis.

Chung-Hao Chen: survey of the SDGs in annual reports, approaches of financial institutions, ESG market performance analysis, WBCSD Taiwan interview.

Solène Schuster: examination of sustainability policies in France and Europe, review of sustainability approaches in France and Europe.

Rehnuma Salsavil: survey of educational institutions' approach to sustainability.

Maria Qazi Azmi: examination of sustainability policies in markets in Asia, the US, and Europe.

We are grateful to them for their efforts and helpful contributions to this book.

Acronyms

BOMA 360	Building Owners and Managers Association International
BREEAM	Building Research Establishment Environmental Assessment Method
CDP	Carbon Disclosure Project (former name of CDP)
CPG	Consumer packaged goods
CSR	Corporate Social Responsibility
DJSI	Dow Jones Sustainability Index
ESG	Environmental, social, and governance
ETF	Exchange-traded fund
FFBB	Future-Fit Business Benchmark
FMCG	Fast-moving consumer goods
GHG	Greenhouse gas
GIIN	Global Impact Investing Network
GRESB	Global Real Estate Sustainability Benchmark
GRI	Global Reporting Initiative (Standards)
ICT	Information and communications technology
IM4E	Impact Management for Everyone
IMM	Impact measurement and management (GIIN); or impact multiple of money (Y Analytics)
IMP	Impact Management Project
ISO	International Organization for Standardization
KPI	Key performance indicators
LEED	Leadership in Energy and Environmental Design
MDG	Millennium Development Goals
OECD	Organisation for Economic Co-operation and Development
PRI	Principles for Responsible Investing
ROI	Return on investment
SASB	Sustainability Accounting Standards Board
SBT	Science-based targets
SDGs	Sustainable Development Goals
SRI	Socially responsible investing
TBL	Triple Bottom Line
TCFD	Task Force on Climate-related Financial Disclosures

UNCTAD	United Nations Conference on Trade and Development
UNFCCC	United Nations Framework Convention on Climate Change
UNGC	United Nations Global Compact
UNSIF	United Nations Development Programme SDG Impact Finance
VC	Venture capital
WBCSD	World Business Council for Sustainable Development

Foreword

Years ago, when I was a graduate student focusing my research on the intersection of business and sustainability, one of my colleagues attempted to give me sage advice. "Sustainability is a fad," she warned. "You would be better off focusing on dot coms." That was 1999.

Now, to be fair, information and communication technologies have impacted and disrupted the business world in ways few could have imagined. But so has sustainability. And, regrettably, the science around the impacts that social and environmental issues are having on all aspects of our lives today—not at some distant point in the future—has become an inescapable reality that only threatens to build exponentially over time.

Even a decade ago, too often one had to defensively justify why social and environmental issues had any relevance to managerial decision making. Social and environmental issues were the domain of philanthropy and government policy. Times have changed. Today, the question "What is the private sector's unique role in achieving sustainable development?" is more relevant and complicated than it has ever been.

As we accumulate more knowledge about how companies impact and are impacted by grand challenges like climate change, poverty, and ecosystem degradation, the domain of business and sustainability becomes more fragmented, complex, and specialized. It also becomes more salient to all aspects of business operations, from sourcing to marketing, from operations to investment.

In line with this evolution, sustainability is no longer a niche interest for a passionate few or the responsibility of a small group of specialized employees on the margins of the company. CEOs, COOs, CFOs, CIOs, CMOs, senior management, and a growing share of labor are grappling with whether and how sustainability will be the foundation of their organization's ability to competitively create value through the products and services they sell, the employees they recruit and retain, and the customers that they attract; or whether sustainability will be the source of their organization's undoing through the disruption of their firm's value chain, the obsolescence of their company's products, services, and business model, and the erosion of the economic foundation on which their industry was built.

With *Leading Sustainably*, Trista Bridges and Donald Eubank provide an important review of where we have been, capture the complexity of the field as it stands today, and frame a path forward that leaders can use to manage the organizational and market factors which impact a company's ability to evolve and grow in a marketplace where attention to social and environmental issues has fast risen to the level of table stakes.

Implicit throughout the book is the message that business-as-usual is no longer an option. Not because companies "ought" to address sustainability concerns, but because research results and performance outcomes are quickly making clear what the investment community has come to realize in their own right in recent years—sustainability is where the growth lies; it is *where the money is.*

The world is being taken over by generations raised on the realities of income inequality, climate change, and potential mass extinction. Those same youth are better connected with one another around the globe than at any time in history, and they are growing louder in their calls for change, not wanting to inherit a world where change is too late.

They know business has a unique role to play in addressing our challenges, they want to see business assume that role and responsibility, and they are going to do their best to hold the sector accountable through what they purchase and where they work.

The United Nations Sustainable Development Goals (UN SDGs) have become a popular mechanism by which more people are understanding the systemic complexity of sustainability issues. Yet, despite the fact that more people are thinking about and engaging in the sustainability discussion in the business world, fewer people seem to have any sense of how we got to where we are today.

To that end, Trista and Donald provide a compelling review of how the SDGs are not merely a set of overlapping goals with a myriad of potentially confusing indicators. They frame the SDGs rather as a culmination of decades— if not more than a century—of effort to make capitalism a constructive engine of economic, environmental, and social well-being.

Building on that point of view, they recognize the strategic implications of sustainability for companies—that there is no one solution that can be applied to all firms.

The competitive challenge of business requires managers to understand not only the materiality of sustainability with regard to their companies, but also the additionality of what their companies can bring to the marketplace that is distinct, impactful, and ultimately valuable to consumers, stakeholders, and shareholders alike. This requires leaders to develop strategic vision, and find ways to marshal the skills and resources necessary for their companies to realize that vision through change and innovation.

Drawing on extensive research and interviews, the authors acknowledge that the successful examples we have indicate that neither top managers nor individual companies can do this alone. As outlined throughout this book, effective change requires commitment and collaboration within and across the organization through leadership and employee engagement. But it also requires commitment and collective action through partnerships with other firms, government, civil society, academia, and the multilateral community.

Trista and Donald's framework for achieving a more sustainable business model can guide the reader who wants to implement change within their organization. Their advice is clear: understand both those issues that matter to your firm, as well as those issues that can be impacted by your company; engage employees from top to bottom of the organization to ensure you have the right, motivated talent and team; commit to action and get wins on which you can build additional success; carefully prioritize how you build momentum within the firm; and create alignment so that sustainability is not some niche issue within the company but forms the basis on which your company competes successfully in the marketplace.

In short, they tell us, get started, learn, experiment, discover, try, fail, and try again until we get it right because we have nowhere to go but forward.

Dr. Mark Milstein
Director, Center for Sustainable Global Enterprise and
Clinical Professor of Management
Cornell University
Ithaca, NY
January 2020

Preface: *Pro bono humani generis*[1]

The business world is at a fundamental crossroads. The age of the stakeholder is rapidly superseding that of the shareholder. More than just a buzzword, the idea of the stakeholder recognizes that companies have always existed as an inseparable part of the communities and business networks in which they operate, however vast and physically distant.

Contrary to what the shareholder model often implied, good business decisions have never really been driven purely by profit motives. It is becoming increasingly obvious that what is good for society—and thus, by definition, for the environment—is good for business. This new embrace of responsibility does not preclude the design of efficient, lucrative business models. In fact, when done properly, precisely the opposite is true: Socially responsible and sustainable business decision-making opens up brand new, exciting, profitable—and, in all its meanings, sustainable—revenue streams.

Today's reckoning is not purely an altruistic choice made by businesses; new demands from various civil society organizations and the consensus-driven initiatives of the United Nations have been shepherding along the changes required to make business operations sustainable for years. With the United Nations' 17 Sustainable Development Goals (UN SDGs) and the implementation of the Paris Agreement, these constituencies have outlined new expectations for not only how governments function, but also how businesses must operate in a sustainable society.

The SDGs—more than 50 years in the making—provide a comprehensive framework for understanding all aspects of social, political, and business actions. They are powerful statements of human ambition for a fair, just, and sustainable society. Many in the business and investing world today are calling them "a gift", as the SDGs can provide a framework to quickly and effectively guide businesses' efforts to align their operations with the meaningful goals that society desires.

The successful businesses of tomorrow will be the ones that embrace this new framework today.

*****

Business evolves continuously. Since the first publicly traded joint-stock corporation was formed—generally agreed to be the Dutch East India

Company in 1602[2]—we have seen many changes. The Industrial Revolution led to modern assembly line production. The rise of service-economy businesses in the 1970s unleashed new forces in marketing, consumerization, and a focus on customer service. More recently we've seen digitalization transform almost every corner of industry.

While these evolutionary business bounds have generally correlated with progress in the social realm, businesses and society—including the environment—have experienced massive growing pains along the way. A variety of human-caused disasters have had real-world consequences for individuals, communities, and our ecosystems.

As far back as the 1890s, coal smoke and smog were recognized as a health problem. In the second half of the twentieth century, individual businesses were deemed personally responsible for a widespread series of environmental disasters and health scandals. Industrial accidents such as the release of the herbicide dioxin by a Monsanto plant in West Virginia in 1949[3] and then by a flavoring and scenting industry supplier outside Milan in 1976[4] were some of the first major publicly recognized disasters that were explicitly caused by individual businesses. Amoco and Exxon were responsible for major oil tanker spills, Amoco in the Cádiz spill of 1978 off the coast of France[5] and Exxon in the Valdez spill of 1989 in Alaska.[6] In the tragic 1984 Bhopal disaster in India, the accidental release of the toxic chemical methyl isocyanate at a Union Carbide plant killed thousands in the immediate aftermath and continued to cause negative effects, including further deaths, for tens of thousands later.[7]

Some hazards were more inherent to the products a company sold. A campaign of lawsuits against big tobacco companies exposed the dangers of smoking cigarettes. Sugar was the next substance targeted, in a major wake-up call for food and beverage companies.

In the early days of industrialization, apparel companies and other businesses were powerfully reprimanded for unacceptable treatment of employees, leading to labor laws and union organizations designed to protect workers. But in the 1990s, consumers learned that rather than being stamped out, the predatory practices had simply been shipped overseas to developing countries. Top brands such as Nike, Gap, and later Adidas, Uniqlo, and even Apple, had to respond to the discovery that their products were being produced in "sweatshops" with abusive conditions for their workers. Fair trade campaigns uncovered similar problems in agricultural production, from exploitive payment structures to problems as horrifying as human trafficking, slave labor, and forced child labor.

As recently as the start of this century, individual consumer product failures have caused havoc to businesses as well as society and the environment. In 2008, Nestlé's baby formula products in Hong Kong and China were discovered to contain melamine, a toxic compound that causes kidney failure.[8] High levels of lead were found in Maggi noodles that were made and sold in India in 2015.[9]

These are only a few of the known examples. Such human and environmental tragedies were the disastrous result of business actions. In many ways, including as public relations catastrophes, they exposed businesses to the kinds of massive existential risks that could be the death knell for a company. Their wake-up call is clear. *Businesses must find ways to do better in order to maintain the public's trust and be good citizens of the world if they want to remain viable.*

*****

The concept of "sustainability" as we think of it today has been developing over many years. It made its first meaningful appearance to the general public in the 1970s due to concerns about the state of the earth's environment. The UN embraced the concept and brought it into a series of conferences meant to improve living conditions worldwide, which were launched in 1972 with the UN Conference on the Human Environment.

Moving away from a "savior" aid model to an "enablement" model, members of the UN began to recognize that social development and environmental protection require balancing needs with available resources, and, increasingly, taking a circular view of how the two interact.

Confronting the health, social, and environmental risks of their businesses in the 1990s, entrepreneurs, executives, and investors recognized the need to find a new way to work, and *sustainability* entered their vocabulary. The newly founded World Business Council for Sustainable Development provided guidance to help them examine their social, environmental, and economic impacts when assessing their performance (the predecessor to today's environmental, social, and governance, or ESG) and find more effective, efficient, and profitable ways to operate in society. At this point, we begin to see the shift away from the shareholder-value-only model of Milton Friedman to the contemporary embrace of stakeholder engagement.

Taking a stakeholder view helps businesses navigate a more sophisticated market of enlightened consumers who have a newly heightened awareness of the impacts of their purchasing decisions and hold a more skeptical and savvy perspective on companies' actions. Since the 1990s, these consumers have not only been supported by smart purchasing guides such as Consumer Reports, but they are also informed and educated by passionate and media-friendly non-profit organizations (NPOs) that have taken it upon themselves to investigate business practices and report on bad behavior. Throw in the Internet's instantaneous view across the world, and you can no longer assume that any of your corporate actions are invisible to your customers.

*****

Just in the year that we have been writing this book, issues surrounding sustainability have moved even more dramatically to the front and center of consciousness around the world.

Last year, the UN Intergovernmental Panel on Climate Change concluded that we have just over a decade to prevent the worst outcomes caused by global warming and climate change. In response, around the globe, young people—your customers—have been regularly marching in the streets by the millions—literally—demanding that their elders pay attention, recognize the problem, and take action to mitigate the anticipated damage that is becoming increasingly evident.

And the COVID-19 outbreak has shown with absolute clarity the terrifying reality of what a shared, global crisis looks like, both as a health disaster but also as a penetrating view into what happens when social responsibilities are not correctly valued and addressed. The coronavirus may have halted the economy, but the failure of businesses, just as much as governments, to properly manage their relationships with all of their stakeholders is what will slow it from recovering as quickly it needs to.

This book proposes important ways that corporations can lead in a very substantive way to reign in the causes of the climate crisis and realign themselves with their stakeholders. The actions corporations take in this regard will also substantially benefit their own businesses. The opposite is equally true: Those corporations that choose to ignore the changes happening rapidly around them are likely to find their businesses seriously diminished.

*****

Inevitably, then, companies today are asking themselves, "How can we best manage ourselves in such a rapidly changing, multi-stakeholder world?"

It's not easy to answer the question of how to make the transition to a truly sustainable business model. There are plenty of tools that use traditional shareholder measurements to understand a company's performance. Return on investment is fairly straightforward to calculate, and a great indicator for shareholders. Today though, when we talk about ESG and sustainable business models, there aren't yet sufficiently robust, mutually-agreed-upon frameworks for a multi-stakeholder world.

At its heart, this is a discussion about knowledge and capabilities. We believe that the first step in switching from a shareholder model to a sustainable stakeholder model requires businesses to increase their understanding of what exactly sustainability is—how it *has* evolved and how it *is* evolving, about what companies *are doing* and what they *can do* to make the shift to a more sustainable business model.

Today, the SDGs are perhaps the most powerful, thorough, and broadly accepted explanation of what it generally means to be sustainable. But their targets and indicators are directed primarily at governmental policy making. To become effective tools for business they must be translated into a business context. This is possible, and ambitious academic, policy, and business partnerships are creating comprehensive tools for management to apply SDG-aligned thinking to their own operations and strategy.

*****

Realistically, we don't think every business will see and embrace the value of a sustainable business model, let alone understand how to achieve one. Some—or, to start, many—may think of the idea as risky, and not grasp the potential upside. While we appreciate that, we also have seen—increasingly more commonly—that many businesses sincerely *want* to make the transition, or, if nothing else, simply feel pressured to do so. And we do believe that this latest evolution is not a fad. It has acquired a long history, has been tested and proven, and is unstoppable. It is now clear that being a sustainable business has become a basic requirement for operating in society today. If you can't put the minimum stakes on the table, you won't be in the game.

We have spoken with executives, operations managers, and sustainability officers in multinationals, small and medium-sized enterprises, and start-ups; with social impact, ESG, and SDG investors; with sustainability service providers, academics, and thought leaders; with policy makers, international organization professionals, and non-profit actors and many other thought leaders. We have seen and worked with many companies that want to improve on what they are already doing to become even more sustainable, yet they still haven't determined the best way to take their efforts to the next level.

Through our findings from these discussions we hope to provide more transparency on what is going on, and present our own views on how companies can rapidly transition toward more successful and sustainable business models. However, first and foremost, we hope this book will bring everyone together on the same page.

By the end of the book, you should have a thorough understanding of the five steps that we have discovered are commonly necessary to enable the transition to a sustainable business model. You should have a good grasp of the transformations going on in measurement, reporting and managing impacts, and related changes across finance and industry. We'll provide insights on the concrete steps that businesses can take to accelerate these transformations. And in our "Mission-driven" vignettes, you will learn about companies that were built-for-sustainability from the ground up.

We hope that these insights will inform your activities in your own business and improve your contributions to your teams' efforts.

Although current times can feel worryingly uncertain, we are heartened by the growing awareness around the world that it is time to change our consumption patterns and lifestyles. In our investigations, it was truly encouraging to learn what companies are working on today. We believe that business will be a pivotal actor in enabling this change—that business could be as many told us along the way, the most powerful engine driving change on this planet.

Still, shifting business in general toward sustainability is a monumental task. How to accelerate business on this path is the critical question.

In this book we aim to provide some answers to this burning question, and solutions for how to move your organization forward in the journey toward achieving a sustainable business model. And while it is important to remember that reimagining how business works is more of a journey than a race, we can't ignore the fact that rapid changes are happening at an *accelerated* pace these days. Significant environmental and societal shifts are underway in response to our monumental challenges.

In the following pages, we hope you enjoy exploring with us how businesses can keep and increasingly are keeping pace with these changes and succeeding in this journey.

In the spotlight: mission-driven companies

During our research, we spoke with a wide and diverse range of people working to move our society toward sustainability. From education to finance, NPOs to the corporate and start-up worlds, everyone we've spoken with have been catalysts in this transition.

There's one group of organizations in particular that are 100 percent "all in". Mission-driven businesses are laser-focused on bringing fully sustainable innovations and business models to sectors that have struggled profoundly to do so on their own. These companies' visions may seem idealistic, but all of the mission-driven organizations that we've interviewed are achieving remarkable societal—and in many cases, financial—impact.

In 1994, John Elkington coined the phrase "Triple Bottom Line" (TBL). He sought to encourage fundamental change of the economic system itself, with companies shifting toward a model that takes into account the full cost of business by balancing "people, profits, and planet".[10] While the process of business migrating toward a TBL model has been slow, recent research has shown that companies and brands with "purpose" are far outpacing both sector and economic growth in markets like the United Kingdom and United States.[11] The TBL revolution is here, with a generation of companies now held up as models to follow by even their non-mission-driven peers.

With many no more than 15 years old, these companies represent business's new generation and are pioneers for what business post-2030 could look like. Coming of age as the post-World War II market-driven economic model has come under immense strain, these companies believe that delivering a product that delights customers while also being sustainable is broadly achievable. But this isn't just a belief. It's a belief system that they've translated into viable and profitable companies with breakneck growth.

In a series of five vignettes titled "Mission-driven" appearing throughout this book, we will illustrate what makes these companies models for what we hope the future of business will be.

Prologue: Vision 2030—where could we be?

A note first: Let's imagine where we would be in the year 2030 if everything goes right. If the ideas presented in this book are implemented. That may be a big "if", but let's say that by harnessing the SDGs as guidelines and calls-to-action, and responding with purpose to the COVID-19 crisis of 2020, corporations have played a major role in:

- Lifting the majority of society out of poverty and its tragic outcomes
- Redirecting business to reduce harm in all spheres and contribute to the benefit of all stakeholders
- Uniting countries, international organizations, and the business world in partnerships that address climate change and the achievement of peace, justice, and strong institutions

Imagine that nations have fulfilled their Nationally Determined Commitments in the Paris Agreement, and then raised their ambitions in order to stop global warming at a rise of 1.5 degrees. Imagine that they then began to reverse the rise in the volume of the gases that they are releasing into the atmosphere, the gases that are changing the climate. Imagine that in response to COVID-19, they have accelerated their re-alignment with their stakeholders. Imagine that they have imbued their core relationships with a renewed sense of the value of their employees, contractors, suppliers, and customers, and the communities in which they operate.

But fair warning: Please don't think us naive. We are painfully aware that this is a major endeavor that the world is embarking upon, recognizing that it is necessary for self-preservation. There is some heavy lifting ahead. Achieving the lofty goals of the SDGs and the Paris Agreement will require a massive effort. Recovering from COVID-19 and reimaging the post-pandemic world will take dedication, discipline, and whole- and cross-industry efforts. Changing how business is done, corporation by corporation, small business by small business, will take serious work and commitment.

For the sake of argument, though, let's allow ourselves to imagine the results if we do. Imagine that in the year 2030, an executive sits back to review their company's yearly business planning and thinks of all the progress they've made in the past decade, the challenges, the advances, the positive outcomes, and the new landscape of the business world.

*****

What a great year 2030 it has been. We've experienced a wealth of lessons since the conclusion of our 2030 Agenda Business Plan; some hard, some revelatory. Many targets were hit along the way, putting us in a stronger position, and many were adjusted to reflect what we discovered as we advanced. In total, however, the exercise of imagining, 15 years ago when we first began to conceive of the plan, what it would mean for our company to exist today in the year 2030 has been an outstanding success. Anticipating the responses that we would have to make to a rapidly changing business, social, and, indeed, physical environment has positioned us to survive—business as usual as well as crisis—while our competitors have struggled to adapt, been pushed to the side by newcomers in the market, or had to close up shop completely.

This period has been a story of not only recognizing the risks, but also about finding new business opportunities as our company moved to a more sustainable business model. Some of the new business and service lines that we developed during the transition are now our market leaders, while some of our old mainstays are no longer any part of our product portfolio.

I remember the meetings back in 2017, 2018, and 2019, when many on our teams, and even those in management, were skeptical about the forecasting and "back-casting" that we used to create a strategy for survival in a future world. They questioned our numbers and assumptions, but the champions of the strategy carried the day by clearly defining scenarios that we were likely to encounter.

Our approach considered demographics, resource availability, social change, climate and health models, and technological developments. This started with the assumption, based on the best UN forecasts for the 2030 landscape, that the world's population would rise to 8.5 billion people and the middle class would continue to expand. (As progress was made on the UN SDGs, this population boom was certainly driven in part by the greater access to health care, lower birth rate and childhood mortality, and greater longevity that resulted from progress toward the goals.) We then predicted that these changing demographics would result, obviously, in an increase in demand across all product and services sectors to provide for the needs of the newly economically empowered. And, on the flip side, we recognized that we would be in a race to secure the natural resources required to meet sales demands.

These assumptions inevitably forced us to consider how the physical environment could provide for such an increasing appetite for basic consumer needs. We saw that our sources of supply for agricultural, material, mineral, and other natural resources were already strained, highly degraded, or based on out-of-date, environmentally detrimental practices. Adding another billion consumers that expected to enjoy the same high material standard of living as their predecessors—for as long or longer—was never going to be easy on the biosphere.

To compete in this new landscape of rapidly evolving supply (or lack of supply) and demand would require whole new ways of operating.

At the same time, we had to assess our operations in the context of the increasingly real impacts of the climate crisis, which were unavoidably apparent to those of us who were paying attention. You have to remember that at the time there were still people who denied this was even happening. Despite the first catastrophic series of "100-year hurricanes" happening on a *yearly* basis, and the alarming acceleration in the melting of the Arctic ice mass, the reality and potential impact of the climate crisis did not become commonly accepted until around 2019.

Naysayers were still trying to distract the public—some, perhaps, naively, but more often than not disingenuously for an ulterior agenda—by pointing to the startlingly cold temperatures of the Polar Vortex that pushed further south into the United States and the European Union as a contrary indicator. Soon, of course, it became obvious that these "vortexes" had been unleashed on those areas by the very melting at the pole.

In terms of public awareness, everything changed in 2019 with the first global climate protests, and the first major climate change lawsuit to reach trial in the United States. Led by student movements that were set in motion by the focused and angry message of Swedish high schooler Greta Thunberg, the student actions were supported by other new civil society movements such as Extinction Rebellion that reached out to professionals of all ages. These forces coalesced into the largest simultaneous protests ever held on a global scale.

Not only did people around the world who hadn't thought much about the climate suddenly find themselves forced to engage in meaningful discussions on the issues, but businesses also couldn't help but stand up and take notice.

Companies that were publicly blamed by the protesters viscerally felt the threat to their businesses and, whether they had already started to make efforts to become more "sustainable" or not, found themselves shamed into accelerating their actions for the sake of their own survival. Few industries were spared the protesters' ire, as we realized that every issue suddenly had an advocacy group or other civil society organization keeping track of what the key participants in any particular market might be responsible for.

Just as these movements were quietly building over the years, legal efforts to hold responsible the parties that caused the climate crisis, whether governments or business, were being explored by activists, indigenous groups, and young students. It started with cases that sought damages from oil companies, and which revealed that these businesses had had years of foreknowledge of climate problems and actively spread disinformation about their scope, or with litigation against national governments that sought to accelerate the passing of climate-related legislation. New tools that linked the effects of climate change to the causes—called "attribution science"—meant that it was harder for businesses to claim that they had no responsibility for rising seas on the coasts or even the desertification of farmland. Company board members realized that they had to protect themselves from legal liabilities that could be caused by their business choices, and the easiest way to do so was to chart new courses that avoided corporate activities that were vulnerable to lawsuits.

Comprehensive responses didn't materialize overnight, but the message was received, and subsequent Paris Agreement negotiations accelerated their conclusions. Activists of all stripes corralled uncooperative countries, industries, and companies and persuaded them to make real commitments to actions to halt and reverse the rising temperatures resulting from their worst policies or commercial activities.

In contrast to when our company started on its journey, middle school students studying geography today are no longer confused about the difference between the Arctic and Antarctic—it's obvious that the landmass in the south is still there, while the once frozen locale of the North Pole is a tragically diminished version of its former self. Not to be glib, but think if you will of the old Christmas elf Santa having to join the ranks of other climate migrants if the impact of businesses and nations on the environment is not further reduced. How would you explain that to a kid?

The outbreak of COVID-19, in some ways, eclipsed all this as a hard wake-up call. As the disease spread like a wildfire around the globe, it put a heightened spotlight beyond the "usual" environmental issues onto evolving social ones. As companies and investors had tried to transition to more equitable and sustainable business models, it had always been more difficult for them to get their heads around the *S* in the environmental, social, governance concept of "ESG"—especially given prevailing political trends in some countries to try and empower the most muscular and free-market versions of capitalism imaginable.

Suddenly, with the halting of the economy, it became glaringly obvious how vital a role business played in protecting its own employees, customers, and communities to make it through these difficult times together. This was seen most clearly in countries with fragile social safety nets, where, without the help of their companies, employees might literally not survive to come back to work without there being a business model in place that recognized, respected, and valued their essential role within the organization.

But even before that, for our own business, the melting polar caps had clearly shown that the world had already overrun the 1.5-degree rise in temperature that we set as the baseline scenario within which we would have to prepare to operate in our 2030 Agenda Business Plan. It is impossible to overstate how important this scenario was back then as a major point of reference for understanding what it would mean to operate as a viable organization in 2030 and beyond.

From a business perspective alone, rising seas and melting ice was problematic. But the impact that the climate crisis would have on all aspects of farming and transportation was an even greater concern for our business lines that depend on agricultural production. Evaluating 2-, 3-, and 4-degree scenarios in addition enabled us to envision what would be required to maintain production, especially by finding innovative substitutions and re-engineering manufacturing systems for reduced inputs in the cases where we didn't think that we could secure dependable resources and supply chains.

We also understood that environmental changes resulting from a 1.5 degree or more rise in temperature would have major impacts on humans as well. Climate migration and related public health disasters would become a great disrupting factor in the future of the organization, so we had to consider how we worked with the communities that were the source of our workforce. This meant that we not only relocated manufacturing sites based on forecasts about changing waterlines, but we also considered the effect this would have on resident communities and where they would be.

The 1.5-degree scenario also had a major impact on our production design. By 2019 it was clear to anyone paying attention that global warming was caused by the incredible amount of carbon dioxide that humans had released into the atmosphere in the roughly 200 hundred years of the industrial era. Scientists described the graph measuring the amount of carbon in the air over the past 600,000 years or so as a hockey stick—a long straight line on one end leading to a sudden upward spike in recent years. The earth had only once before experienced such disastrous conditions.

Approximately 252 million years ago, during the Great Permian Extinction, massive volcanos set fire to underground deposits of coal and oil, filling the skies with so much carbon that it killed off the majority of land and marine animals, plants and coral, and led to the greatest extinction ever of insects.

So if you want a worst-case scenario, we have an actual historical one in the story of the Permian, which is also known as the "Great Dying". We haven't reached that point yet in what has come to be known as the Anthropocene—the current geological age characterized by the dominant impact of human activities on the earth's ecology. All the way back in 2017 scientists had warned us that "biological annihilation via the ongoing sixth mass extinction" was already underway. They're still trying to determine today how much the efforts to reverse negative climate impacts and halt harmful business activities have been able to create the conditions necessary to help repair, at least in part, some of the damage done.

Sorry to get dramatic there, but it was becoming clear to us that as well as considering our own survival as a business, we had to take responsibility for our contribution to the increasing volume of carbon dioxide and other greenhouse gases (GHGs) in our atmosphere. As a result, we determined that for the 2030 Agenda Business Plan all products that we produced had to be carbon neutral in the manufacturing process; had to emit the minimum possible GHGs throughout their lifecycle, including end-of-life; and, where possible, actually capture carbon in their production or even operation, using it as a source material where possible.

Thinking this way was a revelation that allowed us to avoid a lot of the pain that other organizations suffered as countries ramped up their ambitions and regulations for meeting their commitments to the Paris Agreement.

The arrival of the SDGs was the second powerful motivator—and tool—that enabled us to avoid risks and find new business opportunities. Launched in 2015 with much fanfare, the UN framework's catchy collection of colorful icons and short aspirational goals—"End poverty," "End hunger," "Good health"—was quickly embraced by leading businesses as the best way to talk about their efforts to be sustainable. Following the inevitable backlash against the hype, and accusations of "rainbow washing" that were bandied about by skeptics, there was an inevitable acceptance and recognition that real work had to be done to make the SDGs meaningful for business. These efforts revealed the goals to be a substantive and proper guide to how to operate in a society that contained a wealth of ideas on how businesses could set and achieve ambitious targets, as well as the opportunities to be had through making it happen.

Industry associations, non-profit think tanks, and what came to be known as "sustainability service providers", deserve credit for leading the way in helping businesses discover, develop, and employ the business opportunities in the heart of the SDGs.

Our company started by mapping how our activities at the time contributed to the goals, and then selecting to focus on a couple of the SDGs that we thought were most relevant to our business. This became a key element of the 2030 Agenda Business Plan. Quickly it became apparent, though, that this was hardly a meaningful place to start. First off, in terms of mapping the SDGs, any company could make the same claims about how their business-as-usual activities made the same contributions. Secondly, the natural interconnectedness of the framework—via relations that had positive and negative impacts between goals—meant that it was impossible to focus on a couple of goals without considering them all. Besides, as an organization operating in the real world, touching communities both near and far—including our employees, customers, investors, and other diverse stakeholders—at the end of the day it was impossible to ignore any of the goals.

Ultimately, we had to embrace a position that took them all into consideration in our decision-making processes, and our plan quickly became stronger for it. The end-to-end perspective that this forced us to take taught us so much about our own organization that we were able to recognize problems way in advance of our competitors and to support the segments of the business that were driving the greatest growth. To do this, we had to look beyond the SDGs to a variety of reporting and management tools that were rapidly becoming the standards for business strategy and operations.

By 2018, it was taken for granted that you had to report on the minimum "first-generation" of sustainability indicators. These included pay equity, carbon dioxide and other GHG emissions, energy use, water use, waste generation, rate of employee turnover, and rate of employee injury. Investors had made sure of that with their new expectations of what represented a quality business.

From there, measurement and business model orientation became much more sophisticated with new international accounting standards for materiality from the Sustainability Accounting Standards Board (SASB), disclosure requirements from the Taskforce for Climate-related Financial Disclosures (TCFD) that revealed whether executives were considering a host of risks—physical risks from climate change, market and technological risks from economic systems in transition, as well as reputational, legal, and policy risks—and a selection of well-designed methodologies for measuring and managing the impact of your business activities such as the Future-Fit Business Benchmark and the Impact Management Project. Once we got the hang of these tools and started to benefit from their insights, we moved on to more philosophical visions of our business's place in society.

For the 2030 Agenda Business Plan, we decided to use the Planetary Boundaries concept proposed by the Stockholm Resilience Center (SRC) as the framework for developing specific assumptions for our access to natural resources and our own environmental impact. This helped us to move to a Circular Economy model that taught us to minimize both our inputs and our outputs in the production process, as well as in our overall operations as a business.

As we went along in the process of preparing for the future conditions that we had assumed in our forecast, we realized that fundamentally realigning our relationship with society was vital for our business to survive given the projections that we were making.

One way we reconsidered our relationship with society was by looking at where we stood in terms of the stock of renewable and non-renewable resources such as plants, animals, air, water, soils, and raw materials that we depended on, our "Natural Capital". Our new understanding of the company's reliance on the resources needed to achieve a flourishing and healthy society led us to certify the company as a B Corp, widely known today as an organization whose mission and operations meet the highest standards of performance against environmental, social, and financial measures.

To tell the truth, though, we struggled all the way through 2021 with executing the rollout of the 2030 Agenda Business Plan. First off, for a time we didn't even know if we'd survive as a business because of COVID-19. Luckily the work we had already done around sustainability prepared us better than some of our competitors, and we decided to double down on our sustainability efforts as we saw this as the only way to operate in the post-COVID-19 paradigm.

Yet it was still difficult to develop a commonly accepted idea across the organization of the value of the concepts that we were building. And understandably so—for years the majority of those entering companies were doing so with the straightforward understanding that business was there to create profit for shareholders; everyone else was along for the ride and, if they were hardworking or lucky, as big a bonus as they could get for themselves based on what they did to increase that profit.

This view was so deeply embedded in business that few people inside companies critically questioned how business was done, or imagined that it could be done differently without requiring onerous sacrifices on the part of individuals and organizations alike.

I'm proud that in the early days we took this as a rallying cry for setting out to prove that assumption wrong. While we encountered pushback on our changes in the 2030 Agenda Business Plan, we found that a robust internal communication program, built around business cases and the long-term value of transforming into a sustainable organization, was able to convince enough employees across the operation of the need to change. And, in the end, of course, most everyone was happier for the change.

We didn't get everyone to come along, unfortunately, and those who couldn't find a way to share our new vision, well, they "self-selected" and left of their own accord when they saw that the majority were committed to this new way of doing business. More encouragingly, in the process of disseminating our new ideas in the 2030 Agenda Business Plan, sustainability champions stepped up unbidden and asked to help drive the program. I think that the opportunity woke a part of them that was looking for something more meaningful and satisfying than the old paradigm.

This dynamic itself actually helped us in the short run, as we quickly found out that the new generation of employees entering into the workforce had been exposed to ideas around sustainability and even the SDGs from an early age. Their expectations of an employer were radically different than what we saw from the 1980s up through the first decade of the 21st century. By redirecting our strategy and operations, communicating the changes publicly, and realigning ourselves with societal values, we were able to attract the best and brightest talent. These people are now the managers that I depend on to develop and drive our business strategy.

You could say that the transformation in the thinking of our workforce and the new tools and methods we were applying led to a revolution in business planning and setting strategy. It used to be that, in both our yearly reviews and at the identification of new projects, "Sustainability" was a checkbox at the end of the process, the last thing we asked ourselves about before we pulled the trigger. Looking back, it's incredible to think that you might ask at the end of the process, "OK, so we're ready to go—is it sustainable?" Would anyone go back through six, nine, however many months of planning to the drawing board and say, "Well, I guess we'll just start over again?"

With the new tools and frameworks, we now had ways to assess choices and make decisions at the outset based on the sustainability of options. As we started to adopt these methods, we opened up our thinking via those really top-level concepts like the Circular Economy, the Planetary Boundaries, and the Natural Capital model, and were then able to drill far down into our value chain in all directions to avoid problems before we created them. Because of the huge productivity gains they were delivering, questions around sustainability became the first thing that we considered in new ventures, and they helped us to avoid innumerable risks that we had begun to identify and uncover new opportunities that we might not have otherwise recognized.

It was an exciting time to be learning about new concepts, to rethink the ways that we had been trained to do business, and discover better ways of operating. Achieving first wins by applying them in sustainability initiatives made our teams feel even better about the work we did together as an organization. While it did take a lot of education internally to help our people across the organization understand the purpose and value of doing this, the effort paid off and you could feel the whole company shift, almost as a whole. And people liked it.

From 2020, we started to fully incorporate sustainability metrics beyond those first-generation indicators—the pay equity, waste generation, rate of employee injury metrics that I mentioned before—into our business planning activities. At first these were clearly singled out as "sustainability issues" in the items lists, then they became a standalone section. Today they are so broadly incorporated within our business planning requirements and activities that they have in a sense actually disappeared.

Recently, in fact, I can't help but notice that we don't talk about sustainability as much as we used to. I think it's become so ingrained in the way that we do business that "being sustainable" is synonymous with "being a business".

As concepts around sustainability have become integral parts of functional roles such as accounting, operations, supply chain management (naturally), marketing, HR, and even sales, the idea of standalone sustainability "officers" has become redundant. We take it for granted that these concepts underpin our fundamental existence as a company—when we say "business", we mean *what we do and how we operate in society as a sustainable organization*. Put simply, we do business for good, but we can just say today that we do business.

Compared to 15 years ago, back when the 2030 Agenda Business Plan was launched in 2015, we are in a far better place. The company is healthier and better positioned to survive for another 15, 30, 50 years; we are more certain of our positive contributions to society; and our organization has a renewed vigor and a more secure "social license to operate", as they say. There is less uncertainty in our business planning activities, and it's become easier to make business decisions because we can base them on material issues on which we have a deep and sophisticated understanding and line of sight.

Making the change wasn't always easy, but I can say today that, for our business, for my career, for my own sense of satisfaction, and for my knowledge that we are serving society in a meaningful way, it was the right path to take. I look forward to continuing this journey in 2031 and beyond.

Notes

1 "For the good of all humanity".
2 Stringham, Edward Peter (2015). *Private Governance: Creating Order in Economic and Social Life*. Oxford University Press, p. 39.
3 Rushe, Dominic (2012, February 24). Monsanto close to "Agent Orange" settlement with US victims. *The Guardian*. Retrieved from www.theguardian.com/world/2012/feb/24/monsanto-agent-orange-settlement-west-virginia.
4 Davis, Melton S. (1976, October 10). Under the poison cloud. *New York Times*. Retrieved from www.nytimes.com/1976/10/10/archives/under-the-poison-cloud-the-toxin-that-escaped-from-an-italian.html.
5 Walters, Joanna (2014, March 24). Timeline: most notorious marine oil spills in history. *The Telegraph*. Retrieved from www.telegraph.co.uk/news/earth/environment/10717493/Timeline-most-notorious-marine-oil-spills-in-history.html.
6 Taylor, Alan (2014, March 14). The Exxon Valdez oil spill: 25 years ago today. *The Atlantic*. Retrieved from www.usatoday.com/story/news/nation/2014/03/21/exxon-valdez-25th-anniversary/6707983/.
7 Taylor, Alan (2014, December 2). Bhopal: The world's worst industrial disaster, 30 years later. *The Atlantic*. Retrieved from www.theatlantic.com/photo/2014/12/bhopal-the-worlds-worst-industrial-disaster-30-years-later/100864/.
8 Wiggins, Jenny (2008, December 3). Nestlé defends melamine record. *Financial Times*. Retrieved from www.ft.com/content/599aa718-c16f-11dd-831e-000077b07658.
9 Ferreira-Marques, Clara, and Kalra, Aditya (2015, June 5). Maggi withdraws all noodles in India after state bans and lead scare. Reuters. Retrieved from www.reuters.com/article/us-india-nestle-idUSKBN0OL03720150605.
10 Elkington, John (2018, June 25). 25 years ago I coined the phrase "triple bottom line". Here's why it's time to rethink it. *Harvard Business Review*. Retrieved from: https://hbr.org/2018/06/25-years-ago-i-coined-the-phrase-triple-bottom-line-heres-why-im-giving-up-on-it.
11 B Lab (2018, March 1). B Corp analysis reveals purpose-led businesses grow 28 times faster than national average. Sustainable Brands. Retrieved from https://sustainablebrands.com/read/business-case/b-corp-analysis-reveals-purpose-led-businesses-grow-28-times-faster-than-national-average.

1 How we got here

The story of sustainability and the SDGs

"A charter for the people and planet in the 21st century"

Let's step back from that ideal future we just outlined and start with an introduction to all the currents that led up to the Sustainable Development Goals—commonly known by the acronym "SDGs"—and the growing movement of companies applying them to their own business models.

To be honest, you don't have to read this chapter to understand what comes after in our surveys of where businesses are, how they are measuring and managing their progress, and what are the best corporate practices around the SDGs that we have discovered. You could skip it and still learn about what is most important to your career or your business in light of the launch of the SDGs.

But, if you want to know *why* the SDGs and sustainability in a corporate context are not just mere buzzwords or flashy trends, you will want to dive into this chapter at some point during your time with *Leading Sustainably*. Here we outline two things: why the SDGs represent the culmination of a transformation of how governments, international bodies, civil society, and for-profit businesses understand their responsibility to communities on the earth, and how businesses are embracing sustainability to improve their own operations and performance.

We'll try not to get too wonky, but you know how it is when wading into the weeds of international treaties and conferences, or of the origins of intergovernmental organizations and such. And if you do pass by the "How we got here" section for now, and then have nagging questions about what this is all about, please come back to hear the full story later.

What are the SDGs?

First off, here's a simple rundown of what the SDGs actually are—their structure, if you will: The Sustainable Development Goals are a "comprehensive, far-reaching and people-centered set of [17] universal and transformative Goals"[1] for society that were jointly developed and agreed upon by the representatives of all United Nations (UN) member countries in the 2015 declaration "Transforming our world: The 2030 Agenda for Sustainable Development".

The goals can be categorized as specifically addressing the earth's biosphere, society as a whole, or the economic sphere.

The SDGs are numbered and listed in order of their agreed-upon priority, i.e. the most pressing are ending poverty (1) and hunger (2), while peace, justice, and strong institutions (16) and partnerships for the goals (17) are important but come later (though they, of course, can help in the achievement of higher priority goals).

And the goals have a deadline, the year 2030, when the UN targets achieving each of them under the 2030 Agenda for Sustainable Development.

These goals were based on work done in a series of conferences that date back almost 50 years and were put into their final form in an inclusive UN consultation process that was held over five years. They were created by consensus and unanimously agreed upon by every UN member state.

Now it gets a little more complicated: Underneath the goals are 169 targets that elaborate on what they hope to achieve and 232 indicators that show how to measure progress. These targets and indicators are expressed at a country level, with common, standardized metrics that can be applied across all nations. In this, they act as a guide for countries on what they should be working on to improve internally and where they can create relevant policies to make progress on the goals.

The UN states that the "SDGs and targets are integrated and indivisible, global in nature and universally applicable, taking into account different national realities, capacities and levels of development and respecting national policies and priorities".[2] While the organization strives to support implementation of the goals, how countries will formulate policies and actions to achieve the SDGs is left up to them to decide for themselves. Also, they are non-binding. Each country determines its own ambition, and proposed follow-ups and review processes are voluntary and country-led. Though there are no obligations or penalties, voluntary national reviews are scheduled to be held every summer at the UN's High-level Political Forum, the annual meeting in New York to assess progress on the UN's efforts, where countries can choose to report on their advancement on the goals.

Over the course of the countdown to 2030, the UN will assess overall progress of the agenda internally, and the structure of the goals can be updated and evolve as lessons are learned. Practically speaking then, the purpose and value of SDGs is in being a kind of framework that supports a common understanding of how countries are performing on managing the most serious human questions of our age.

Every year, progress on each goal is being independently tracked and reported on by a partnership between the German foundation Bertelsmann Stiftung and the UN's Secretariat of the Sustainable Development Solutions Network, headed by renowned economist Jeffrey Sachs. Bertelsmann presents the performance of each country ranked in comparison with each other, with an analysis of their individual progress on every goal within their own borders.

And to be honest, as of 2020, countries individually and as a whole have been failing to make the necessary progress on the targets of the SDGs to achieve the goals by 2030. This recognition, only five years into the effort, should goad countries into upping their ambition and reaching beyond their borders through financing, new technology applications, capacity-building, and better trade and policies. Which leads us to the seventeenth and final goal: global partnership.

The seventeenth goal is considered essential to success in that it should bring "together Governments, civil society, the private sector, the UN system and other actors … mobilizing all available resources".[3] These partnerships are necessary to share knowledge and assist in practical implementation efforts, and to share the cost for achieving the goals by 2030, which is estimated to be between $5 trillion and $7 trillion according to the UN Conference on Trade and Development (UNCTAD).[4]

Currently there is an investment gap in developing countries of about $2.5 trillion. While a large percentage of that gap can be made up from sources within those countries, the remainder will have to come from private investors or from Overseas Direct Aid, which at present annual levels is at a tenth of what is required. UNCTAD has proposed that the gap can be closed by the partnership between the home countries of private investors, state-owned firms, and sovereign wealth funds, and host countries, transnational corporations, and multilateral development banks.[5]

In our research for this book, we have discovered that investors of all stripes—social impact investors, insurance fund managers, infrastructure funds, and more—are having real conversations about the opportunities found in investing in the SDGs and are actively and ambitiously creating targeted funds to do so. How quickly they may fill the gap we cannot say yet, but they see doing so as not only helping themselves to avoid business risks caused by failures to achieve the goals, but also as a chance to develop new profitable business opportunities based on them.

We have seen that such managers of capital have the interest and will to invest, and that at the same there are projects that *want* to be in investors' pipelines, though it appears that there is some disconnect between the two sides that needs to be bridged. This is a matter of communication, expectations, and acceptance of risks, which will ultimately need to be explored, understood, and addressed to close that funding gap.

*****

While countries may be failing to move forward fast enough in their policies and actions, there are now businesses that, like such investors, are ahead in their efforts to align their strategies and operations with the opportunities and business cases for the SDGs. That is what this book is about, and we will show you how industry leaders, backed by enlightened capital, are making sustainability a priority and driving the implementation and success of the SDGs.

And to be honest, this is not necessarily a new trend—there has been an acceptance of sustainability as being a powerful tool for businesses to improve their operations dating back to at least the 1990s. It is just now, with the launch of the SDGs, that the importance and uses of sustainability thinking have become easier to recognize and discuss in the public sphere.

So, let's see how we got here.

The path to the Sustainable Development Goals

The rise of international consensus, environmental consciousness, social development, and business-for-good

The origins of the SDGs at the UN can be directly traced back to the UN Conference on the Human Environment held in Stockholm in 1972. While the conference was originally designed to focus on humans and the natural environment, the conversation among national delegations quickly delved into issues of human rights and the relationships between developing and developed nations. This tension between human concerns and environmental concerns has been at the core of all subsequent conversations on the subject of development, including the 2019 round of the UN's Paris Agreement negotiations held in Santiago, Chile.

At the conclusion of the 1972 Conference on the Human Environment, the convened parties produced a final document that outlined 26 principles and 109 recommendations for action specifically on environmental issues, and supported, as well, fair international and domestic policy developments. In its essence, this endeavor already encapsulated the main themes that would be woven together into today's vision for the SDGs: progress, inclusion, fairness, and prosperity in addressing environmental, social, economic, and developmental subjects.

The full back story of the SDGs, though, is one of multiple threads of twentieth-century social, economic, environmental, and business developments coming together at an international level to create powerful new ways of understanding and taking action in our world. A combination of philosophical and political ideals, market initiatives, environmental movements, new economic and social thinking, humanistic moral imperatives, and historical reassessments of empires and colonies fed into an evolution of the mission at the UN.

Broadly speaking, you could say this evolution represented a global movement at the UN away from international peacekeeping as a first priority, to a shared vision of *progress* for all—a recognition that peace is only possible when society is fair for everyone and communities manage their natural resources as stewards to prevent environmental degradation.

At the same time, the global consensus represented by the launch of the SDGs is intertwined with the evolution of corporate philosophy and practices, in particular with a specific understanding of the responsibilities of business that goes back to the mid-twentieth century. In reaction to rapid industrialization, businesses began to reestablish social and environmental principles in their internal operations that earlier were sometimes put aside as the mechanisms of capitalism accelerated throughout the century.

Starting from an idea in the mid-nineteenth century of the social responsibility of businesses—way before the concept of Corporate Social Responsibility (CSR) as we know it today—a public discussion arose during the expansion of the industrial revolution that included a focus on environmental and community issues. These ideas coalesced in the later 1990s into a well-defined set of criteria that companies needed to understand, report, and improve upon: their environmental, social, and governance, or ESG, positions.

From the decade in which ESG first appeared till now, the idea has transformed from being a generally-agreed-upon but loosely defined concept with which to identify businesses' obligations to society, to one that has a robust ecosystem of principles, frameworks, and standards bodies for understanding, measuring, reporting, and defining strategy around ESG issues and the broader—and highly relevant—practice of sustainability in a corporate context.

In order to understand the creation of the SDGs and their importance to businesses, our interest here then is in the origins of sustainability as it is practiced in a *business* environment, of international agreements, of the concepts of human rights and sustainable development, and of truly meaningful partnerships between the UN and the corporate world.

It is worth noting clearly from the start that the majority of the international efforts that produced the new global perspective we see today are based on *international consensus* rather than international governance. They were not attempts to create a "world government"; rather, they brought diverse nations of the world together in agreement on subjects that were of vital importance to all of them, and are typically formulated as principles to follow, not rules to govern. This stands true today with the SDGs.

This framework is thus consensus-driven and voluntary, not unilaterally mandated, and therein lies its power—the SDGs are essentially a codified admission that we are all in this together and we need a strategy for the planet. Businesses today are showing they understand this interdependency, and often can act more quickly to improve upon it than many other parties in the world.

"A world connecting"

Let's begin a quick swing through the history of international agreements by stopping briefly with German philosopher Immanuel Kant, who wrote the essay "Perpetual Peace" at the end of the eighteenth century.[6] "Perpetual

Peace" establishes a philosophical vision of an international union, the kind of vision that would underlie the founding of the UN. It's an admittedly hopeful proposal that includes the rejection of standing national armies and the transformation of every country into a republic. It's a realistic one, too, in that Kant proposes a federation of free states rather than an international government, acknowledging that countries fear, and would continue to fear, accepting the concept of an overriding "law of nations".[7]

It was also ahead of its time. Although we see the first international unions, both political and commercial, appear in the nineteenth century, these were mostly confined to Europe and North America, and they would take a while to gain momentum.

To start, the Congress of Vienna in 1814 was the first collective gathering of some 200 representatives of European states to jointly determine international treatises. Previously countries had hashed out such agreements one-on-one via delegations and official, hand-delivered letters. The congress was called to reconfigure Europe after the defeat of Napoleon, and is generally considered to be the origin of the modern political era in the West. Think of it as a first real-world step forward toward the idea of an international union.

The congress brought together Germany, Belgium, France, the Netherlands, and Switzerland to form the Central Commission for Navigation on the Rhine, which, according to Harvard professor and historian Akira Iriye, is believed to be the first modern intergovernmental agreement.[8]

Still, war continued to plague Europe, and in 1863 the International Committee for Relief to the Wounded was called to determine how to care for those injured in conflict and to protect the medics who assisted them. The conference resulted in 12 participating countries signing the Geneva Convention, the first international agreement on the standards of international law for humanitarian treatment in war. The standing committee for the effort, renamed the International Committee of the Red Cross in 1876, would itself become one of the first international non-governmental organizations, an original NGO.

The second half of the nineteenth century saw a rapid growth in such international NGO-type groups. "Although a small number—one survey mentions five—of such organizations may have existed prior to 1850," notes Iriye, "most studies agree that it was in the last decades of the century that many more (numbering about ten every year during the 1890s, for instance) were established."[9]

The earliest international intergovernmental efforts to cover business-like practices followed the Red Cross' founding, with the establishment of the International Telegraph Convention in 1865 and the Universal Postal Union in 1874. These agreements were designed to remove the need for individual treaties between countries by replacing them with international commercial standards. It's natural that communication activities would be the first to look across national borders, and in their creation both organizations helped accelerate the growth in international groups and agreements. (Both, too, have continued their work to this day.)

Building on the first Geneva Convention, the Hague Conference of 1899 was an initiative of Czar Nicholas II of Russia that was held to determine what was acceptable in the *conduct* of warfare. The first Hague Conference, and a second in 1907, are important because they were the earliest significant agreements to be ratified by a selection of "major powers" that represented every region of the world. At this point, we are looking beyond the West, with representatives from China, Japan, and modern-day Thailand in attendance in 1888, and countries from every continent except Africa signing on to the various conventions by 1907.

Parties from 26 countries attended the first conference, and 46 delegations joined the second, with nearly 50 nations signing on to some portion of the resulting agreements before the onset of World War II. The Hague treaties, and the preceding Geneva Convention, were the first successful global compacts on international law made to determine commonly accepted "political" behaviors across nations and regions.

By 1907, the creation of the Union of International Associations (originally the Central Office of International Associations) in Brussels was clear evidence that the number of NGO-like international organizations was now high enough to warrant yearly coverage of their activities. The association continues to report regularly today on NGO activities in its *Yearbook of International Organizations*.

Given the history of the last century, it's fairly obvious that this connecting of countries and like-minded people and enterprises across borders didn't result in an environment of greater understanding. Instead, outbreaks of international violence and domestic exploitation and inequalities created dangerous times in the first half of the twentieth century.

The League of Nations created in the aftermath of World War I was an attempt to build on ideas from the Hague and Geneva agreements to strengthen the possibility for peace. The league's focus was on preventing warfare in the first place through disarmament. It, too, famously failed in this effort, but did, in the process, give birth to the International Labor Organization (ILO).

Though originally conceived of before the war, the ILO was founded at the same time as the league in 1919 with a mission to improve laborers' living and working conditions. While the politically focused league was unable to create an effective structure to do what it set out to do, the ILO has had greater success by addressing conditions in the working world. It became part of the UN in 1946 and has lasted to this day.

Rather than pursuing political means to disarm nations in conflicts, as the League of Nations attempted, the ILO believed that the key to securing peace was by creating a fair playing field for citizens of all countries, and it strived to guide countries toward guaranteeing humane conditions for workers. The Preamble of the ILO Constitution explicitly addresses this mission, stating that "universal and lasting peace can be established only if it is based upon social justice".[10] This focus on social causes is a forerunner of the UN's twenty-first-century mission to enable sustainable development to create fairness across societies as one means of preventing conflict.

Around this time, the business world took a major step in uniting—and thus expanding—markets with the founding of the International Federation of the National Standardizing Associations in 1926. Renamed the International Organization for Standardization after a hiatus during World War II, ISO's aim is to set standards for products and processes in commercial markets.

This has supported the development of a harmonized market across national and regional boundaries by guaranteeing a common expectation of the quality and safety of diverse products from various sources of production. The growth and acceptance of the ISO set the stage for today's globalization, freeing markets from their local characteristics by establishing expected standards based on best business practices.

A turning point with basic rights for the "Developed" and the "Developing"

The historian Iriye marked World War II as an inflection point in the development of "transnational connections" in his book *Global Community: The Role of International Organizations in the Making of the Contemporary World*. At this historical stage, the world turns from connecting to becoming truly interdependent.

We might posit that this change starts in America with the idea of internationally promoting a certain standard for basic human rights. Near the beginning of America's involvement in World War II in 1941, Franklin D. Roosevelt, the 32nd president of the United States, gave a State of the Union speech that came to be known as "The Four Freedoms". Roosevelt included "Freedom from want" as the third Freedom on his list when describing those core values of American democracy that should be extended abroad and used to determine the country's political and military actions.

Freedom from want is presented in a description of "opportunities for adequate medical care", social equality and security, and equal opportunity and the protection of civil liberties.[11] Not only would the speech inspire the foundation of the UN, but First Lady Eleanor Roosevelt led a UN commission five years later that built upon these very ideas to propose the Universal Declaration of Human Rights in 1948, with 48 of 58 UN member states voting in favor of adoption (and the remainder abstaining).

Roosevelt's successor, Harry Truman, was the first to publicly put forward the idea that a vast segment of the world was "undeveloped", at his second inauguration in 1949. Truman outlined a division between developed countries that had acquired advanced industrial and scientific techniques, and those underdeveloped nations that were "living in conditions approaching misery". He said that "Their food is inadequate. They are victims of disease. Their economic life is primitive and stagnant. Their poverty is a handicap and a threat both to them and to more prosperous areas."[12]

The creation and structure of the SDGs is also fundamentally informed by the evolution of such thinking on the distinction between developed and developing countries.

With great ambition and a fair shake of idealism, Truman proposed during his inauguration that Americans:

> should make available to peace-loving peoples the benefits of our store of technical knowledge in order to help them realize their aspirations for a better life. And, in cooperation with other nations, we should foster capital investment in areas needing development.
>
> Our aim should be to help the free peoples of the world, through their own efforts, to produce more food, more clothing, more materials for housing, and more mechanical power to lighten their burdens. We invite other countries to pool their technological resources in this undertaking ... Such new economic developments must be devised and controlled to benefit the peoples of the areas in which they are established. *Guarantees to the investor must be balanced by guarantees in the interest of the people whose resources and whose labor go into these developments.*[13]

How this worked out in reality can be held up for debate. That is, whether it was an unfair categorization of half the world as being "not up to par", or a bold and generous effort toward achieving greater shared prosperity—or a series of painful lessons in good intentions and the onset of neocolonialism.

The reality was that the unraveling of colonial empires and the impact of World War II had left behind a legacy of countries that had their native social infrastructures destroyed, their natural resources often depleted or strained, and their home economies left dependent on external entities. Truman's response was to call for developed countries and companies to go out and to do good, while doing business.

In practice, what became "Development Theory" went through several stages before the current focus on sustainability, as it struggled to find a fair and effective way to achieve its grander stated goals. At first, developed states—whether or not they were following Truman's call to action or obeying their own internal dictates, swept up in the natural evolution of modern capitalism—promoted and enabled a sometimes haphazard rush to industrialize developing countries.

In the language of the Cold War years, these non-industrial developing nations were, at first, considered to be "Third World" countries, meaning they were outside of the sphere of both Western capitalism and Soviet Communism. In practice, large infrastructure projects planned in Third World countries built out the roads, plants, and transportation hubs that were thought to be necessary for a modern industry.

Without the appropriate institutions in countries to make such projects operational, or sometimes even access the necessary raw materials, these strategies were not always successful. A series of different theories were thus applied to seek the right model, including Structuralism, Dependency, Basic Needs, and Neoclassical theory. In the 1960s and 1970s, the focus turned from industrialization to the development of human capital and the delivery of economic and social aid. With Neoclassical theory in the 1980s, the direction of development settled on a more, you could say, controversial promotion of unlimited free trade.

With the current consensus behind the 2030 Agenda, all of this is being displaced by the SDGs' concept of sustainable development. And, while the concept of developed and developing nations, generally thought to be that between the "West" and the rest of the world, still exists, a new more sophisticated understanding has redefined the blocks of countries as the "Global North" and the "Global South". The Global South is generally made up of countries that experienced colonialism, calling out the debt owned by colonialist powers to their former territories.

This divide makes clear that countries are at different starting points, that they should be responsible for different amounts of impacts, and that some deserve an admission of the debts owed to them, if not, even, a full or partial repayment. Such thinking informs the language in many of the principles in declarations from the UN conferences that have built up to the SDGs, where it is recognized that different countries have different abilities and responsibilities to respond to any recommendations and calls for action.

This orientation therefore is in the background of conversations around international projects such as the Paris Agreement and the 2030 Agenda, which ask for no one to be left behind and everyone to be on board the efforts. The Rio Declaration on Environment and Development of 1992 thus formulated the idea that "The developed countries acknowledge the responsibility that they bear in the international pursuit of sustainable development in view of the pressures their societies place on the global environment and of the technologies and financial resources they command."[14]

*****

To step back for a minute then, looking at the evolution of thought on international development in the post-war years, the proper origin of the SDGs could be said to even predate the specific aims of the 1972 Stockholm Conference on the Human Environment. The 17 goals themselves are really the logical conclusion of the founding principles of the UN itself in 1945 by the 51 original members, nourished in the light of a growing public awareness of the downsides to the development of the modern industrial world. The basic vision of the SDGs is contained in Article 25 of the UN's Universal Declaration of Human Rights, that "Everyone has the right to a standard of living adequate for the health and well-being of himself and of his family, including food, clothing, housing and medical care and necessary social services."[15]

There's only one Spaceship Earth: the limits come in view

Let's pause our thoughts on the evolution of thinking at the UN and take a look now at the first appearance of widespread environmental consciousness in the public from back in the 1950s and 1960s, and the beginning of environmental movements.

Conservation movements began in the 1800s and continued to gain momentum through the mid-twentieth century. In Britain such movements started with protections for birds, and in the United States with an appreciation of the natural beauty of the country's "Wild West", leading to the passing of government acts to preserve flora and fauna and prevent pollution of air and water. Concern with the natural led as well as to the creation of non-governmental organizations that advocated for such policies, including the Royal Society for the Protection of Birds (1889) and the Sierra Club (1892).

By 1948, conservation groups had gone global with the founding of the International Union for Conservation of Nature, followed not long after by the World Wildlife Fund in 1961.

Problems with acid rain, smog, and polluted water systems had been identified as far back as the mid-1800s, but with the continuing, rapid industrialization of the United States after World War II, businesses increasingly found themselves in the crosshairs for being the cause of the deteriorating natural conditions for wild and human life alike.

American marine biologist and author Rachel Carson powerfully raised some of the first questions about the environmental cost of industrial practices in her 1962 book *Silent Spring*.[16] The result of deep research and peer review by scientific colleagues, *Silent Spring* revealed the environmental and public danger of the widespread use of the chemical DDT and other pesticides in the United States.

It's safe to say that Carson won no friends in the chemical industry, but she did create a new awareness in a public forum that led to rise of a host grassroots environmental movements. The inspiration for the founding of both the non-profit Environmental Defense Fund in 1967 and the US Environmental Protection Agency (EPA) in 1970 can be attributed to the impact of her work.

A series of environmental disasters in the United States, including the New York smog of 1966, 1969 Santa Barbara Oil Spill, and 1969 Cuyahoga River Fire, predated in the United Kingdom by the London smog of 1952, were another source of high-profile evidence of the dangers of unchecked business and civil practices. With the creation of the EPA and the European Economic Community's first Environmental Action Programme in 1973, government acts and regulations began to address not just environmental conservation and the use of pesticides, but other pressing problems of the time caused by human impact and industrialization.

Their purview included waste-water pollution; solid waste policies; vehicle emissions; smog and air quality; pollution caused by oil; acid rain; the destruction of the ozone layer; the control of chemicals and toxicants; and forest, sea, and fisheries management. This would lead to controls on industry that were formulated in the first environmental policies and regulations.

A recognition of the fragility of nature when faced with our rush to industrialize nations inspired the concept of "Spaceship Earth", mentioned in essays by twentieth-century educators and thinkers Kenneth Boulding and Buckminster Fuller.[17] The use of the framing "Spaceship Earth" by these two polymaths reflected a fundamental change in perspective from the one that was originally assumed in economics—that of the earth having an endless supply of natural resources available to a manageable population of humankind—to one where we had to live within the boundaries and limits of the planet. It was a shift in thinking from an open-systems view to a closed system, or, as native Hawaiians say, "The canoe is the island, the island is the canoe."

Boulding and Fuller understood that with an expanding population and an accelerated demand for resources of all kinds, it was necessary to be stewards of the planet who would maintain a natural balance with the environment so as not to exceed what was available for present and future generations alike.

In 1968, the Club of Rome started a methodical exploration of what it meant to be living on a planet with finite resources. The group was formed when academics and business people came together to understand the interrelation of modern social and environmental problems and how best to solve them. The Club of Rome members used computer simulations developed by Jay W. Forrester to explore environmental scenarios outlining the finite nature of natural resources and how this would impact human activity. They documented their findings in the groundbreaking book, *Limits to Growth*, in 1972.[18]

In *Limits to Growth*, the club stated that if society did not change its business-as-usual practices, in a hundred years the world would experience "overshoot and collapse".[19] The authors described "sustainability"—in one of its earliest appearances in this kind of context—in a discussion of ecological and economic stability as a "state of global equilibrium" that was the goal of a world model based on a "policy to control growth deliberately":

We are searching for a model output that represents a world system that is

1. sustainable without sudden and uncontrolled collapse; and
2. capable of satisfying the basic material requirements of all of its people. [20]

The dire warnings in *Limits to Growth* inevitably attracted critical responses about the authors' methodology and intentions, but the fundamental idea sparked a lively public debate about the cost and limits of progress. The book has sold tens of millions of copies, the Club of Rome is still spreading its message, and the acceptance of natural limits continues today in the concept of the Planetary Boundaries from the Stockholm Resilience Centre.

The same year, controversial population researcher and ecologist Garrett Hardin published an article in the journal *Science*, "The Tragedy of the Commons",[21] that brought attention to an old concept of the management of common lands. First documented by economist William Forster Lloyd in the United Kingdom, the idea of the commons is found in traditions and law in Europe in the 1500s, and may go back further as an archetypical management system of shared resources in locations around the world. In Bali, for example, the management of rivers and streams was once handled by a complex set of relationships and rules to make sure families received a fair portion for their farming and daily life.

Hardin's thesis in "The Tragedy of the Commons" (that common land management is bound to fail, hence the "tragedy" of the title) was ultimately rejected, but its correction put new energy into the conversation around environmentalism. The concept of the commons deals with the mechanics of how to live within a world of limited, and, most importantly, shared resources. Up to this day, much of the thinking that followed *Limits to Growth* has used the idea of the commons to try and find solutions that create a sustainable model for an expanding population and world economy.

While *Limits to Growth* and "The Tragedy of the Commons" were focused mostly on sustainability in the context of the environment, the book inspired a series of thinkers in other fields to explore the outlines of what a sustainable *society* would look like. This included modern religious thinkers, who put forward powerful moral arguments.

For God's sake, let's be sustainable (or, let's recognize business is the problem)

The World Council of Churches (WCC) opened a conversation at the start of the 1970s about the role of sustainability in society, in, of all places, Iron Curtain-era Eastern Germany. The WCC held a couple of conferences, first in Bucharest and later in Boston, that culminated in a 1979 report, *Political Economy, Ethics and Theology: Some Contemporary Challenges*, that outlined their understanding of the importance of sustainability. The report is a fascinating, clear-eyed, and insightful document in and of itself, and includes an early indictment of the negative role business can play in people's lives.

The report writers not only saw that companies were encouraging customers to become their worst selves in the market, they also determined that such businesses were embracing and promoting unsustainable practices and attitudes.

From their religious vantage point, which in truth mirrors much of the humanistic universal vision of the UN, the WCC identified an "enlarged frame of reference" that included three concepts—justice, participation, and sustainability—

that they believed were required to understand the future of society.[22] Looking just at their idea of "sustainability", the WCC laid out the negative impacts on society of unfettered a capitalism that was lacking in self-discipline:

> At first glance, unsustainability may seem to arise primarily from increasing consumerism and the rate of economic growth alone. But closer examination reveals as well the confluence of forces which drive the system toward an ever-increasing accumulation of capital in private and state hands without social control. Competitive industrialization, without societal goals defined by the community, leads to the increasing misuse of science and technology, a fostering of a constantly enlarging demand for consumer 'goods', supported by a never-ending stream of new products answering a mix of real and artificial needs. All this leads to a narrow kind of economism, with the result that people are tempted to limit their horizon to mere economic objectives, contributing, therefore, to an increasing alienation of people. When the competition accumulation and the quest for profit orient the administration of science and technology, the result is the exploitation of natural resources (the material environment) within the short-time horizon of return on capital, be it private or public, rather than within the long-time horizon appropriate to the interests of humanity and the whole of society.[23]

Among the solutions that the WCC suggested to increase world justice, participation, and sustainability was to assess "the consequences of further world economic growth ... on natural resources and on the physical and human environment". This was a moral call to action to take the analysis of the *Limits to Growth* seriously.

Robert Stivers, a professor of religion, worked in a similar vein as the WCC in "The Sustainable Society: Ethics and Economic Growth". The 1976 book set out a vision of "an economy sustainable indefinitely in terms of resources and population, a new political system, and a new ethic".[24] As an "eco-theologist", Stivers claimed no knowledge of the physical and demographic limits to material growth, and concerned himself instead with what a new ethic social would look like.

"Care allied with technology and growth can produce striking gains", he wrote in an essay on the sustainable society, finishing with a call for further research on science-based solutions and policy making that understood that "stewardship means limits, appropriate size, holism, justice, and diversity".[25]

Business and sustainability has an early moment

Who the first person was to ask "What it would mean to a business to exist in a sustainable society" is, for our purposes, the most interesting question.

In the 1970s in Woodlands, Texas, oil company owner and real estate developer George P. Mitchell launched a series of conferences that took the ideas of growth raised by the Club of Rome and expanded on them in the

United States. The first of three Woodlands Conferences started in 1975 with the theme "Limits of Growth", proceeding to "Alternatives to Growth" two years later and finally "The Management of Growth" in 1979.

Harlan Cleveland of the Aspen Institute, an early sponsor of the conferences, had

> observed that fifteen years ago it would have been unthinkable to have a conference on growth as large as the one at Woodlands, because growth was our secular religion. Growth has to be planned and practiced and pursued—not interrupted by protests and placards, nor slowed down by querulous queries such as 'Growth for what purpose?' or 'Growth for whom?'[26]

Coming from a business perspective, growth was desirable, so how could it be managed sustainably? Indeed, protestors who did show up for the conference were "pro-growth and wanted to know 'why are we trying to stop growth'", reports Jurgen Schmandt in his history *George P. Mitchell and the Idea of Sustainability*.[27] (Don't worry, for the purposes of this book, we're not going to wade into that debate.)

Political science professor James C. Coomer reported on the conclusion of the 1979 Woodlands Conference, in a publication he edited called *The Quest for a Sustainable Society*,[28] which detailed how to reimage society in a resource-constrained world. The book features the work of 13 experts on different aspects of the subject, and—most importantly for our investigation —contains a chapter titled "Business Organizations in the Sustainable Society" by Dillard B. Tinsley. This the first time that we find someone directly linking the practice of sustainability to a business context.

A professor emeritus of management and marketing at Stephen F. Austin University in Texas, Tinsley explored then the exact same territory and the same questions that businesses should be addressing at the start of their sustainability journeys in the very year that we are writing. He proposes in his first paragraph that:

> Successful transition to a sustainable society will require meaningful participation by all segments of society. If the varied talents and resources of the business community are to be effectively mobilized in this transition, business managers must be given a clear picture of how businesses will operate in a sustainable society. It is not enough to assert that the economy as a whole will be structured in a particular manner or that resources will be allocated according to certain priorities. Business managers desire to know how the values, goals and operations of their organizations will be affected. How will business interact with its customers? What will be the role of managers and other employees? What will be the criteria for judging employee performance?

Tell us about it. This is exactly what we are still grappling with today and what we explore in this book, based on conversations with the business managers who are paving the way.

Tinsley finishes his list by saying that "Business managers will very likely resist transition to a sustainable society, at least until such questions are answered."[29] In today's environment, though, business managers are not passively waiting for someone to answer the questions for them before they move forward. They are actively interrogating and defining the interactions, roles, and criteria in order to accelerate that transition to a sustainable society. Frankly, they see no other choice.

Coomer and Cleveland felt the same in 1979, when writing that, "The quest for the sustainable society is finding ways to make complex decisions that do not require government to handle all aspects of governance for a necessarily pluralistic society in an increasingly interdependent world."[30] It took a while, but forward-looking businesses are picking up the mantle of leadership today that the Woodlands Conferences called for all those years ago.

As for progress on sustainability and business in the 1980s, most of the energy from these conferences went into debating the nature of economic growth and, in the best cases, creating an intellectual framework to justify the need to become sustainable. Developing actual actions to preserve natural resources and create sustainable models would have to wait. A fourth Woodlands Conference was held in 1982 with the theme "The Future and the Private Sector", but in attempting to attract participants from the business rather than academic world, the event stalled and the impact that the organizers hoped to have on business was minimal. In the end, Tinsley's contribution on companies' role in sustainability was an outlier in the conversation, and the next meaningful public step forward for the meeting of sustainability with business would not come until the Rio Summit in 1992.

"Global interdependence"

Now let's go back for a minute, and examine the thread of the UN as it starts to embrace thinking about sustainability and how to define the concept.

The UN was founded to *pursue peace and progress*. This is in contrast to the preceding Hague Conference and Geneva Convention, which explicitly tried to *manage* the inevitable occurrence of warfare. The first two objectives under Article 1 of the UN's charter are "To maintain international peace and security" and "To develop friendly relations among nations." While the initial assumption was that the organization's mission would therefore be peacekeeping, the reality was that this was and is an incredibly complex and difficult thing to do in practice.

During the Cold War years, achieving a consensus on where the UN could be called in to act as an international policeman and how it could reduce the friction between countries with such different agendas as China, the Soviet Union, and the United States was a thankless endeavor. The lack of a standing army of its own, as well, hindered the UN's ability to deploy itself into conflicts. Which may be for the best, for that is a fraught area to consider as the organization itself has been open to accusations of a kind of neocolonialism in some efforts.

In the 1970s, the UN efforts in the practical pursuit of *progress* increased, embracing the more complex and nebulous objectives 3 and 4 of Article 1: "international co-operation in solving international problems of an economic, social, cultural, or humanitarian character" and "harmonizing the actions of nations in the attainment of these common ends".[31] UN summits around that time focused on identifying and discussing environmental and social issues, including planetary conditions, food supply, and discrimination against women.

The concept of "sustainable development" officially entered the conversation in the 1980s with the release of the World Conservation Strategy in 1980 from the International Union for the Conservation of Nature. The importance of sustainable development was cemented, though, with the publication in 1987 of the final report from the UN's World Commission on Environment and Development, *Our Common Future*.[32] This was the result of four years of research on the international spread of industrialization that had been driven by developed nations, and the impact of such industrialization on developing countries.

Better known in UN circles as the "Brundtland Report", the document looked at economic issues from the context of the environment as a two-way street, determining that problems in one area begat problems in the other, and vice versa. To do so, the writers drafted the definition of sustainable development that is commonly used up to today:

> Sustainable development is development that meets the needs of the present without compromising the ability of future generations to meet their own needs. It contains within it two key concepts:
>
> 1. the concept of "needs", in particular the essential needs of the world's poor, to which overriding priority should be given; and
> 2. the idea of limitations imposed by the state of technology and social organization on the environment's ability to meet present and future needs.[33]

From here out, discussions of the environment and social and economic development become more robust, constructing the firm foundation that leads to the SDGs and the Paris Agreement on global reductions of carbon emissions in the atmosphere. With the Brundtland Report's clearly articulated concept of sustainable development, and a new focus on economy tied to the environment, the UN Conference on Environment and Development (UNCED) in Rio in 1992 forcefully presented the next steps for the UN and the business world to take.

Three major developments that would have a significant impact on the business world came out of the conference, better known as the Earth Summit or the Rio Summit: The Rio Declaration on Environment and Development (and the accompanying Agenda 21), the UN Framework Convention on Climate Change (UNFCCC) and the Business Council for Sustainable Development.

The Rio Declaration proclaims 27 principles that outline how sustainable development should proceed in the world. Starting with the first principle that "Human beings are at the centre of concerns for sustainable development. They are entitled to a healthy and productive life in harmony with nature",[34] the declaration emphasizes the humanism that must underlie international development efforts. The document contains no specific goals, but it was accompanied by the release of Agenda 21, which proposed a number of voluntary actions to achieve progress along the outlined principles.

Recommended objectives and actions are broken out in sections titled Social and Economic Dimensions; Conservation and Management of Resources for Development; Strengthening the Role of Major Groups; and the actual Means of Implementation. Combined, these two documents act as a kind of first draft for the 17 SDGs, and saw success varying according to region. They could not, however, be said to have really ignited the popular imagination of what was possible, especially as Agenda 21 was a dense, technocratic text.

On the other hand, the adoption of the Framework Convention on Climate Change led quickly to the creation of the Kyoto Protocol in 1997 and ultimately the Paris Agreement in 2015. Both Kyoto and Paris outline actual ways of meeting the mutually-agreed-upon commitments of the UNFCCC treaty. Inevitably, with these agreements' policy recommendations and mechanisms for setting greenhouse gas emissions reduction targets, all businesses will ultimately feel the impact of these attempts to create a sustainable natural environment and, you could say, a sustainable business environment as pertains to energy usage in all forms.

The third major development, the founding of the Business Council for Sustainable Development, was the one most immediately connected to the corporate world. Swiss businessman Stephan Schmidheiny was asked by the then Secretary-General of the UNCED, Maurice Strong, to assemble a committee to bring in the voices of business into the conversation on sustainability and the environment.

Schmidheiny brought together 48 international CEOs for "confidential and pre-competitive" conversations on the subject, which resulted in the publication of *Changing Course* at the Rio Summit.[35] *Changing Course* covers a wide range of business subjects, from markets, trade, energy, financing, innovation, and technology to leadership and management of change, and presents case studies on best practices (much like this book in your hands now).

The book argued against the Club of Rome's assumption that the limits to growth were determined by resources, saying that instead the problem was that there was a "scarcity of 'sinks' ... that can safely absorb wastes".[36] To address this, businesses were working on ways to avoid waste and pollution by turning to greater energy efficiency and what we would call today Circular Economy concepts.

Changing Course describes such actions as "eco-efficiency", and even proposed the start of a "triple EEE" rating—environment, efficiency, and enterprise—that could be provided to investors and banks, much like what we are seeing today with ESG reporting, sustainability indexes, and other new frameworks and benchmarking efforts that we will discuss later.

Ben Woodhouse, then Director of Global Environmental Issues at Dow Chemical, believed even at that time that the "the degree to which a company is viewed as being a positive or negative participant in solving sustainability issues will determine, to a very great degree, their long-term business viability".[37] This is the foundation of what we still believe today—though it is not enough to be simply "viewed" as such—and we will outline in this book how the public and corporate spheres have evolved since the release of *Changing Courses* and the founding of what continues today, with upwards of 200 member companies, as the World Business Council for Sustainable Development (WBCSD).

*****

The thinking behind the WBCSD was reflected in another milestone for business and the environment in 1992: the launch of the first environmental management standard, BS 7750, by the BSI Group. Later adopted by ISO as the ISO 14000 family, these standards provide "practical tools for companies and organizations of all kinds looking to manage their environmental responsibilities".[38] They are a voluntary way for businesses to show their various stakeholders the seriousness of their commitments to the environment. Achieving ISO 14000 certification can help companies understand their own operations in a more powerful way than competitors who might not have such a certification, placing ISO 14000-certified businesses at an advantage. According to ISO, today there are more than 300,000 certifications to ISO 14001 across 171 countries.[39]

Bringing it all together and addressing the risks

No single person can claim to be the originator of the ESG concept, but 25 years ago serial entrepreneur John Elkington coined the term "Triple Bottom Line" (TBL) to put at the center of the conversation the idea that companies should examine their social, environmental, and economic impacts when assessing their performance.[40] Elkington popularized his concept, which he also presented as a focus on "People, Planet and Profit", in the 1997 book *Cannibals with Forks: The Triple Bottom Line of 21st Century Business.*[41]

TBL was key in changing the way we think about sustainability in two important ways. First, it introduced the idea that companies should focus on stakeholders rather than shareholders. In the modern business era, the objective of "maximizing shareholder value" had been considered, up until that point, the gold standard of best practices in business.

Elkington sought to shift the focus away from pure value maximization for shareholders to understanding how value is created for *all* of a company's stakeholders (which do include, of course, shareholders as well).

Second, TBL laid the foundation for new kinds of accounting, integrated reporting, materiality, impact measurement, impact investing, and the like.

The problem for companies that wanted to embrace TBL concepts was that while it is easy to measure financial inputs and outcomes, it is more difficult to quantify social and environmental aspects. The TBL approach thus required new frameworks and metrics in order to assess the value of environmental and social impacts.

Organizations and associations that support the evolution of sustainability as a discipline, such as the Sustainability Accounting Standards Board (SASB), Global Impact Investing Network (GIIN), Global Reporting Initiative (GRI) and Dow Jones Sustainability Index (DJSI), trace their origins back to Elkington's TBL-based ideas and work. Many of the concepts and entities that TBL spawned are now core to the work of sustainability. CSR officers around the world, and newly named sustainability officers, are increasingly being asked to participate in key business functions such as strategy, finance, and marketing.

A new mission for the UN

Starting in the late 1990s under then Secretary-General Kofi Annan, the UN increased efforts again on its mission of *progress*. Annan called on the UN to empower people around the world to make their own lives better. He believed that doing so could directly tackle the causes of war, those being, generally speaking, inequality, lack of resources, and an absence of agreed-upon law.

Part of Annan's strategy was to engage business and labor, as well as civil society groups, in a "global compact" to follow ethical practices and standards. Annan proposed an official network, to be called the Global Compact, to business leaders at the World Economic Forum's annual meeting in Davos in 1999, rekindling a relationship with business that had existed at the founding of the UN but disappeared during the Cold War years.

The Global Compact's mission is to mobilize businesses to follow the network's ten principles and advance the SDGs and other societal goals. The Global Compact was founded on nine principles for business to commit to, which cover human rights, labor, and the environment; later a tenth principle was added for corruption. These ten principles act as a kind of precursor to the SDGs for businesses, setting a baseline of how they should act as corporate citizens. More than 12,000 signatories today consult with the Global Compact on how to implement the SDGs.

The same year as the launch of the Global Compact, Annan added a new "freedom" to the UN's concept of human rights with the release of a policy report

Table 1.1 Millennium Development Goals

Millennium Development Goals, 2000–2015

Eradicate extreme poverty and hunger
Achieve universal primary education
Promote gender equality and empower women
Reduce child mortality
Improve maternal health
Combat HIV/AIDS, malaria, and other diseases
Ensure environmental sustainability
Develop a global partnership for development

Source: Image courtesy of Read the Air (www.readtheair.jp).

for the Millennium Summit in September of that year, the "freedom of future generations to sustain their lives on the planet". That report, *We the Peoples: The Role of the United Nations in the 21st Century*, was the culmination of UN conferences held throughout the 1990s on the organization's mission, challenges, and security activities. They led Annan to conclude, as regards the newly defined freedom, that "we are plundering our children's heritage to pay for our present unsustainable practices".[42]

The Organisation for Economic Co-operation and Development (OECD) had in the same time period formulated its own International Development Goals. It subsequently partnered with the UN to launch in 2000 the precursor to the SDGs, the Millennium Development Goals (MDGs). These were eight simply formulated goals, such as "Achieve universal primary education", and other reasonably manageable targets that were given a deadline for completion by 2015.[43]

At the conclusion of the MDG program in 2015, the UN's then Secretary-General Ban Ki-moon announced that "The MDGs helped to lift more than one billion people out of extreme poverty, to make inroads against hunger, to enable more girls to attend school than ever before and to protect our planet."[44] In addition to reducing extreme poverty, the UN reported that preventing deaths by malaria and increasing access to improved drinking water saw significant progress across the world, and primary education completion increased, though it fell short of becoming universal.

Judged on a country level, of course, the results varied on a majority of the eight goals, with some nations and regions outperforming others. A 2018 review of the MDGs' achievements by the US think tank Brookings Institute reported that "Low-income countries and sub-Saharan African countries registered positive acceleration on a majority of the indicators assessed and accounted for much of the world's post-2000 accelerations", while "middle-income countries typically registered larger cumulative gains than low-income countries but had less acceleration overall".[45] (Brookings goes on to estimate that "21 million lives were saved due to accelerated progress", but called into question some of the value of the MDGs in making it possible to meet targets that it thought would be achieved anyway.)

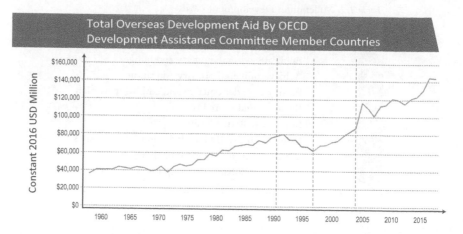

Chart 1.1 The launch of the Millenium Development Goals helped reverse the trend of fall-
ing Overseas Development Aid (ODA) collected from the OECD's Development
Assistance Committee countries. By 2015, ODA was reaching all-time highs of
more than $130 billion.

Source: © OECD / Image courtesy of Read the Air (www.readtheair.jp).

Beyond their own internal targets, the MDGs had two other important
successes. Overseas Development Aid (ODA) by members of the OECD's
Development Assistance Committee countries had been dropping in the
1990s, from a high of $80 billion in 1996 to a low for the decade in 1997 of
$62 billion. In the build up to the launch of the MDGs, total ODA increased
in support of achieving the goals, returning to $83 billion by 2003 and
reaching $121 billion by the end of the decade (see Chart 1.1). Upon the
completion of the MDGs in 2015, ODA was at $130 billion.

Tracking of progress on the MDGs also added a new mechanism to propel the
goals forward. Many people were doubtful at the time of the value of measuring
countries' performance, which meant that their relative progress could be
compared. There were questions whether it would be acceptable to the parties,
whether it would encourage or discourage them, and how effectively it could be
done.

In the end, though, the ability to compare countries' progress created
a positive feedback loop that goaded them on to higher levels of ambition. In
this sense the measurements, which were essentially a way to rank
performance, turned the project into a kind of competition where no one
wanted to appear to be not doing as well as other members of their cohort.

Now it is a competition

With the SDGs, the country ranking has now been formalized as a feature in
the tracking of national performance, as we mentioned earlier at the start of

this chapter, with Bertelsmann Stiftung and the Secretariat of the Sustainable Development Solutions Network partnering to release a free, yearly *SDG Index & Dashboards* global report.

The report grades each country individually on its performance on each of the 17 SDGs, creates a blended score on a scale of 1 to 100 (based on arithmetic and geometric means), and ranks all countries against each other in a master list. In 2017, Sweden, Finland, Denmark, and Norway took up the top four spots, achieving scores in the low to mid 80s, with the rest of the top ten rounded out by European countries and Japan. On the other end of the scale were the Democratic Republic of Congo, Niger, and Chad, with Liberia in last place with a score of only 42.8.

In total, the report functions as a way to see how the world is doing collectively in its ability to meet the 2030 deadline to achieve the goals. And right now, for the record, it doesn't look good if countries don't become more ambitious in their national efforts.

And this is where it becomes interesting. If you work for an organization that values the SDGs as a guide for how to conduct business (for whatever good reasons —let's not get into that now), you've set internal targets, and now you are making a business decision about where to locate a new facility or find a new supplier, do you choose the Czech Republic or Slovenia? Argentina or Chile?

A better ranking on the SDG Index becomes a competitive advantage for these countries. A Swedish attendee at the second annual World Circular Economy Forum in Yokohama laments that the event was co-hosted in Japan by Finland rather than his own country. And then a Sweden delegation appears in Taiwan to tout its abilities in helping countries achieve sustainable production. It's become a competitive market for countries to show off their sustainable brand, and that is transforming the programs of national trade initiatives.

The SDGs as a way forward for business

So let's come back to the world of business. While governments and international institutions were ramping up their ambition in addressing the world's most pressing problems, there was a parallel effort going on in the corporate world.

Since the formation of the WBCSD at Rio and the formulation of TBL by Elkington in the 1990s, business has been steadily coming around to the view that sustainability is critical to its own strategy and operations, not as an add-on but in a *core* function. This embrace of sustainability has started with Circular Economy concepts in factories and production lines, and appears in CSR efforts and market positioning based on a company's thought leadership in the field. And now it's starting to go deeper into business organizations.

In the past, the journey has often begun when an organization decides to become involved in philanthropic activities. This then is folding into CSR programs in order to bring them closer to the control of their business managers and budgeting concerns. Such a path leads to the realization that these new concepts that an organization is working with can also benefit its core business itself by opening up new opportunities and helping to avoid business risks.

Now the SDGs are rapidly becoming accepted as a beneficial framework for transitioning businesses toward sustainability. While they are not built for business, the SDGs are clear, comprehensive, and well supported, and have been universally promoted and standardized. In the next chapters, then, we will show why—and how—businesses and investors see the thinking that underpins the SDGs as the way forward in their journey to sustainability.

We must note, finally, that as this book is being finished in the midst of the COVID-19 crisis, there is a lot of uncertainty about how things will look over the next couple of years. Nonetheless, we are convinced that the learnings, concepts, and ideas that you will find here will give businesses the critical tools that they need to succeed in this new world.

Notes

1 United Nations (2015). *Transforming our World: The 2030 Agenda for Sustainable Development*, Article 2.
2 Ibid., Article 55.
3 Declaration for the 2030 Agenda for Sustainable Development.
4 UN Conference on Trade and Development (UNCTAD; 2014). *World Investment Report 2014*.
5 UNCTAD (2014). *World Investment Report 2014 Overview: Investing in the SDGs: An Action Plan.*
6 Kant, Immanuel (1795). Perpetual Peace: A Philosophical Sketch (Zum ewigen Frieden. Ein philosophischer Entwurf).
7 Ibid.
8 Iriye, Akira (2005). *Global Community: The Role of International Organizations in the Making of the Contemporary World*. University of California Press.
9 Ibid., page 11.
10 International Labour Organization (1919). Constitution, Preamble.
11 Roosevelt, Franklin D. (1941, January 6). Four Freedoms. Available at www.our documents.gov/doc.php?flash=true&doc=70&page=transcript.
12 Truman, Harry (1949, January 20). Inaugural Address. Available at https://avalon. law.yale.edu/20th_century/truman.asp.
13 Ibid. (emphasis added).
14 UN (1992, August 12). The Rio Declaration on Environment and Development of 1992.
15 UN (1948, December 10). Universal Declaration of Human Rights, Article 25.
16 Carson, Rachel (1962, September 27). *Silent Spring*. Houghton Mifflin.
17 Fuller, R. Buckminster (1969). *Operating Manual For Spaceship Earth*. Southern Illinois University Press; Boulding, Kenneth E. (1966). The Economics of the Coming Spaceship Earth, in H. Jarrett (ed.), *Environmental Quality in a Growing Economy*, pp. 3–14. Baltimore, MD: Resources for the Future/Johns Hopkins University Press.
18 Meadows, Donella H., Meadows, Dennis L., Randers, Jørgen, and Behrens, William W., III (1972). *The Limits to Growth: A Report for the Club of Rome's Project on the Predicament of Mankind*. Potomac Associates, page 158.
19 Ibid.
20 Ibid., page 158.
21 Hardin, Garrett (1968, December 13). The tragedy of the commons. *Science*, Vol. 162, Issue 3859, 1243–1248.
22 Commission on the Churches' Participation in Development and the Department on Church and Society of the World Council of Churches (1978). *Political*

Economy, Ethics and Theology: Some Contemporary Challenges. Pages 8. Retrieved from https://core.ac.uk/download/pdf/29409948.pdf.
23 Ibid., page 8.
24 Stivers, Robert L. (1976). *The Sustainable Society: Ethics and Economic Growth.* Westminster Press. Page 187.
25 Stivers, Robert (1979). The sustainable society: Religious and social implications. *Review of Religious Research*, 21(1), 71–86. doi:10.2307/3510157.
26 Coomer, J. (1980). Third Biennial Woodlands Conference on Growth Policies: The Management of Sustainable Growth, held at the Woodlands, Houston, Texas, during 28–31 October 1979. *Environmental Conservation*, 7(1), 79–80. doi:10.1017/S0376892900006858.
27 Schmandt, Jurgen (2010). *George P. Mitchell and the Idea of Sustainability.* Texas A&M University Press, page 51.
28 Woodlands Conference on Growth Policy & Coomer, James C. (1981). *Quest for a Sustainable Society.* Published in cooperation with the Woodlands Conference by Pergamon Press, page 164.
29 Ibid., page 164.
30 Ibid., Foreword, page xi.
31 UN (1945, June 26). UN Charter.
32 UN (1987). *Report of the World Commission on Environment and Development: Our Common Future.*
33 Ibid., page 41.
34 UN (1992, August 12). Rio Declaration on Environment and Development, page 1.
35 Schmidheiny, Stephan, Business Council for Sustainable Development, and Timberlake, Lloyd (1992). *Changing Course: A Global Business Perspective on Development and the Environment*, Volume 1. MIT Press.
36 Ibid., page 9.
37 Ibid., page 11.
38 ISO. ISO 14000 Family—Environmental Management. Retrieved from www.iso. org/iso-14001-environmental-management.html.
39 Ibid.
40 MindTools (n.d.). The Triple Bottom Line: Measuring your organization's wider impact. Retrieved from www.mindtools.com/pages/article/newSTR_79.htm.
41 Elkington, John (1997). *Cannibals with Forks: The Triple Bottom Line of 21st Century Business.* Capstone.
42 United Nations (2000). "We the Peoples: The Role Of The United Nations In The 21st Century" presented to General Assembly by Secretary-General. Retrieved from www.un.org/press/en/2000/20000403.ga9704.doc.html.
43 UN (2000, September). United Nations Millennium Declaration.
44 Jones, S. (2015, July 6). UN: 15-year push ends extreme poverty for a billion people. *The Guardian.* Retrieved from www.theguardian.com/global-development/2015/jul/06/united-nations-extreme-poverty-millennium-development-goals.
45 McArthur, John, and Rasmussen, Krista (2018, March 5). Taking stock (once more) of the Millennium Development Goal era. Brookings Institute. Retrieved from www.brookings.edu/blog/up-front/2018/03/05/taking-stock-once-more-of-the-millennium-development-goal-era/.

Our definition of sustainability

In a business context, *sustainability* is a continuous process in which an organization strives to reduce and ultimately eliminate its negative impacts on societal and environmental resources, and increase the benefits that it provides society in the course of its commercial activities, while maintaining or improving its profitability and market performance.

When integrated into business practices, sustainability can increase operational excellence and productivity, or be leveraged as a strategic differentiator to help companies carve out a unique, competitive position.

The Sustainable Development Goals (SDGs)[1] establish a framework for achieving this model of sustainable business.

Note

1 The SDGs are the heart of a global agenda, agreed upon by international social consensus, that establish the most pressing social and environmental issues of our age, set ambitious goals for alleviating them, and provide a high-level roadmap for making progress toward hitting those targets.

2 For profit, purpose, and survival

Why business is embracing
sustainability

A confluence of pressures are forcing businesses to embrace sustainability: new customer expectations, the threat of competition from mission-driven upstarts, investor expectations determining the cost of capital, the climate crisis and the need for resilience, competitive advantages and the potential for lower costs, a race for talent, a new focus on a proper relationship with the full range of stakeholders, and generally a growing understanding that you should be able to do well financially by doing good. That's a laundry list of things that would keep an executive up at night. Yet this collection of forces should not be considered to be an obstacle to companies going about their core missions—rather, there are real, positive business cases for why addressing them actually helps organizations to do so.

In recent years, business managers and executives have been wrestling with new volatility, uncertainty, complexity, and ambiguity in the marketplace, generally referred to by the acronym VUCA (volatility, uncertainty, complexity, and ambiguity). A large part of that heady mixture of confusing conditions is caused by the new market forces listed above that businesses are facing today. The good news is that responding to the sources of such pressures makes an organization much leaner and more responsive to new opportunities, as well as being better prepared to defend its market share and position against competitors.

Organizations that prioritize sustainability are achieving growth rates greater than that of peers in their sectors, while companies that have harnessed environmental, social, and governance (ESG) criteria to gain a better visibility within their operations are outperforming their competitors in the stock markets. And businesses that educate the public about the pressing issues facing their industries create a loyal customer base that they can depend on.

When meeting these challenges, businesses can achieve new profits, find a purpose that resonates with society, and prepare themselves to survive in the long run by becoming sustainable organizations.

Where to start? Address the "why"

While in theory the arguments are evident for an organization to embark on a transformational journey to adopt a built-for-sustainability—or even Sustainable Development Goals-based (SDG-based)—model, the reality is

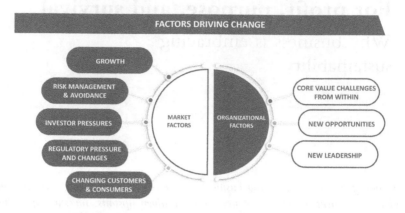

Figure 2.1 In our research, we found that there are eight factors that are forcing companies to change and adopt more sustainable business practices. Three are internal, organizational factors, and five are external, market-driven factors.

Source: Image courtesy of Read the Air (www.readtheair.jp).

that companies first need to make a clear business case for their key stakeholders.

Many companies will immediately try to quantify the financial impact (both cost and revenue) this fundamental shift will have on their business model. But there are other equally important factors that lay the foundation for the business case and ultimately address "why" an organization would make this shift.

These fall into two categories: organizational factors and market factors (see Figure 2.1).

Many of these factors will need to be present before most organizations decide to make this fundamental shift in their business model. Let's take a detailed look at how several of these factors are forcing companies to rethink their traditional "business as usual" models, starting with a look at how consumers have changed in recent years.

"So what have you done for me lately?"

In most of our lifetimes, businesses have not truly been thought of as forces of good. Though a company may have been providing low-cost nutrition to underfed populations or breakthrough medical cures to seemingly intractable medical problems, that didn't mean that its production methods or market practices matched its more positive impacts on society. As our short history of environmental disasters and health scandals in the preface shows, some of these companies were directly responsible for dramatic human disasters, often impacting the very customers that they were serving or the labor forces upon which they depended.

The blame for short-sighted business decisions, corner-cutting, and operational failures can be squarely placed on the shareholder view of the business world. Longer-term visions that actually preserved and grew capital sustainably were obscured by a perverted sense of shareholder value that championed investor returns measured by quarterly growth.

The new focus on the stakeholder, as opposed to the shareholder, is meant as a remedy to failing to balance profits with a company's social purpose, a failure whose cost is the survival of an organization itself.

But the dangers to a business today are not just about maintaining a clean record in serving its customers and avoiding damage to the environment. Companies large and small are in the spotlight more than at any point in history, and there are high expectations for how they act. As citizens have become more skeptical of governments, many take the view that companies are better actors for societal change.

The Trust Barometer from communications firm Edelman, which has tracked changes in people's trust of various institutions around the world for almost 20 years, noted in its most recent survey that among the general population, 52 percent trust business, nearly on par with the trust level of non-governmental organizations (NGOs) at 53 percent. Trust for government and the media, in contrast, stands at just 43 percent.[1]

As is often said, "With great trust comes great responsibility." Customers are also looking at companies more closely to see if their mission, activities, and products align with the customer's own. This desire to support "companies with purpose" is even stronger among Millennials, those born from roughly around 1981 to 1996, and Generation Z, born from generally 1997 to 2012.

A recent study by American Express found that 76 percent of Millennials said that businesses need to have a genuine purpose which resonates with people.[2] Yet, while trust is now higher for business than government, companies should be seriously concerned that Millennials' view of business is dimming, with only 47 percent agreeing in Deloitte's annual global Millennial Survey that "Business leaders are committed to helping improve society", a 15-point drop from the previous year.[3]

Generation Z's views on this topic are even more pronounced, with a recent survey from Cone Communications finding that 94 percent of that generation believe companies should address social and environmental issues, versus 86 percent of the general population.[4]

These new attitudes translate into purchasing decisions. There is still more work to be done around the trade-offs that consumers are willing to make between the cost and built-in sustainability of a product or service, but early indications show that younger generations are willing to put their money where their mouth is.

Hospitality giant Hilton commissioned an in-house survey to understand how Millennial and Generation Z customers viewed the question of paying more versus doing good, doubting at the start that there was much tolerance for higher-cost holidays. In contrast to such expectations, the results were startling, showing this consumer segment had strong preference for sustainable tourism operations despite higher price tags.

And it's not only younger generations; in some categories, the whole market is shifting. Research from New York University's Stern Center for Sustainable Business released in June 2019 by Professor Tensie Whelan and scholar Randi Kronthal-Sacco, "Actually, Consumers Do Buy Sustainable Products", showed that "50% of CPG (consumer packaged goods) growth from 2013 to 2018 came from sustainability-marketed products."[5] Whelan and Kronthal-Sacco report that "products marketed as sustainable grew 5.6 times faster than those that were not. In more than 90% of the CPG categories, sustainability-marketed products grew faster than their conventional counterparts."

The new Sustainable Share Index from the Stern Center reveals that sustainability-marketed products delivered nearly $114 billion in sales in 2018, a 29 percent increase over 2013 volume, and predicts that the segment will grow by 2023 to more than $140 billion. Whelan and Kronthal-Sacco discuss the winners and losers in this new environment, pointing out how Unilever and PepsiCo's visionary pivots to sustainable practices and products have been rewarded—despite shareholder skepticism—while companies such as Kraft Heinz that have not embraced product development in this space are suffering.[6]

Given these findings, mainstream investors should ultimately come around to the business point of view that such market-savvy corporate leadership has already recognized.

Companies that cater to these new preferences will win in the marketplace, but they need to take real, meaningful steps in their strategies and operations, as consumers will be watching them closely.

The competition is good from the get-go

One category of organization that need not worry about this much are newly arrived "mission-driven businesses" that are moving from being considered niche competitors to becoming mainstream threats.

Mission-driven businesses are laser-focused on bringing fully sustainable innovations and business models to sectors that have struggled profoundly to do so on their own. These are the companies that are accelerating the desire for sustainable products seen in the Stern Center research. Designed to treat all stakeholders fairly from the start, they are perfectly positioned to satisfy new consumer expectations—and it's their incumbent market rivals that need to be on their toes.

John Elkington's Triple Bottom Line (TBL) approach, whose origins we discussed in the previous chapter, spawned a host of companies built from the ground up around a more stakeholder-friendly framework. Not only have these businesses managed to successfully take an integrated approach to assessing their social and environmental impact, but they are also increasingly outpacing the average growth of their respective sectors.

Many mission-driven businesses are B Corporations (or B Corps), a certification that is provided by B Labs, a US-based non-profit to organizations whose mission and operations meet the highest standards of performance against environmental, social, and financial measures. In order for an organization to obtain the B Corp certification, it needs to achieve a passing Impact Score on the B Impact Assessment, which we will discuss at length in the following chapter. Generally speaking, the certification requires that these companies consider the impact of their decisions and actions on their workers, customers, suppliers, community, and the environment.

Recent analysis of B Corp-certified companies found that in the "fast-moving consumer goods" (FMCG) space such businesses grew at an average of 27 percent in 2017 versus a national average of 3 percent for typical FMCG outfits. Complementing the Stern Center findings, research from Nielsen in 2017 found that consumers are not only highly interested in these products, but a full 73 percent are willing to spend more for goods and services that have positive impact.[7]

These aren't all start-ups. Many of these businesses are well past that stage and have built large, multinational, durable companies. Corporations in various sectors are closely following these companies, and some have made moves over the years to acquire these new insurgent firms.

That mission-driven businesses are outpacing the growth of market incumbents shows the risk of a business being complacent in this new competitive environment. And even more so, it implies that there are real advantages to embracing sustainability and a solid business case for operating your organization based on a fundamentally stakeholder-friendly, sustainable stance. Suffice it to say, sustainability can determine an organization's ability to survive in a world where major changes are causing the great VUCA that businesses are experiencing in their markets.

New risk sensitivities drive investment decisions

From a more top-down perspective, changes in the world of investment have created major pressures on businesses to improve their impact on society.

When it comes to how investors are approaching target companies today, there are two big trends: First, mainstream managers of capital have become seriously concerned about climate and other material business risks to their investments; and second, a new class of investor is looking for returns that have as much to do with "social impact" as they do with financial returns— i.e. profit for a purpose.

The focus on the ESG perspective has been how both camps started to address concerns about their investments. The ESG moniker was first articulated in a report commissioned by then United Nations (UN) Secretary-General Kofi

Table 2.1 Mission-driven businesses across sectors, many inspired by John Elkington's Triple Bottom Line (TBL) approach, have been built from the ground up around a more stakeholder-friendly framework. Increasingly, many of these companies are outpacing the average growth of their respective sectors.

Company	Sector
Eileen Fisher	Apparel
Patagonia	Apparel
Kickstarter	Crowdfunding platform
Ben & Jerry's *acquired by Unilever*	Dairy
KEEN	Footwear and accessories
Method Home *acquired by SC Johnson*	Home care
Mrs. Meyers *acquired by SC Johnson*	Home care
Barilla	Packaged food
Danone North America	Packaged food (dairy, water)
Bolton Food	Packaged food (canned)
Aveda *acquired by Estée Lauder*	Personal care, cosmetics
Natura Cosméticos	Personal care, cosmetics
Etsy	Handmade and vintage ecommerce marketplace
Pukka Teas	Teas and supplements
Ragn-Sells	Waste management

Source: Courtesy of Read the Air (www.readtheair.jp).

Annan, "Who Cares Wins", in 2006. Two years before, Annan had invited 55 of the world's leading financial institutions to join an initiative "to develop guidelines and recommendations on how to better integrate environmental, social and corporate governance issues in asset management, securities brokerage services and associated research functions". The concept took off in the first decade of the twenty-first century with the appearance of the first modern investment funds that made their decisions based on a belief that awareness of ESG issues would lead to better financial performance.

Money managers came to see that an internal focus on ESG at a business could lead to a better view into a company's own operations, resulting in reduced costs, improved revenue, and recognition of new business opportunities; reduction of risk to the business from internal and external factors; and an improved public image among employees and customers.

They believed that applying an ESG filter would therefore lead to lower capital risk from their target investments and a chance to outperform the market or other competitors in the sector. This filtered down to companies as an expectation that they should report on their performance through an ESG filter and improve where they were showing signs of risk to their operations.

In the early days of ESG, institutional investors' emphasis tended to be on the "G" as they understood "governance" better than did the environmental and social aspects of the framework. Based on this familiarity, they saw governance as having the strongest direct link to performance. Companies embraced this as well, as it was about improving their view into their own operations, rather than changing their touchpoints to society and the environment.

As the impact of the climate crisis has become more evident, though, institutional investors' perspective has shifted, and the climate has been on their radar for several years as a key material risk to business. The science behind the Paris Climate Agreement made it patently clear that this is a pressing worldwide problem, posing a significant danger to society and the planet unless substantial steps to halt its progression are taken.

Investors have woken up in particular to the potentially calamitous impact of the climate crisis and resulting businesses risks in sectors such as agriculture, beverages and water, commercial fishing, and insurance.[8]

So now there's a heightened urgency among investors to understand companies' exposure to environmental risks and exposure to other materiality risks, such as food crises or social instability, and what their strategies are to avoid or mitigate them. In response, the "E" in "ESG" has been refocused in the past two decades from addressing pollution to being largely defined by the climate crisis.

Capital managers for whom exposure to climate risk is a criteria for placing funds can use ESG reporting to screen investments, and financial institutions have been developing ESG-related investment instruments in recent years to offer solutions to investors that help them reward companies that have greater resilience in the face of climate-related disasters.

On a smaller scale, the demographics of the investment world are changing, with more participation in the market from younger generations and an increase in the number of women working in the field. Much like in the consumer market, the generational shift presents a different set of concerns in making financial decisions. Many Millennial and Generation Z investors are making selections based as much on their values and hope for a better world as on their desire for a return on capital. Generation X leads them both in applying this investment philosophy.

With both institutional and retail investors alike increasing their holdings in ESG-related assets, there's strong evidence that the approach investors take to valuing enterprises is changing. Even institutional investors such as the world's largest pension fund, Japan's Government Pension Investment Fund (GPIF), with $1.1 trillion in assets, and others such as the Dutch National Civil Pension Fund, are increasing their ESG positions or specific ESG or climate-related goals.[9] In total, ESG investing today accounts for approximately $20 trillion in assets under management (AUM) around the world.[10]

On a regional note, while Asia has been thought to lag on climate and the environment, there are strong signs that players in the region will make significant strides, with several nations leading the charge on technologies that will power sustainable transportation infrastructure and renewable energy, and a growing middle class that is increasingly demanding about environmental issues.[11]

It is inevitable that these dynamics will positively influence Asia's investor class as well. Where previously companies could do the bare minimum to show they were taking some action on these risks, investors want to see concrete, and even ambitious, actions by companies demonstrating that they have robust plans in place to deal with various material risks.

With this increased investor interest and investment in organizations that are high-performing on ESG and now SDG criteria, both investors and companies are looking for better tools, methodologies, and frameworks for issues that are often hard to quantitatively assess, which we will discuss in the following chapter.

Impacts of a climate crisis on business

The international consensus that we must take action under the Paris Agreement to reduce greenhouse gas emissions and halt the rising trend in global temperatures is underpinned by a scientific consensus that outlines the dangers of *inaction*: rising oceans, shortages of fresh water and desertification of once fertile lands, the disruption of normal weather patterns and an increasing frequency of extreme weather events, and increasing instances of human climate migration.

The scientific mobilization to understand the current state of the environment and the potential impact of these changes is massive and unquestioned by a near-total majority of the scientific community. To ignore these forecasts is to accept an equally massive risk to the survival of your business.

Add to that the impacts of continuing globalization and population growth, and there is the real possibility that the business environment will experience significant disturbances in supply chains, resource availability and pricing, and access to critical materials—essentially the opposite case of the rosy picture we painted in the Prologue.

Don't cross the line

The Planetary Boundaries model from the Stockholm Resilience Center (SRC) shows the limits of how humans can impact the environment today without upsetting the ecological balance irreparably. In a corporate context, the Planetary Boundaries illustrate what an organization needs to keep in mind to be resilient.

SRC defines resilience as "the capacity of a system, be it an individual, a forest, a city or an economy, to deal with change and continue to develop". Drawing on its science-based approach, the framework then

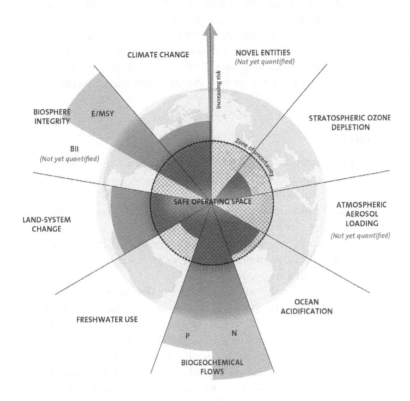

Figure 2.2 The Planetary Boundaries.
Source: J. Lokrantz / Azote, based on Steffen et al. 2015.

identifies nine planetary boundaries within which the planet is in a "safe space for human development".[12]

Recent studies have shown that due to human actions, four of the nine boundaries have already been crossed: climate change, loss of biosphere integrity, land-system change, and altered biogeochemical cycles (i.e. for phosphorus and nitrogen; see Figure 2.2). SRC advocates for the private sector, via development of new products and services and direct investment, to implement more ecologically sound practices to reverse these trends, for the sake of the whole of society and, subordinately, for its own survival.

For companies in the food, beverages, ingredients, and agricultural sectors, this conclusion easily resonates. The danger—to their fundamental business models—of crossing the Planetary Boundaries for genetic diversity, phosphorus, and nitrogen should be obvious, and should motivate them to take actions to prevent the worst-case scenarios, while seeking to find alternatives to their own practices that are currently causing the boundaries to be broken.

The interconnectedness of this framework also makes a strong case that organizations in other sectors as well should take an approach that helps them understand how their actions impact the environment and how they relate to SDGs beyond those that appear, at first glance, most directly relevant to their business.

It's only natural

Businesses in the apparel, food and beverage, forest products, finance and a host of other industries can see this with even clearer contours when they look beyond the more commonly recognized forms of capital—financial, human, manufactured, social, and intellectual—and take into consideration their absolute dependence on natural capital.

Natural capital refers to the stock of renewable and non-renewable resources, such as plants, animals, air, water, soils, and raw materials, that combine to bring benefits to people.

The Natural Capital Coalition, supported by the World Business Council for Sustainable Development (WBCSD) and many others, outlines how *all* businesses depend on natural capital to some extent and consequently experience risks or opportunities as a result of their own positive or negative impact on it (Figure 2.3). Thus, it is essential that businesses understand their impact and dependencies on natural capital and adjust defensively in order to continue to be viable operations as we face more complex environmental conditions for companies.

A final note on the climate crisis: Like ESG, companies will not only feel pressure from this factor within their internal operations; the first experience they will have with climate crisis issues will most likely come from outside as investors struggle to understand this risk. The latest development in this subject has been the creation of specialized reporting practices on exposure to climate risks by the Task Force on Climate-related Financial Disclosures (TCFD).

An initiative chaired by Michael Bloomberg and made up of major investment funds, international commercial banks, other asset managers, and multinational corporations, the TCFD has created a set of recommendations for how a company can measure and disclose the potential dangers to its business from climate risks.

Like ESG, by measuring these factors, the next logical step is to determine how to manage them. Companies need to seriously consider the impact of changes in the physical environment to their business, as well as the necessary adjustments that they will have to make due to the energy transition that is ongoing to address climate change. If they don't, investor expectations will ultimately push them to do so.

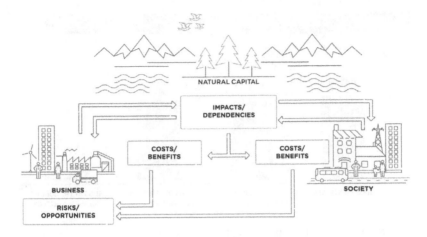

Figure 2.3 The Natural Capital Model.
Source: Natural Capital Coalition (CC BY-NC-ND 4.0).

> [The financial sector] see the necessity of a large-scale energy transfer, what we don't know is the extent to which this will happen as a transformation of existing companies or a gradual building down of existing companies and building up of new ones,

explained Martin Skancke, Chair of the Principles for Responsible Investment Board and member of the TCFD's Financial Stability Board, at the 2019 TCFD Summit in Tokyo. He added:

> It will probably be a mix of both, some businesses will be able to transform their business models and make money in a low-carbon economy, others will not. [...] The TCFD framework, really, to me, provides the information set that investors need to make that informed decision.

Read between the lines, and the message is clear: Investors want to know if you are paying attention, because they won't be betting on companies that aren't going to make it to the other side of the energy transition or through the climate crisis.

Far to go

So how are companies faring in understanding the business case and taking actions to start their sustainability journeys?

The organizations we spoke to largely said that their companies are broadly embracing the SDGs and, more generally, sustainability. Rather than reveal

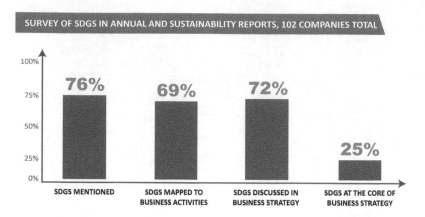

Figure 2.4 Sample of global companies' approach to the SDGs.
Source: Image courtesy of Read the Air (www.readtheair.jp).

great progress in achieving sustainable business models, though, we were under the impression from these discussions that work in these fields tends to happen at an earlier stage of an organization's journey.

We surveyed annual reports, which we saw as the most important document for communicating an organization's mission and strategy, of a range of businesses that were considered sustainability leaders. We found that the vast majority of companies we studied are now mentioning sustainability and the SDGs in their annual reports, have mapped the SDGs to their business activities, and are discussing these subjects in relation to their strategy (Figure 2.4).

However, very few businesses have put sustainability and the SDGs truly at the core of their business strategy. To assess this, we looked at what whether they are developing or were already offering products and services that are "sustainable"; if they're moving to operationalize sustainability in their strategy and operations via supply chain modifications, supplier validation, and other initiatives; or if they see sustainability as a driver of growth and cost efficiencies going forward. Only 25 percent of the companies surveyed showed indications that they were doing so.

Our conversations with companies supported these findings. While we spoke with many leaders in the field of sustainability and discussed their ambitious visions and plans, it was apparent that almost none of them could be considered to be operating as fully sustainable organizations. Thus, it was clear that sustainability is not yet fundamental to business models; this is a journey that companies are on and no one has mastered it yet. At best, the majority of companies are at the stage of priority- and vision-setting for sustainability strategies, and they are struggling to move to the next level.

Based on this and other observations, we determined nine key takeaways from our investigations, and one overall assessment of where we are today, which is that *we have far to go*.

The nine takeaways

We know that there *is* a step change going on in the business world when it comes to its stance on sustainability. Yet we also quickly discovered in our conversations that there are a host of issues that businesses are struggling with—in common—across industries. Some of these struggles illustrate concisely where progress in this transformation is today, others reveal the main motivators for pursuing sustainable business models, and, finally, some highlight the key areas on which companies should focus their efforts.

Our nine major takeaways, which we outlined in a paper for the Official Conference Proceedings of the Asian Conference on Sustainability, Energy & the Environment, are that:

1. Sustainability is not yet fundamental to business models—this is a journey companies are on and no one has mastered it
2. Companies are trying to move beyond having a "vision" for sustainability to fully *systemizing* their initiatives
3. Companies are struggling to measure and assess performance on sustainability and the SDGs—there are a lack of *widely-agreed-upon* frameworks and tools, which deters companies from fully moving their business toward sustainability
4. Investors are acting as enlightened managers of capital to light the way and drive adoption
5. Greenwashing is increasingly not possible—cheap talk that promotes a green image when you haven't changed core business practices that have a negative impact on the environment or society, is easy to uncover with new frameworks and benchmarking, while civil society and related organizations are paying rapt attention to what companies are saying and what they actually do
6. There is a race for talent, who are becoming pickier about a company's position on sustainability
7. Within organizations, employees desire to understand sustainability and how it will impact their work
8. The supply chain is a major focus of sustainability efforts; there is great room for progress here
9. Collaboration and partnership are essential to success; efforts required are too complicated to do alone[13]

You can glean from the first through third takeaways how well companies are doing in their efforts. There's a spectrum of progress, and organizations are at different points along the way in their journeys. Yet most companies still have a long way to go in incorporating sustainability in their business models.

As regards the SDGs, while there are many companies that have both determined which of the 17 goals are the most important to their business and formulated a vision of where they want to be on either a selection or on all of the 2030 goals, the next step of building a strategy around that vision and communicating it in a meaningful way throughout the organization is a stumbling block for all but the best-positioned of organizations. Knowledge is lacking, and creating messaging on sustainability that can be understood, embraced, and acted upon by their teams is a challenge for even the most advanced organizations. (Below we discuss knowledge transfer about sustainability within an organization, and in the next chapter we will explore at length the question of how to measure and assess performance on sustainability and the SDGs and which frameworks to consider.)

That said, motivators for businesses to push forward with sustainability initiatives are not lacking. Investor expectations, the risk of greenwashing, and a race for talent are all urgent issues that companies must address.

While we have touched upon investors and issues around greenwashing in earlier discussions in this chapter, the race for talent is worth dwelling on for a moment. Just as consumers are becoming pickier, so are employees. Newer generations of potential new hires are looking for businesses that share their more sophisticated values on environmental and societal impacts. We also quickly recognized in our research another major factor, one that is clearly related to our point above about a lack of knowledge in organizations—that there are far too few experts in the field of sustainability today to fulfill the demand for having such people fill functional roles in the company.

Companies need to understand that such knowledgeable talent, the very kind of people that are needed to advance companies, want to be in businesses that they themselves recognize to be leaders in sustainability, businesses that are sincere in addressing environmental and social issues. Sustainability practitioners that already have a grasp on the concepts around this subject are vital to your success in this endeavor. Companies that are underperforming in this field are at risk of being unable to attract them to join.

Businesses should focus on three principal takeaways when they move to overcome obstacles to their progress, the final three on the list. First, they should empower employees to make sustainability-driven decisions by spreading the requisite knowledge across their organizations. This requires educating their employees on sustainability concepts that are relevant to their organization. Doing so is not only an opportunity to advance the enterprise as a whole, it also ensures that you are able to hold onto the best talent.

Next, we found in our conversations that the supply chain presents great opportunities for sustainability wins. And working within your supply chain goes hand-in-hand with the final focal point for progress: partnerships. You can't expect to do this alone—partnerships are vital to success, whether they are with other sustainability-aligned businesses such as your suppliers and customers, NGOs and various civil society groups, local and national governments, or others. We'll cover the importance of partnerships more in our later chapters.

The way forward

So how can you move beyond the "Far to go" takeaways? Our point of view is that there are five steps that organizations proceed through as they look to transform to a sustainable business model (see Figure 2.5).

At each step in the Five Steps to a Sustainable Business Model, there are distinct milestones that we believe companies on this journey must achieve to proceed to the next (see the box "The Five Steps to a Sustainable Business Model").

The Five Steps to a Sustainable Business Model

1. **Base-level understanding**

   - Senior management awareness
   - Building of a sustainability team
   - High-level objective-setting

2. **C-level engagement and initial choices**

   - CEO support and buy-in for a business model shift
   - Aligning current activities to SDGs
   - Materiality analysis to inform sustainability priorities
   - Initial target-setting for priority areas
   - Reporting (e.g. Global Reporting Initiative, ESG)

3. **Actions and first wins**

   - Launch and roll-out of initiatives
   - Partnerships for action (i.e. civil society, international organizaions)
   - Active communications (internal and external)
   - Intra- and inter-industry engagement and recognition
   - Progress tracking along initial targets

4. **Cross-organization priority-setting and buy-in**

   - Clarity on current position and direction (i.e. versus best-in-class players, other competitors)
   - Understanding of impact on all SDGs (although priorities may be structured around a few)
   - Roll-out of clear key performance indicators (KPIs)
   - Sustainability integrated into product or services portfolio
   - Building cross-organization sustainability knowledge and capability, via leadership development and training

5. **Alignment and process integration**

   - Sustainability strategy = business strategy
   - Clear action plan—deliverables, timings, responsibilities—to support strategy

---

- A common platform
- Values and principles
- Integrated approach to business choices, planning, product development, and reporting
- Systems (technologies and processes) in place to enable regular tracking against new KPIs
- New KPIs embedded in employee review and incentive systems

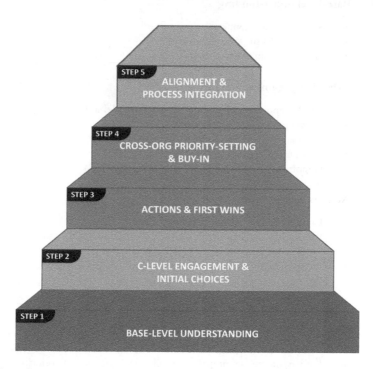

Figure 2.5 The Five Steps to a Sustainable Business Model represents the common organizational evolution of a company that sets off on its journey to integrate sustainability into its processes and align itself with the SDGs.
Source: Image courtesy of Read the Air (www.readtheair.jp).

Although some may be skeptical about the volume of chatter from businesses about the SDGs and sustainability, we believe that the enthusiasm is sincere. A growing number of businesses around the world have a true desire to arrive at

Stage 5 of the process we've laid out above. However, while there's many catalysts to change, as noted earlier in this chapter, there are a few important blockers, namely:

1. *Measurement:* How can we measure sustainability and progress against the SDGs from a business context? How do we understand companies' impact in a broader sense—for stakeholders and society?
2. *Finance:* How can companies transition to a sustainable business model within a financial system that emphasizes and rewards short-term results? Are the financial markets starting to embrace sustainability as a driver of value? How can we mainstream sustainable finance?
3. *Organizational capabilities and "getting there":* What capabilities does a sustainable business model require? What are the best-in-class examples and success stories from which we can draw inspiration? What are some practical tips companies can follow to accelerate their transition?

Over the next few chapters, we will explore these blockers in more detail. But before we get there, here's a final anecdotal note on making the business case to adopt a sustainable business model. The same example kept coming up in various conversations that we have had about whether businesses that are responding to the pressures we have listed above were actually outperforming their sector peers: If you had invested in European utilities in 2009, your investment today would be worth about $0.20 on the dollar (and this is true in general of the European power market).[14] These companies missed out on the prevailing "environmental trend" in the market—the disruptive impact of renewable energy on their power markets—and for this they lost in the long run. Companies and investors that make this mistake and ignore prevailing environmental and social trends in the corporate world are at risk of the same.

Whether or not, along whatever selected metric, we find a way to quantify the value of adopting a sustainable business model at this point, the bigger picture tells us that the winners of tomorrow are those that are paying attention to the current direction of business advances and taking action today.

The pressures are real, yet the solutions are available. In the next chapter we'll look at how to start measuring your company's social and environmental impacts so that you can figure out ways to manage them, enabling your business to get these new organizational and market forces under control.

Notes

1 Edelman (2018). 2018 Edelman Trust Barometer. Retrieved from www.edelman. com/sites/g/files/aatuss191/files/2018-10/2018_Edelman_Trust_Barometer_ Global_Report_FEB.pdf.

2 American Express (2017). Redefining the C-Suite: Business the millennial way. Retrieved from www.americanexpress.com/content/dam/amex/uk/staticassets/pdf/AmexBusinesstheMillennialWay.pdf.
3 Deloitte (2018). 2018 Deloitte Millennial Survey. Retrieved from www2.deloitte.com/content/dam/Deloitte/global/Documents/About-Deloitte/gx-2018-millennial-survey-report.pdf.
4 Cone Communications (2018). Cone Gen Z CSR Study: How to speak Z. Retrieved from www.conecomm.com/research-blog/2017-genz-csr-study.
5 Whelan, Tensie, and Kronthal-Sacco, Randi (2019). Research: Actually, consumers do buy sustainable products. *Harvard Business Review*. Retrieved from hbr.org/2019/06/research-actually-consumers-do-buy-sustainable-products.
6 Ibid.
7 Nielsen (2017, October 12). Nielsen Global Survey of Corporate Social Responsibility and Sustainability. Retrieved from www.nielsen.com/us/en/press-releases/2015/consumer-goods-brands-that-demonstrate-commitment-to-sustainability-outperform/.
8 Viles, Aaron (2016, April 9). Climate change by industry: Who is most at risk? *DeSmog*. Retrieved from www.desmogblog.com/2016/04/09/climate-change-industry-who-most-risk.
9 Bernow, Sara (2017). From 'why? to 'why not?' Sustainable investing as the new normal. *McKinsey*. Retrieved from www.mckinsey.com/industries/private-equity-and-principal-investors/our-insights/from-why-to-why-not-sustainable-investing-as-the-new-normal.
10 Kell, G. (2018, July 31). The remarkable rise of ESG. *Forbes*. Retrieved from www.forbes.com/sites/georgkell/2018/07/11/the-remarkable-rise-of-esg/#1f7d29c16951.
11 Girvan, C. (2018, July 13). Why change is expected in Asia's ESG profile. Fund Selector Asia. Retrieved from https://fundselectorasia.com/why-change-is-expected-in-asias-esg-profile/.
12 Stockholm Resilience Center (2014, April). What is resilience? An introduction to social-ecological research. Retrieved from www.stockholmresilience.org/download/18.10119fc11455d3c557d6d21/1459560242299/SU_SRC_whatisresilience_sidaApril2014.pdf.
13 Bridges, T.S., and Eubank, D.M. (2019). Far to go: Nine takeaways from a survey of businesses' progress on the journey to achieving the Sustainable Development Goals. *The Asian Conference on Sustainability, Energy & the Environment (ACSEE2019) Official Conference Proceedings*. Retrieved from https://papers.iafor.org/submission50531/.
14 Based on authors' notes taken while attending the TCFD Summit in Tokyo, October 2019.

Mission-driven vignette 1

Toad&Co

A better approach to apparel

Although the apparel industry has long been plagued by practices that are harmful to society, there are many brands, particularly in the outdoor apparel sector that have been some of the most credible and prominent voices on sustainability.

These companies were some of the first to build sustainable apparel businesses and raise their voices to support conversation and clean clothes activism such as living wages and workers' rights. In many ways, they were the founders of a movement, launching the first call to arms to clean up the apparel industry. In addition to Patagonia, which is well-known for its commitment on these critical issues, Toad&Co was another early leader who paved the way to creating the more enlightened apparel sector that exists today.

Beginning in 1991 in Telluride, Colorado, Toad&Co (initially known as Horny Toad) grew in its early years with some key ideas that were fairly unique at the time for the industry. Although environmental sustainability is deeply integrated into its products and everything it does, from early on it never abandoned the idea that its clothing could at the same time support an active lifestyle and be fashionable. This way of thinking was unique as the worlds of "fashion" and outdoorwear, let alone sustainable apparel, existed in very different worlds.

Choosing to integrate these elements was a smart choice that enabled it to expand to new consumer groups, especially women, who were frequently under-represented consumers in outdoor and activewear apparel sectors.

Beyond reaching new consumers, the company also knew it wanted to bring transformative change to the industry. With the environmental mantel already successfully taken up by Patagonia, Toad&Co's leadership decided to bring in a stronger social element to their business. Their first thought was to recycle fleece scraps from their manufacturing process into blankets for the homeless. As it was long before the dawn of the rise circular economy, the idea was deemed to be unworkable as there was no NGO or company that could support this type of activity.

Figure 2.6 Toad&Co, a pioneer in fusing fashion, outdoor apparel, and sustainability.
Source: Toad&Co.

They did, however, find an NGO called Search Inc. that was focused on looking for ways to provide people with disabilities meaningful work as a way to help them integrate into normal life. The Toad&Co team answered their call, developing several specialized programs including building a logistics warehouse where people with disabilities locate items in the warehouse and prepare them for shipment. More than 20 years on, they now provide vocational training and paid work opportunities for between 150 and 200 people each year at the warehouse, perhaps the company's proudest achievement.

Toad&Co is pushing to make its company even more sustainable in the global sense, continuing its programs that support those with disabilities and expanding its initiatives that focus on the environmental sustainability of its product line. Whether incorporating innovations such as TENCEL, which is made from certified sustainable eucalyptus trees; simply designing products to last; or supporting renewed apparel, it explores ways to shore up sustainability across its supply chain.

With a younger generation more aware of the pressing need to protect the environment, it is encouraged by the increasing public engagement on this issue:

> I never expected sustainability to be a true differentiator (for consumers); I thought for consumers it would be more of a tie-breaker. But this has

changed. Fifty-seven percent of consumers will make the decision to buy or boycott a brand based on its social mission. This is up 30 percent in the last year. And this carries over to values. A lot of young people want to work for companies that stand for something.

Gordon Seabury, CEO

While encouraging, Toad&Co knows that there are other groups much less attuned to the urgency of addressing environmental problems. As a response, it launched one of its most successful initiatives to date, the "Go Nude or Wear Sustainable" campaign, at an Earth Day event in 2017. The campaign was so successful that the company embarked on an awareness-building tour to more than 40 cities across the United States in a pop-up shop/trailer.

After years of steady growth and success, it is now looking to expand abroad, hoping that new markets and new generations, who are increasingly concerned about the direction of our society, will find a kindred spirit in Toad&Co.

3   From ESG to the SDGs

Methodologies for measuring and managing impact

How to move from measuring materiality to managing impact

The field of measurement and reporting on sustainability in business is rapidly evolving. New tools are not only changing how companies assess and disclose their performance, they are creating new ways for organizations to take the next step toward building their core strategies around sustainability. Businesses are hungry to understand and apply such methods, partially due to the launch of the United Nations' Sustainable Development Goals (UN SDGs), but more generally because of a recognition on their part that they must fundamentally change their relationship with society and the environment.

Yet the question of which reporting and measurement methods a company should use to understand its sustainability situation can be daunting. A wide range of options makes the decision even more complex. In this chapter we discuss the choices that businesses have to perform the most relevant reporting today; the approaches that are most useful to understanding how your company exists within its marketplaces, value chains, and communities; and how these methods enable businesses to manage their impact and transform their strategy, operations, and even business models. And, finally, we will look at how the SDGs are uniting all these threads into a whole new integrated approach to business.

We hope that this chapter will act as a useful reference that you will return to and look within for guidance when measuring your organization's impact. You may not want to read it all in one stretch, but instead treat it as a resource center that you can refer to when you are searching for the next step in measurement and management or looking for more context on how to develop and implement strategies.

The launch of the SDGs has inspired a complete change in the thinking around environmental, social, and governance (ESG) concepts; Corporate Social Responsibility (CSR); and the other threads of corporate sustainability practices. Now, with the best researched methodologies and new innovative tools, companies can make business cases for sustainability reporting and strategy development. They can adopt whole systems approaches to understand how their companies exist within society and the biosphere. And there are a wealth of options that they can choose from to drive operations transformations today.

Basic sustainability-reporting activities have been well established for a while now. Such reporting has quickly become a de facto part of businesses' annual schedule, whether as CSR communications, standalone sustainability reports, or integrated reports that combine financial and sustainability accounting. ESG reporting is significantly changing investor relations practices and can have meaningful strategic implications for companies, but, at this point in the evolution of the sustainability field, we believe that what is most striking today is what happens *after* companies release their sustainability reporting to investors.

We therefore will investigate here the new ecosystem of frameworks and standards that leading companies are applying as they move beyond the risk-related concerns of ESG and take the next steps that allow them to manage their impacts and more completely put sustainability in a core position in their business planning and strategy.

Where are we today?

In the last chapter, we discussed in our "nine takeaways" the host of common issues that businesses are struggling with across every industry. Considering the overall progress of businesses becoming more sustainable, we saw that sustainability is not yet fundamental to business models, companies are still trying to figure out how to fully systemize their initiatives, and they are having difficulty in measuring and assessing performance on the SDGs due to a lack of widely-agreed-upon frameworks and tools.

Many companies have discussed the SDGs internally and, either on their own or with expert help, mapped their current business activities across to the 17 goals. Based on these efforts, many have also identified the SDGs that are the most important to their business and formulated a vision of where they want to be on a selection or all of the 2030 Goals. (We consider "SDG priority- and vision-setting" as the second stage in our SDG Action Cycle, which we will explain in depth in Chapter 7.)

Hilton, for example, has been a long-time partner of the UN Global Compact (UNGC), supporting its efforts to bring business into conversations on sustainable development. When looking at its own reporting, Hilton realized, from having been on the front lines with the UNGC, that it had to align *everything* that it was doing to the SDGs, and then decide which ones in particular to double down on. The company used the work that it was already doing with the Global Reporting Initiative (GRI) Standards, the Science-Based Targets it had set for carbon emissions reductions, and its assessment for inclusion in the Dow Jones Sustainability Index (DJSI) to take a first pass at where it was on each SDG.

After mapping its activities to all 17 SDGs, the hospitality giant decided to focus on a subset of goals where it thinks it is able to make significant impact, such as on youth unemployment. The company sees the value in doing this exercise for many reasons, but especially because it operates in a lot of frontier markets where SDGs issues are daily realities, and the 2030 Goals help to localize and contextualize its sustainability efforts for people. Hilton has since committed to cut their environmental impact by half and double its social impact investments in alignment with the SDGs by 2030.

A struggle to measure and assess performance

The next steps after mapping and deciding priorities—those of building a strategy around that vision, communicating it in a meaningful way throughout the organization, and assessing the impact of sustainability programs—are stumbling blocks for all but the best-positioned of organizations, and a challenge to even the most advanced.

As regards assessing impact, measurement of the results of sustainability initiatives and progress toward hitting sustainability targets consistently came up as a challenge for both large and small companies with whom we spoke. In order for businesses to move in a more sustainable direction, it is clear that they need to be able to measure, track, and communicate their progress (or lack thereof) on sustainability in general and the SDGs in particular for key stakeholders.

Unfortunately, while there are more and more frameworks and tools aimed at addressing this challenge, for now there is a lack of agreement on *which* frameworks and tools should be the industry standards. Without this validation, many companies are failing to take the necessary steps to fully move their businesses forward toward greater sustainability.

Despite this uncertainty, it is unavoidable that once organizations have decided to embark on an organizational transformation to implement a fully sustainable or SDG-based model, they must select a set of concepts, tools, and frameworks. This is necessary in order to enable them to make important decisions and define the key actions that they will need to take to achieve sustainability internally or align their processes with the SDGs.

As the question around which methods to use can be a daunting one given the wide range of options that exist, we believe that most organizations will test a variety of methods before ultimately settling on the one or ones that best suit their organization's unique culture, mission, capabilities, product portfolio, and people.

ESG as the origin of sustainability measurements

The best place to start on reporting and measurement methods is with ESG, the principles of corporate responsibility that grew out of John Elkington's Triple Bottom Line.

While many companies today discuss the TBL concept of People, Planet, and Profit in their sustainability initiatives, the most prevalent conversations in businesses around measurement and reporting on the impact of companies on society and the environment in general use ESG as the starting point, including thinking around the impact of companies on the SDGs. The utilization of ESG, though, is not necessarily due to businesses embracing the concept—instead it is because of managers of capital using ESG criteria to gain insight on how companies are operating within society in order to make better investment decisions.

Indeed, the investment angle has brought the most pressure to bear on businesses to improve their impact on society. While some companies and communities have adopted TBL accounting to be good corporate citizens, ESG is fundamentally investor-driven, and the majority of listed businesses inevitably come into contact with the concept via the requirements of institutional investors and money managers who are using ESG frameworks to avoid risk and improve performance against the markets.

In order to understand whether a company was serious about its approach to ESG, investors have had to work toward proper structures for:

- Measuring inputs and outputs
- Collecting and disclosing the relevant data
- Setting standards to follow
- Identifying materiality and financial impact of actions and changes
- Reporting on adherence to standards
- Crafting strategies to implement and improve upon sustainable programs
- Setting goals and targets to encourage more sustainable thinking

This inevitable need has led to the adoption of early sustainability-measurement frameworks such as the GRI Standards.

The focus of investors on ESG issues has subsequently forced businesses to meet these new standards in order to reduce their cost of capital. While it would be nice to think that companies adopting sustainable strategies simply desire to do good for society, the reality is that avoiding risk and maintaining a low cost of capital are the most important drivers, primarily, with the discovery of new business opportunities a distant secondary concern. (We believe that this order is backward—businesses should recognize that that chance to pursue new opportunities is the real driver for embracing sustainability. More on this in chapters 5 and 6.) So, inevitably, listed companies today cannot ignore the requirement to do some kind of ESG reporting through the frameworks available in order to satisfy external stakeholders, not to mention in order to remain competitive against peers in the market who are already advancing such sustainability-related actions.

A robust ecosystem of standards and methodologies has thus developed around the ESG concept to allow professional investors to apply the thinking to their portfolios. In the past decade these ESG principles have become well known in the business world as they have achieved broad acceptance across markets. We will take a quick look at the most widely used frameworks that have been developed for measurement and reporting on ESG issues to satisfy these investor demands and expectations.

First, though, we must note that there are significant limitations to the power of ESG. From a company perspective, while ESG can create good visibility within an organization, it is not optimal in helping a company to determine strategy and fully develop a sustainable business model. We believe that ESG is better for recognizing risks than setting strategy or discovering opportunities. This is what made it attractive in the first place to investors, who are continually conscious of protecting their committed capital. Obviously, ESG tools can and do unearth issues that companies should be well aware of, yet in practice they more directly address the immediate concerns of investors.

Even as investor tools, though, there are concerns about the value of ESG. We believe the biggest problem is the grouping of environmental and social concerns—which are more externally focused—together with governance, which is more internally focused. The two are different things, and while a company might perform well on E and S, it could be failing on G, and vice versa. An overall ESG rating may not make this apparent unless you have the proper data and are looking into it deeply enough. The opposition of these facets creates a lack clarity on the real meaning of the concept as a measurement of true performance on any of the individual issues.

As well, the definition of what is proper business performance on the elements of ESG at some point almost becomes more of a moral question. Different investors will define good behavior differently, weakening the value of an ESG assessment to an outside observer. We can't take an individual fund manager's ESG perspective to be representative of whether a company is truly sustainable, or is a good environmental or societal actor.

Clever ways to address both of these concerns are being developed via ratings, rankings, standards, and benchmarks, while investor knowledge of how to actually read ESG assessments will need to become more sophisticated as such reporting metrics become the norm.

One final note on ESG: When we think of moving from an ESG perspective to the new SDG vision, it is important to understand that ESG frameworks do not translate cleanly in a one-to-one manner to the SDGs. There is overlap, but there are also gaps. Also, the SDGs are targeted at *national* policy makers, not at business entities. We do believe, though, that the gaps between ESG reporting and the SDG framework will be quickly be resolved to the satisfaction of companies and investors.

A host of academics, non-governmental organizations (NGOs), business and investor associations, government ministries and agencies, and commercial interests are all feverishly working to map the understanding of business actions that is made possible by ESG-style reporting across to the comprehensive vision of the SDGs. Partially this work is achieved by digging further down into the goals' 169 targets and 232 indicators, some of which already capture business-friendly strategies and metrics.

It is fortunate that the introduction of the SDGs with the 2030 Agenda for Sustainable Development comes at such a moment when investors and businesses are themselves looking at their contributions to or against a host of social, environmental, and self-governance issues and struggling to understand their performance. This introspection is helpful for business as the impact of the SDGs should inevitably be felt in the corporate world—with the UN's 2030 Agenda putting pressure on national governments to meet the targets of the SDGs by the year 2030, a variety of policy changes and incentives across industry sectors should come into place to induce companies to contribute to achieving the goals.

So let's consider the range of different frameworks, protocols, standards, and benchmarks that can now expressly help companies understand and report on their current status concerning sustainability in an SDG world. We should keep in mind, too, that though the nature of such measurement approaches and businesses' preference for one over another is in flux, it would be an understatement to say that companies must engage in whatever way they can today to prepare for the new expectations for how they should operate. As these ways of looking at how a company operates sustainably become more broadly accepted—to the point where they are taken for granted as a business requirement—it will be more difficult for companies to hide behind bold declarations while taking minimal actions.

The basics of ESG reporting: first measurements

Let's take a quick look at the most standard measurement frameworks used for ESG reporting—the GRI Standards and the GHG Protocol (Greenhouse Gas Protocol)—plus requirements by sustainability indices and stock exchanges, before moving on to newer, more advanced and powerful tools to develop sustainability strategies for your business.

Many companies that have started their sustainability journeys will be familiar with GRI and the GHG Protocol already. Both are typical first steps for companies that are starting their sustainability journey and, while providing relevant data for investors, are also essential to understanding where your company is today and assessing the impact of any initiatives you take. ("Understand the context" and "Assess impact" are the first and the final stages in Chapter 7's SDG Action Cycle.)

Without identifying fundamental sustainability concerns and measuring them, no one would know where to start. Both GRI and the GHG Protocol make it possible to perform the minimum of sustainability reporting by focusing on the most fundamental indicators of a company's ESG situation:

1. Pay equity (payroll)
2. Carbon emissions and other GHGs
3. Energy use
4. Water use
5. Waste generation
6. Rate of employee turnover
7. Rate of employee injury

At this point in the evolution of sustainability in the business world, reporting on these seven metrics can be considered the "table stakes" required to be taken seriously as a modern organization. GRI and the GHG Protocol together make it possible to cover your bases at such a minimum level.

Global Reporting Initiative Standards

GRI is an independent NGO founded in 1997 that offers three universal standards—Foundation, General Disclosures, and Management Approach—and three standards for reporting information on an organization's material impacts on the Economy, the Environment, and Society. This helps an organization to map out its full profile of stakeholders. These free reporting frameworks take the form of Requirements, Recommendations, and Guidance that are applied to produce a standardized sustainability report.

With GRI reporting, all stakeholders can see whether these company impacts are positively or negatively contributing to the goal of sustainable development. Reporting organizations can upload their results into a public Sustainability Disclosure Database hosted by GRI to "contribute to the comprehensive pool of data used by a variety of stakeholders".[1] The tools to assess and report in the GRI format are easy to use, with reporting more descriptive than quantitative, open-ended in its self-reporting expectations, and limited in the number of items to disclose in each topic. The standards apply across industry sectors, making for an uncomplicated baseline for sustainability disclosure.

The GHG Protocol

The GHG Protocol Corporate Standard has a narrower focus, providing a number of industry-specific tools for measuring and reporting on carbon dioxide and other GHG emissions. GHG reporting has been at the top of the minds of investors, banks, and company managers that want to reduce their impact on the environment and their risks from environmental disasters caused by the onset of the climate crisis, which the scientific consensus recognizes as being caused by GHG emissions into the atmosphere. Such reporting on emissions is thus, in a sense, the proverbial "low-hanging fruit".

The GHG Protocol process is illustrative of how many such standards and frameworks understand sustainability. The protocol follows a well-considered and methodical series of steps:

1. GHG Accounting and Reporting Principles
2. Business Goals and Inventory Design
3. Setting Organizational Boundaries
4. Setting Operational Boundaries
5. Tracking Emissions over Time
6. Identifying and Calculating GHG Emissions
7. Reporting GHG Emissions[2]

These steps can be taken across a range of activities inside and outside your business, grouped as Scope 1, 2, and 3. Scope 1 includes all direct emissions within your business from fuel combustion, production, and company vehicles. Scope 2 is determined from the usage of energy purchased by outside power generators. And Scope 3 includes all indirect emissions that might occur outside the immediate business operations, from extraction and production of purchased materials to transportation via non-company vehicles for supply and delivery, and the use of outsourced products and services. Often Scope 3 emissions make up the bulk of a business's GHG responsibilities.

The GHG Protocol recognizes that context is everything when it comes to measuring emissions, and offers a number of calculation tools that are cross-sector, sector-specific, and country-specific, as well as standards and tools separately for countries, cities, and projects. It is important to note, though, that the GHG Protocol is designed for a company to compare its performance over time and *not* to compare its performance against other businesses—each business determines its own final method for evaluating its emissions according to the protocol principles and guidelines, meaning that final reports cannot truly be compared across different organizations.

Given the importance of reducing emissions—as an end in and of itself as well as to protect companies from policy changes that will impact them upon the eventual finalization of the Paris Agreement's rulebook —the GHG Protocol is part of a whole microcosm of carbon-related corporate initiatives that represent an end-to-end approach for measurement, disclosure, decision-making, setting strategy, and driving change through principled investment.

This realm includes CDP (formerly known as the Carbon Disclosure Project), which hosts a shared system for emissions reporting by like-minded companies, and CDP's Science-Based Targets initiative, a partnership with the UNGC, World Wildlife Fund (WWF), and World Resources Institute. As the name says, the Science Based Targets initiative helps companies to set realistic internal targets for reducing the emissions for which they have calculated they are currently responsible. (As well, in the investing world, there is the Portfolio Decarbonization Coalition, cofounded by the UN Environment Programme Finance Initiative, which asks institutional investors commit to decarbonizing their portfolios.)

Sustainability indices and listing requirements

There are two other meaningful ways of enabling investors to understand your company's ESG status, both market-related.

Many stock exchanges today include requirements that companies provide a basic ESG disclosure on an annual basis. This can take the form of GRI and GHG Protocol reporting or extend beyond it with specific local requirements. Companies can harness this for their own reporting activities.

HSBC, for example, follows the stock listing rules for both the London and Hong Kong exchanges to establish a foundation for its sustainability strategies.

The UN Sustainable Stock Exchanges (SSE) initiative now provides a yearly ranking on how well exchanges are doing promoting transparency and providing high-quality ESG reporting. This in turn is leading many exchanges to adopt the GRI methodology as a recommended sustainability-reporting requirement (as the Singapore Stock Exchange does) or mandatory one (as the Taiwan Stock Exchange does) for their listed companies.

Listed companies today also prize being included in sustainability stock indices as an indicator of their sustainability bona fides. The DJSI is the gold standard of such indices, with a roster made up of the elite of the sustainable business club.

In order to be added to the DJSI, companies are annually required to submit a "Corporate Sustainability Assessment" to RobecoSAM, a Dow Jones partner and an investment specialist focused exclusively on sustainability investing. The RobecoSAM questionnaire is painstaking in its ESG coverage, but worth the effort as companies covet the better investment profile with lower cost of capital from being included in the indices, plus the public bragging rights.

Beyond the basics

While ESG is fundamental to sustainability reporting, what we believe are most important for the purpose of this book are methodologies that move beyond the risk disclosure posture and reporting requirements of ESG frameworks to new tools that allow for strategic decision-making and business planning. We want to highlight the practical ways that you can put sustainability at the core of your strategy.

So let's dive first into SASB, a framework that straddles the divide between ESG's risk avoidance and new forms of opportunity discovery.

It's a material issue

One of the most important new important measurement frameworks to come up in our discussions with companies, especially in the United States, are the relatively new sustainable accounting standards—launched in 2011—from the independent non-profit Sustainability Accounting Standards Board.

SASB takes a quantitative, industry-specific approach to measurement and disclosure of performance metrics. The approach is used to concisely identify and focus on *material* sustainability issues that clearly have an impact on the risk profile, finances, or business performance of an organization. These may include impacts on the cost of materials, products, and services; cost of capital; assets and liabilities; and intangible assets.

The concept of materiality is a powerful way to account for the value of environmental and social actions. In accounting, *materiality* is understood generally as any data that would affect investors' decisions about a company. In practice, materiality can become a powerful tool for company management to determine sustainability strategies by unearthing the most important issues, vulnerabilities, and opportunities within their business that are directly related to their relationships with society and the environment.

SASB's strength comes from creating a shared language around materiality among investors, CFOs, and regulators so that sustainability can be discussed in an accounting context. And while this makes the standard important for investors, it has as much relevance for determining long-term business strategy in and of itself. Often the difficulty with implementing sustainability as a practice inside a company is that the concepts can feel nebulous and hard to translate into practical terms; or, alternatively, such sustainability concepts are expressed in technical environmental measurements that non-experts have a hard time quantifying in monetary terms.

SASB helps to bridge the divide by applying the language of accounting to sustainability, and encouraging financial values to be assigned to material issues around environment and society. SASB metrics, described in standard units of measurement, can clearly reveal the financial impact of a range of environmental and social company issues on various standard accounting line items of an income statement, balance sheet, or cash flow statement.

SASB's free online Materiality Map tool identifies the most important disclosure issues by industry. The map features ten sectors (which each have four to 15 subsectors): Health Care, Financials, Technology & Communication, Non-Renewable Resources, Transportation, Services, Resource Transformation, Consumption, Renewable Resources and Alternative Energy, and Infrastructure. Each subsector, which total 77, may require reporting on up to 26 possible sustainability risk dimensions that are grouped under five themes: Environment, Social Capital, Human Capital, Business Model and Innovation, and Leadership and Governance. To quantify the subjects under its coverage, the SASB process includes indicators from hundreds of familiar organizations, including the GHG Protocol, GRI, CDP, and US government agencies such as the Environmental Protection Agency.

The SASB sustainability accounting framework and disclosure system is quickly becoming a standard on the path to reporting on and achieving meaningful sustainability results. Investors that have monitored the material sustainability issues of organizations find that those with a superior performance on these topics are more competitive than their peers, and members of SASB's Investment Advisory Group now hold more than $20 trillion in assets under management in companies that perform the audit.

Like GRI and the GHG Protocol, SASB is useful for understanding where your company is today and assessing year-on-year the impact of any initiatives you take. What is material to your company will change over time as your organization evolves based on your understanding and assessment, so the strategic value of establishing your baseline and keeping tabs on materiality is immense.

SASB, as well as GRI and the GHG Protocol, are also used under the umbrella of other reporting initiatives to capture the information that they each look to disclose on particular subjects. These include the Corporate Reporting Dialogue, which brings these three together with CDP, the International Organization for Standardization, the International Integrated Reporting Council framework (<IR>), the Climate Disclosure Standards Board (CDSB) and others; the Natural Capital Protocol Framework; and the Task Force for Climate-related Financial Disclosure (TCFD). Adoption by TCFD, an investor-led initiative spearheaded by Michael Bloomberg, has in fact spurred GRI and SASB to harmonize their approaches. This collaboration should be completed by 2021, greatly simplifying the reporting processes on environmental and social impact, contributions, and materiality. Companies outside the United States that are familiar with reporting via GRI should be prepared to see and utilize more of the SASB materiality approach in the near future.

The age of the SDGs: how they advance measurement and where to start

So far we have looked at reporting methods and sustainability frameworks that have been in use in the last decade or longer. Depending on location and industry, these are proven methods that have been used by sustainability pioneers to take their first steps toward understanding the health of their organizations and to set a vision for where they can go. Now we will look at a collection of new frameworks that are complementary to the SDGs. These frameworks are advancing how companies can understand their sustainability footprints—how they can measure and manage their impacts—to make smart decisions in the age of the Global Agenda 2030 and to design strategies they need to have to get to where they envision going.

We have discussed how John Elkington's development of the TBL concept inspired the creation of entities such as the SASB, GRI, DJSI, and the Global Impact Investing Network. Yet Elkington has expressed disappointment that TBL became simply another accounting tool. In an article in the *Harvard Business Review* in 2018, Elkington writes:

> The original idea was wider still, encouraging businesses to track and manage economic (not just financial), social, and environmental value added—or destroyed. This idea infused platforms like the Global Reporting Initiative and Dow Jones Sustainability Indexes, influencing corporate accounting, stakeholder engagement and, increasingly, strategy.

He adds: "But the TBL wasn't designed to be just an accounting tool. It was supposed to provoke deeper thinking about capitalism and its future, but many early adopters understood the concept as a balancing act, adopting a trade-off mentality."[3]

The SDGs may offer an antidote to this complaint, with the framework's broader context and more natural fit with how businesses think strategically about opportunities. The SDGs offer an opportunity to extend the TBL way of thinking beyond the domains of accounting and finance to that of *purpose*, which can then roll down to strategy, operations, and community engagement in a more meaningful way.

The united way

The SDGs have indeed resonated strongly with many business organizations, causing them to examine how to align their current business activities around one or more of the 17 SDGs, and, if their current business activities are inadequate, move to new ones. As shown in our previous chapter, in our recent review of annual and sustainability reports of more than 100 leading companies from around the world we found that the bulk of these organizations have prioritized the SDGs that they feel are most relevant to their business, mapped current business activities to them, and made a connection to company strategy. Still, when it comes to truly integrating their medium- to long-term business strategy in the SDGs, only a handful have done so.

Nevertheless, some companies have found ways to start to act.

All or one?

Businesses that do engage in the process of understanding how they perform against and contribute to the SDGs are immediately confronted with a critically important question: Should they focus on one or a handful of SDGs to examine further? Or should they do so across all 17 goals? In our research, this question has been a hot topic of debate among sustainability directors and practitioners since the SDG's launch.

In order to avoid what is being called "SDG washing", or more poetically "rainbow washing"—in which organizations eschew the hard work of aligning their strategy, their supply chains, and other activities to the SDGs and opt only to focus on the SDGs at a very superficial level—we believe that companies should move to assess their performance on *all* of the SDGs as a first step in the process.

Companies shouldn't focus their analysis only on the SDGs that they deem to be most relevant for their business; instead, they should aim to analyze their performance on all 17 SDGs in order to get a full picture of their organization's impact. That said, it is fine if they choose to focus their activities initially on a selection of the SDGs that they think are most relevant to their core operations—they just shouldn't do so at the cost of ignoring their possible impact on any of the goals.

From vision to execution

As we have highlighted already, the big question for enlightened businesses today is how to move beyond their mapping and vision-setting exercises to actual assessment of next-generation sustainability performance—including where possible measurement against the SDGs—and improvement of relevant strategies. Several frameworks are emerging that make it realistic to measure an organization's performance on the SDGs, which empowers companies to properly assess the impact of initial sustainability efforts.

We've identified four such frameworks over the course of our research that we found particularly useful: the B Impact Assessment, the Future-Fit Business Benchmark (FFBB), the Five Dimensions of Impact Model from the Impact Management Project (IMP), and Impact Management for Everyone (IM4E) from the UN Development Programme SDG Impact Finance (UNSIF) initiative. We find they are especially helpful in measuring sustainability performance in line with the SDGs. All are structured around an approach that compels companies to examine their positive and negative impacts along key sustainability dimensions, or, in the case of the SDGs, across the 17 goals themselves.

The secret to getting fit: *manage your impact*

The GRI, GHG Protocol, and SASB metrics are practical methods to get started measuring what is most fundamental to understanding social and environmental impacts. They establish the basic context. But as the saying goes, "You manage what you measure," and our interest is the next step of *setting strategy and managing impact.*

The next-generation frameworks that we are now discussing make this possible by moving beyond a check-box measurement process to one where companies can understand how they fit into society and the world in a more holistic manner. These four methodologies help organizations put themselves from the start on the right foot for their sustainability journey by revealing the fitness of their business activities in regards to sustainability and impact on their stakeholders.

The models can answer questions such as:

- How are we performing along various sustainability-related criteria?
- How are we doing versus our peers?
- What are the elements that are most material for our organization and our stakeholders?
- What are the key sustainability issues we should be considering as an organization?
- What is the current context in regard to ESG factors?
- How are we as a business performing in regard to the SDGs?
- Which SDGs are we impacting?

- Which SDGs connect with topics that are most material for our business and stakeholders?
- How do our business activities align with the SDGs?
- What is our actual impact on our stakeholders?
- What is the current state of play as regards climate change, and how do its effects impact our business?

Let's explore how they give organizations a fuller understanding of their SDG performance.

Plan B is Plan A

B Corporations (or B Corps) are companies that have been certified by the US-based non-profit B Labs as organizations whose mission and operations meet the highest standards of performance against environmental, social, and financial measures. In order for an organization to obtain the B Corp certification, it needs to achieve a passing Impact Score on the B Impact Assessment, which is structured around three activities with questioning on a set of subject areas for each activity:

1   Assess: Question areas include governance, workers, community, and environment, such as:

    a. *Governance:* Has the company worked within its industry to develop social and environmental standards for your industry?

    b. *Environment:* Which is the broadest community with whom your environmental reviews/audits are formally shared?

    c. *Community:* Which of the following underserved populations does your business impact or target? If you are a business-to-business focused company, who is the ultimate user of your product or service?

    d. *Workers:* Based on the results of your employee satisfaction assessment conducted within the past two fiscal years, what percentage of your employees are "Satisfied" or "Engaged"?

2   Compare: Compares answers against those of thousands of other businesses to provide a benchmark

3   Improve: Create a customized improvement plan[4]

By submitting to the B Corp assessment and becoming certified, companies are guaranteeing that they are applying a sustainable strategy out of the box. While there is naturally work to be done to determine how to financially succeed in its respective sector(s), as long as a B Corp is fulfilling the commitments it makes in the assessment, it need not worry whether its sustainability strategy is aligned with the goals. (Please note that this certification differs from a legal corporate structure, such as the "benefit corporation" designation that exists in approximately 33 states in the United States and in similar forms in Italy and Colombia; B Labs does, however, actively advocate for the expansion of benefit corporation legal structures throughout the United States and internationally.)

B Corp status is becoming the gold standard for recognizing that a business has been built for sustainability. As of autumn 2019, more than 3,000 companies in 71 countries have been certified as B Corps, with the most well-known organizations including Patagonia, Etsy, Method Home, and Ben & Jerry's. In April 2018, B Corp welcomed its largest member to date, Danone North America. At the time, Deanna Bratter, director of sustainable development at Danone North America, said: "We believe it will be a huge advantage in the long run to embed B Corp criteria and thinking into our organization and business from the very beginning."[5]

You could even say that by attaining B Corp status, companies such as these achieve, in a sense, a *moral* high ground within the business community. In the summer of 2019, the US Business Roundtable released the "Statement on the Purpose of a Corporation" in which member companies announced a shift in their focus from shareholders to stakeholders. The signatories proclaimed that they "share a fundamental commitment to *all* of our stakeholders" (emphasis added by the Roundtable). The letter received mixed reviews, from applause to cries that they were behind the curve or simply stating the obvious, to outright skepticism about their true commitment, and lists of the meaningful actions that they would have to take to make the commitment have any bite.

The response from 33 B Corp CEOs, including those from Danone, Patagonia, and Ben & Jerry's, was a full-page ad in the *New York Times* that said, in essence, *Great, now let's get to work.* These CEOs touted their better model of corporate governance under B Corp certification, asked the Roundtable to help educate investors on the value of this new vision of capitalism, and encouraged them to join forces "to make real change happen". (The Certified B Corporation website lists practical steps that executives can follow to take real action.[6]) By embracing the B Corp philosophy, these CEOs had shown that they were already on the right path, in action as much as words.

How the B Corp model is helpful

The B Impact Assessment is an open, free tool that any business can use to assess its impact on its community, the environment, employees, and customers. According to B Labs, 50,000 companies—20 times the number that have actually received the full certification—have used the B Impact Assessment tool to understand their performance in the field of sustainability. The assessment itself is thorough, challenging companies to provide responses on numerous criteria that any company that has a clear TBL mission would be expected to meet.

Building on its inherent sustainability strengths, B Labs has partnered with the UNGC to extend its online platform and help with direct assessments of a business's performance on the SDGs. The "SDG Action Manager" was launched in 2020 and is designed for companies to track their performance against the SDGs so that they can compare themselves against other organizations, monitor their progress, and improve their impact and ambitions. B Labs is mapping the B Impact Assessment indicators to the SDG targets and indicators with the help of Leeds School of Business's Center for Ethics and Social Responsibility and the University of Colorado Boulder.

As these tools are free and online, they offer companies of all sizes in all locations a low-risk opportunity to get a thorough assessment of how well their business is performing on key sustainability criteria. The learnings that come out of the assessment provide organizations with a clearer picture of where they perform best and areas where they need to improve across their operations and supply chains, and within their fundamental business model.

Having such insights helps organizations to better raise and address questions and choices when they need to make clear decisions around what actions to take—and the plan they need to put in place to execute them—in order to transform their business model into one that is built-for-sustainability or even fully SDG-based.

In shape and built to last

The Future-Fit Business Benchmark is a science-based framework from the Future-Fit Foundation that helps businesses respond successfully to societal challenges. FFBB focuses on a company as a social system that needs to be understood in regard to its activities, its active and passive stakeholders, and its resulting impact. The framework's starting position, then, is that all social systems should safeguard society's long-term viability, by each playing their part in creating an economically inclusive, socially just, and environmentally restorative future.

The FFBB outlines 23 Break-Even Goals that are used to assess whether a company is doing at least the minimum necessary to cause no harm across its entire value chain. Businesses complete a self-assessment on all 23 goals, using a set of progress indicators that can uncover potential blind-spots and highlight where attention is most needed in order for the company to close the gap between where it is now and where it needs to be.[7] In addition, the FFBB identifies a set of 24 Positive Pursuits: societal outcomes that any company may contribute to—even before reaching the Break-Even Goals—which help to speed up the whole of society's progress to future-fitness.

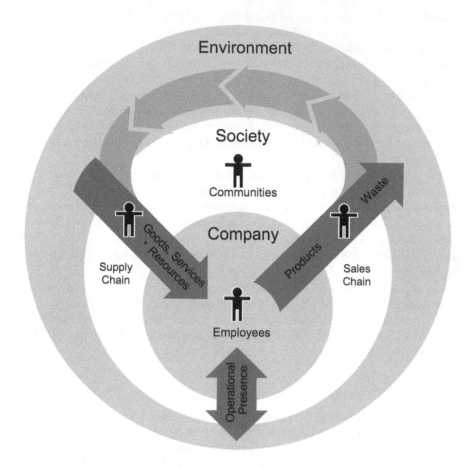

Figure 3.1 The Future-Fit Foundation's vision is that every business can be thought of as a social system that depends on a healthy society, which in turn depends on a healthy environment.

Source: © Future-Fit Foundation (futurefitbusiness.org).

It can be difficult for a company to understand exactly what it must do when it comes to the SDGs' shared vision of the problems in society—how much is "enough", for example, in terms of a business's contribution to SDG13, Climate Action, or SDG1, No Poverty? As the Positive Pursuits and Break-Even Goals very much share the spirit of the SDGs, Future-Fit has mapped the two frameworks across to each other so that any business can identify exactly where it is helping and, albeit unintentionally, hindering society's progress.

Despite being a fairly new benchmark, the FFBB is experiencing rapid uptake among organizations, including The Body Shop, DeBeers, Eileen Fisher, Maersk, and Novo Nordisk.

"We argue that it's fine for companies to focus on one or two or three SDGs," said Susanne Stormer, the Vice President of Corporate Sustainability at Novo Nordisk. (Unless otherwise stated, quotations from named individuals are based on interviews carried out by the authors between June 2018 and April 2020.) She added:

> We do the same, looking at SDG3 (good health and well-being) and SDG12 (responsible consumption). But you still need to consider your impact against all of the SDGs. This is why Future-Fit works, because at a minimum you need to get to break-even and do no harm.

How the Future-Fit model is helpful

The FFBB offers organizations extensive guidance on how they can apply the framework, grounded in leading science and drawing on the best third-party resources available. While its goals are ambitious, the benchmark was developed together with companies of various sizes and from a range of sectors, so it takes a straightforward, business-friendly approach to assessing an organization's current position on the Positive Pursuits, Break-Even Goals, and SDGs. In particular, in order to be practical and meaningful for businesses to apply, the indicators for each Break-Even Goal were designed to be calculable, comparable, complete, concise, and credible.

The Future-Fit approach is a relatively simple exercise that organizations can use to understand their full range of impacts in regard to the SDGs, and, functioning as a measurement tool, to track their contributions to the goals and their performance over time.

What we talk about when we talk about "Impact"

The mission of the Impact Management Project is straightforward and powerful: to build global consensus on how to measure, compare, and report impact. To achieve this, the IMP has united more than 2,000 practitioners "across different perspectives, terminologies and logics"—ranging from investors, asset owners, and foundations to international organizations, policy makers, civil society groups, and more—in agreement on what are the shared norms for impact measurement and management.[8]

As a result of its coalition-building efforts, the IMP has forged a mutually acceptable agreement on what "impact" is, from how we talk about the concept to defining methods for measuring and managing it. Enterprises and investors who then apply these norms to their own impact management practices are able to set goals to reduce their negative impacts and increase their positive impacts. This, in turn, is intended to help maximize their impact performance.

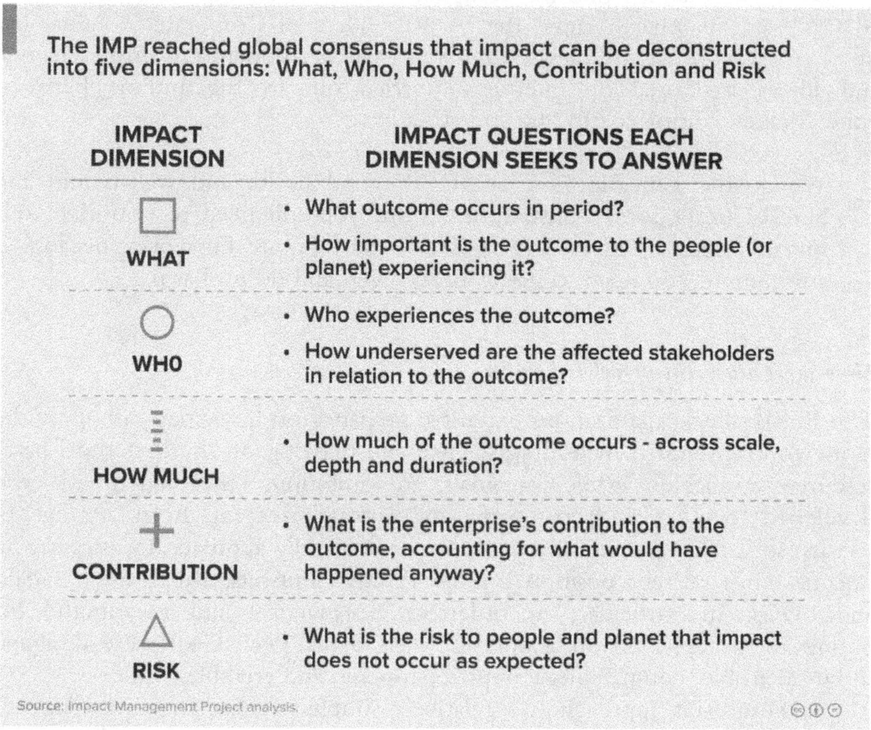

The IMP reached global consensus that impact can be deconstructed into five dimensions: What, Who, How Much, Contribution and Risk

IMPACT DIMENSION	IMPACT QUESTIONS EACH DIMENSION SEEKS TO ANSWER
☐ WHAT	• What outcome occurs in period? • How important is the outcome to the people (or planet) experiencing it?
○ WHO	• Who experiences the outcome? • How underserved are the affected stakeholders in relation to the outcome?
⁝ HOW MUCH	• How much of the outcome occurs - across scale, depth and duration?
+ CONTRIBUTION	• What is the enterprise's contribution to the outcome, accounting for what would have happened anyway?
△ RISK	• What is the risk to people and planet that impact does not occur as expected?

Source: Impact Management Project analysis.

Figure 3.2 The five dimensions of the IMP and the 15 impact data categories that operationalize these dimensions.

Source: Licensed under CC BY CC BY-NC-SA 4.0.

The consensus of the IMP's community of practitioners is that impact can be defined as "a change in positive or negative outcome for people or the planet", and that the nature of such impact can be broken into five dimensions:

What

What outcomes the enterprise is contributing to and how important the outcomes are to stakeholders.

Who

Which stakeholders are experiencing the outcomes delivered by the enterprise and how underserved they are in relation to those outcomes.

Investors' intentions relate to three types of impact: A, B or C

Figure 3.3 The IMP guide to classifying the impact of investments.
Source: Licensed under CC BY CC BY-NC-SA 4.0.

How much

How many stakeholders experienced the outcome, what degree of change they experienced, and for how long they experienced the outcome.

Contribution

Whether an enterprise's or investor's efforts resulted in outcomes that were likely better than what would have otherwise occurred.

Risk

The likelihood that the impact will be different than expected, and that the difference will be material from the perspective of people or the planet who experience the impact.[9]

Additionally, there are 15 categories the IMP has identified that are used to assess performance across the five dimensions of impact (Figure 3.2). This data can then be used to determine where an organization sits within the IMP's "ABCs": *A* for "Acting to avoid harm", as in preventing or reducing significant effects on important negative outcomes for people and the planet; *B* for "Benefiting stakeholders"; or *C* for "Contributing to solutions" (Figure 3.3). The IMP provides a live Impact Class Catalogue of more than 40 investment products that have been self-assessed along the five dimensions of impact as a resource for comparisons to those who contribute their own assessments and as a guide to other asset managers and owners, including funds from Calvert Impact, Neuberger Berman, and Standard Life Investment.

How the five dimensions of impact are helpful for assessing impact performance

It's often too common for observers to focus on the "What" and "Who" dimensions of impact, which look at the outcomes occurring solely to specific stakeholders. By pulling back to include the other three dimensions—How much, Contribution, and Risk—decision-makers can gain a comprehensive view of the impact of an enterprise on its stakeholders and how those impacts can be managed effectively. The five dimensions also enable organizations to understand whether their outcomes are "good enough" by comparing their performance against industry standards.

Finally, the focus on impact and outcomes ties the framework neatly into understanding progress toward the SDGs. Take, for example, job creation: If an organization states that it "has created 100 jobs" without any contextual information, claiming a link to the SDGs can be challenging. Maybe these jobs were given to people who were poached from competing companies; that is, to employees who would still have jobs if they weren't working for this specific company. Maybe these jobs were created in industries that pay above-average salaries, such as investment banking. Or perhaps they were given to individuals who were already wealthy before joining—such cases as these hardly represent an advancement of SDG targets.

If, on the other hand, 100 jobs were created for individuals who were previously unemployed and living under the poverty line, it's reasonable to claim that the creation of these new positions is helping to advance the SDGs. By providing contextual data, the five dimensions of impact clarify which initiatives are truly affecting the most underserved stakeholders.

Being able to measure and benchmark outcomes in this manner and compare them across various activities can powerfully inform decision-making when selecting the best strategies to employ if you are trying to improve your organization's social or environmental impacts. By creating transparency on your positive and negative impacts, the IMP approach can be incredibly useful for goal-setting within an organization and quickly recognizing where it needs to improve its performance based on negative outcomes.

For founders that are looking to build a business from scratch, the five dimensions are a powerful guide too. When establishing new organizations, leaders can use the five dimensions to identify—as their starting point—a real-world business problem that needs to be solved for a particular set of stakeholders who are not yet being offered a solution by another provider; at the same time, the founders can make sure that those stakeholders' own perspectives and requirements are considered from the get-go. Such an approach will go far in helping a company to join the ranks of those mission-driven businesses that we have highlighted elsewhere in this book.

Let's be democratic about it

Karl Richter, Executive Director of social impact investing consultants EngagedX and former Head of Research and Knowledge for UNSIF, has spearheaded a complementary impact-related project to the five dimensions that helps investors move from measuring impact to managing it. Called Impact Management for Everyone, this analytical framework for social impact investing provides plenty of flexibility for an organization to find its own way through this jungle, rather than force it onto a one-size-fits-all path.

Richter's framework harmonizes an investment perspective with an enterprise perspective, including in its vision listed companies that have set voluntary targets or are fulfilling regulations that require improved outcomes, and social enterprises. Thus, IM4E helps align businesses with impact management best practice as much as it does investors. Its straightforward yet comprehensive methodology on impact measurement makes it solidly part of the larger discussion on how to understand and create metrics around impact.

IM4E aims to shift the focus of an organization "from counting 'what' happens to understanding 'why' things happen". This helps you to improve what you measure in the first place, so that you apply the right tools to actually manage impacts. The framework takes an almost humanistic approach by presenting a rubric that includes a "common journey", "different pathways", and reporting (based on the concept of "level of evidence required" from the academic world).[10]

The common journey proceeds through the following steps:

1. Establish intent
2. Identify objectives, metrics, and indicators
3. Define targets and select strategies
4. Measure, collect, and validate data
5. Analyze and evaluate data
6. Report and disclose results
7. Use results to inform decision-making

The execution of these steps is supported across the full range of stakeholders, with each providing whatever outputs are most appropriate to their type of entity and requiring inputs from other stakeholders that satisfy their reporting expectations. These range from "less intense" for the more standardized, quantitative kind of data usually handled by various investor types to the more descriptive, customized reporting that happens in civil society organizations such as non-profit organizations and policy-making bodies.

The discrete pathways that impact management might take on any aspect of an activity are also broken down on a higher-to-lower scale of intensity (see Figure 3.4). On one extreme is the "Agnostic" approach, which doesn't consider impact at all, followed by the first step forward of "Avoid harm"; on the other side we reach the holy grails of "Assess effects" and "Interpret impact".

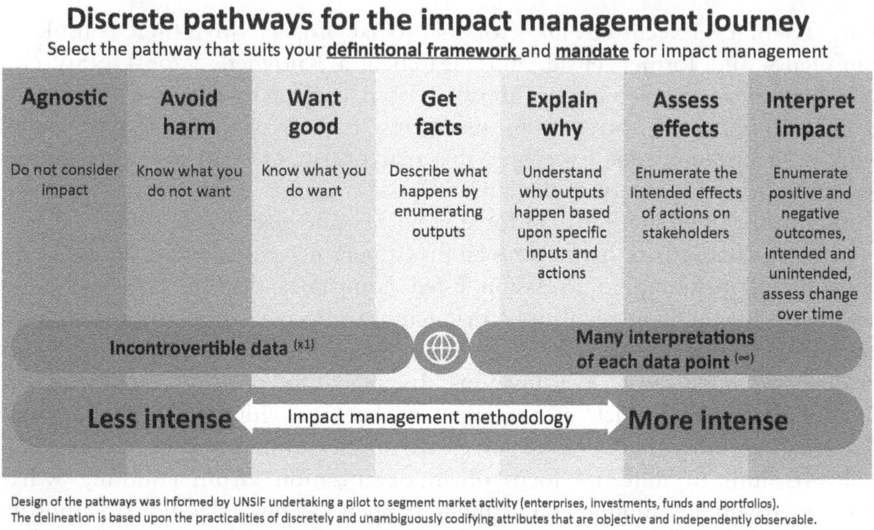

Discrete pathways for the impact management journey

Select the pathway that suits your **definitional framework** and **mandate** for impact management

Agnostic	Avoid harm	Want good	Get facts	Explain why	Assess effects	Interpret impact
Do not consider impact	Know what you do not want	Know what you do want	Describe what happens by enumerating outputs	Understand why outputs happen based upon specific inputs and actions	Enumerate the intended effects of actions on stakeholders	Enumerate positive and negative outcomes, intended and unintended, assess change over time

Incontrovertible data $^{(x1)}$ 🌐   Many interpretations of each data point $^{(\infty)}$

Less intense ← Impact management methodology → **More intense**

Design of the pathways was informed by UNSIF undertaking a pilot to segment market activity (enterprises, investments, funds and portfolios). The delineation is based upon the practicalities of discretely and unambiguously codifying attributes that are objective and independently observable.

Figure 3.4 Discrete pathways for the impact management journey.
Source: Courtesy of Karl Richter.

Thus, while ambition is, ideally, always encouraged, auditors can measure impact within whatever pathway a measurement target currently lies.

When it comes to providing evidence for the validity of the data supplied, auditors also have flexibility as regards their own perspectives, contexts, and reasons for assessing impact; the rigor of data they require; and more. Following the academic research model of "levels of evidence", auditors supply the following types of inputs as is appropriate:

1. Published and peer-reviewed
2. Published in academic or research journal
3. Statistically rigorous analysis
4. Multiple studies or time-series analysis
5. Single case study or story-telling
6. Expert opinion or rating or label
7. Circumstantial evidence or stakeholder opinion

How Impact Management for Everyone is helpful

IM4E is truly the first step toward a major, comprehensive vision of sustainability measurement and management. Sustainability, impact, and the SDGs are being discussed more and more at the executive board level, in a much different way than how CSR has been handled. But these conversations haven't gone far enough yet, as there are things that need to be done first to make them meaningful. What boards really require are standardized impact statements that can accompany their financial statements.

Richter tells us that the purpose of IM4E is "to create a normative framework for the private sector to engage in a way that is appropriate and dynamic, but works for them. One that can be independently validated and rigorous". By doing this, issues that have remained externalities, off balance or profit-loss sheets, will move on to them. This could be brand value that is driven by an improved posture on social issues, or the cost of potentially stranded assets such as fossil fuel-related ventures that are becoming too risky due to carbon emission policies.

To make this possible, it is necessary to address the idea that impact is inherently subjective and to separate between things that are factual—such as levels of carbon dioxide or nutrition—and those that are more subjective. Thus, the goal is to add more scientific rigor in order to empower fact-based measurement and management of impact.

An element of this includes authenticating such claims about an organization's impact, and even creating a "credibility score" for what people claim, in the manner of a credit score. This puts sustainability into the realm of traditional accounting, where there is a whole industry behind such efforts, with major entities—à la KPMG, PwC, Deloitte—signing off on impact reporting. As a result, there would have to be clear standards or metrics for making claims, and reliable, comparable source data to validate such claims. This methodology would make it so that both positive and negative impacts, across the SDGs, were apparent within an organization, rendering "SDG washing" impossible.

For now, for the UN and for fund managers, IM4E aims to provide a standardized framework, improve compliance, and guide data managers to enable common functionality and data interoperability within reporting platforms. For businesses, the model encourages them to back up their claims of prioritizing specific SDGs by making apparent what their actual impact is, and then encouraging them to re-allocate their resources appropriately to achieve measurable results on those specific commitments. Finally, with investors having a clear view into an organization's actual impacts, there will be added impetus coming from managers of capital for businesses to build proper strategies to achieve their self-stated goals.

Anything or everything: time to get started

For any company to discover their state of play, it must determine what specifically to measure within the organization. So far, we have reviewed a number of frameworks and methods for understanding the current status of a company in its sustainability journey, the external risks to businesses today, and the business case for aligning a company with the SDGs.

It is fairly well accepted now that the SDGs have the potential to bring about a step change in how business functions and impacts the world. As sustainability moves from a "nice, right thing to do" to a critical paradigm for business, stakeholders will become increasingly demanding about seeing demonstrated results. We believe that this changes the role that these tools will play—that they will become more and more central to day-to-day operations, shifting their use beyond CSR or sustainability functions to occupying more traditional areas such as marketing, finance, production, and procurement.

That there are such a wide array of approaches available reveals the constant evolution and innovation in the tools and frameworks that best enable businesses to successfully proceed through the Five Steps to a Sustainable Business Model, as well as to progress on the "SDG Action Cycle" that we will discuss in our final words in Chapter 7. Although there are some core approaches that will be considered "table stakes"—the minimum efforts required to play in these areas that the vast majority of organizations will use, such as SASB, GRI, and the GHG Protocol—organizations will need to identify the unique suite of approaches that best suit their unique situation.

Having set measurement standards would certainly help to quickly spread the use of agreed-upon frameworks to a wider range of sectors and business activities. However, assessing and measuring sustainability and performance against the SDGs is still bound to be a complex process. The organization itself, and its people, mission, structure, and more, will be a driver of determining which assessment and measurement approaches will be most appropriate to that business. And as we highlight in our definition of sustainability, this is an ongoing process, and businesses will need to revisit what worked at one stage to determine if it is appropriate for their next moves and strategies.

Having to comb through the available concepts, frameworks, and tools to identify what works best for each organization, and for the stage the organization finds itself in, should not be a reason for inertia, though. Companies we interviewed stressed that as sustainability is fairly new as a business discipline, the contours of their own journey and the methods and tools used to support it will necessarily experience a bit of trial and error initially. How this process plays out will vary from company to company.

Yet it is most important that organizations simply get started and try *something*. This was emphasized by Rebecca Self, CFO of Sustainable Finance at HSBC, during the UN's 2018 High Level Political Forum SDG & Business Forum in New York when she said,

> Don't wait for perfection. Don't get caught up in which framework is the best one for measurement of what you do. There will always be a bit of trial and error in this. Try any of the options available and start to align your reporting with the SDGs however you can. Start today.

How many of these methods to use will also continue to vary by organization. Some such as HSBC use unique approaches such as turning to the aforementioned London and Hong Kong stock exchange listing rules to develop a set of principles. Others, such as Novo Nordisk, opt for an approach based on a new but well-structured framework that relies on the FFBB.

Others still, such as Hilton, chose to use a myriad of approaches at any point in time. When we spoke with Daniella Foster, who was then Senior Director of Global Corporate Responsibility at Hilton, about what the hospitality company uses, she revealed that

> We use everything, because our executives took the opportunity to align with the SDGs seriously enough that we didn't want to miss anything. When you are in hospitality, you inevitably will touch upon every SDG. So were able to secure the funds internally to implement every standard we might consider.

May your organization be so lucky, and if it is not, then proceed with whatever you can today. Many organizations are still at the beginning of their journey. Fortunately, there are many approaches that will enable businesses to guide their organizations through a successful transformation from business-as-usual into a business that is built-for-sustainability.

Notes

1 Global Reporting Initiative (n.d.). Sustainability Disclosure Database. Retrieved from www.globalreporting.org/services/reporting-tools/Sustainability_Disclosure_Database/Pages/default.aspx

2 Greenhouse Gas Protocol (n.d.). The Greenhouse Gas Protocol. A Corporate Accounting and Reporting Standard, Revised Edition. Retrieved from https://ghgprotocol.org/corporate-standard.

3 Elkington, John (2018, June 25). 25 years ago I coined the phrase triple bottom line. Here's why it's time to rethink it. *Harvard Business Review.* Retrieved from https://hbr.org/2018/06/25-years-ago-i-coined-the-phrase-triple-bottom-line-heres-why-im-giving-up-on-it.

4 B Labs (n.d.). Start the B Impact Assessment. Retrieved from https://bimpactassessment.net/bcorporation.

5 B the Change (2018, October 2). The world's largest B Corp on the future of business. Retrieved from https://bthechange.com/the-worlds-largest-b-corp-on-the-future-of-business-673bccda1d54.

6 Certified B Corporation (n.d.). Business culture has shifted. Retrieved from https://bcorporation.net/news/business-culture-has-shifted.

7 Future-Fit Foundation (2018). Future-Fit Benchmark Methodology Guide (Release 2.1). Retrieved from https://futurefitbusiness.org/wp-content/uploads/2019/04/FFBB-Methodology-Guide-R2.1.pdf.

8 Impact Management Project (IMP; n.d.). IMP practitioner community. Retrieved from https://impactmanagementproject.com/impact-management/practitioner-community/.

9 IMP (2018, September 16). What is impact? Retrieved from https://impactmanagementproject.com/impact-management/what-is-impact/.

10 Richter, Karl H. (2018). Impact Management for Everyone presentation.

11 Food and Agricultural Organization of the United Nations (2018). Save food: Global Initiative on Food Loss and Waste Reduction – key facts on food loss and waste you should know! Retrieved from: www.fao.org/3/a-i4068e.pdf.

Mission-driven vignette #2

Re-Nuble

Expanding access to organics through repurposed food waste

Eating naturally isn't a "niche" phenomenon anymore. People are increasingly concerned about what they put in their mouths and their bellies. Consequently, the market for organic foods has grown in leaps and bounds in the United States and elsewhere, making it difficult for farmers and other food producers to meet the growing demand for organic produce and other food products.

Although demand is rising, the price of high-quality and organic food arguably remains too high, making it all too often inaccessible for poor and working-class consumers.

At the same time, the food waste in the world is increasing at an alarming rate. The UN estimates that roughly one-third of the food produced for human consumption, a massive 1.3 billion tons, gets lost or wasted every year.[11] For many years, disposing of waste in emerging markets such as China and Southeast Asia was big business. More recently, these nations have begun to effectively reject their role as the "world's waste repository", causing cities, states, and regions in developed countries to scramble for alternatives.

These are just two of the daunting challenges that are stressing the global food system. Fortunately, there are an increasing number of innovators stepping up to confront these challenges head on. Re-Nuble, a fast-growing start-up leveraging unrecoverable vegetative waste streams to develop innovative, plant-based, and animal-free agricultural technologies for farmers, is one of the most promising.

Tinia Pina, Founder and CEO of Re-Nuble, saw the negative impact that food with low-nutrient density had on the students as a voluntary college preparatory teacher for New York Cares Harlem, and was well aware of the food waste issues that the city was combating. In 2012, Pina conceptualized a business that could address both problems and launched it in 2016.

Figure 3.5 Re-Nuble's repurposing of food waste contributes to society's transition to a viable, cost-effective and more eco-friendly system.

Source: Re-Nuble.

Re-Nuble's organic fertilizer from food waste was first positioned to enhance hydroponic plant growth. It was later reformulated and has evolved into an on-site, customizable nutrient system for farms of all sizes and types, including soilless and hydroponic systems.

In comparison to the synthetic fertilizers that are known for fast-acting yet fast-fading effects, Re-Nuble's organic products deliver an equal nutritional value that is "ionically available". This facilitates more efficient absorption of nutrients by plants as they don't need to expend the energy to convert it. Although organic approaches to fertilizing plants can produce relatively slower growth, they do not "leech out" nutrients nor deplete the plant in the way that synthetics do.

Re-Nuble is not only a stand-out in its space on a product level, but also when it comes to cost-competitiveness. As their core nutrient input product is 15 to 20 times more cost-effective than mineral salts, Re-Nuble's organic nutrients are cost-competitive versus the only commercially used organic alternative, which is up to 69 percent more expensive. This advantage not only encourages farmers to switch, but also aligns with the company's mission: to make nutrient-packed organic food affordable for everyone.

Re-Nuble's sustainability isn't limited to the growth of plants. Its approach to tracking the environmental footprint and social impact of its operation is comprehensive, from monitoring the tonnage of food waste diverted and the number of jobs created to the amount of greenhouse gases produced and the amount of food production enabled. These measurements help Re-Nuble build a convincing sustainability case with the municipalities with whom it collaborates, as well as with the growing number of farmers it serves as customers.

With the concept of circularity embedded into the core of the brand, Re-Nuble continues to strive to use every compound and food molecule of the food waste it has access to in its products. The vision to create a closed-loop agriculture system with no more food waste or chemical additives has led the company in a clear direction as it expands from wholesalers, resellers, and distributors on the East Coast to nationwide. In addition, controlled-environment farmers and those operating in dry climates, whether in the United States or elsewhere, are also interesting growth opportunities that the company is either developing or actively exploring.

Big players in the fertilizer industry are taking note of the trend toward using more natural solutions, with young innovators like Re-Nuble leading the way. As farmers and consumers continue to accelerate their demand for more sustainable and organic solutions, a profound change in the agricultural and food system may come a lot sooner than we think.

4 The transformation of finance

Sustainable investing goes mainstream

Sustainable finance has moved from a niche, vague concept to the top of the agenda for investors across asset classes and geographies. Private equity and venture capital (VC) are considering longer-term funds that diverge from the maximum ten-year fund life approach, and nearly three-quarters of investors now view environmental, social, and governance (ESG) disclosures as very important as data shows that such reporting can help reduce risk-adjusted returns. While our view is that ESG falls more into the realm of risk management rather than opportunity identification, it is an important step in businesses' evolution toward more sustainable business models.

There's clear signs too that we're in the midst of transformation of the perspectives and values of investors themselves. Younger generations and a sizable portion of older generations are advocating for a more sustainable approach. Impact investing, which aims to generate positive, measurable social and environmental impact alongside a financial return, and sustainable investing, now defined as integrating ESG measures into investment decisions, are witnessing unprecedented interest, with such investors taking seriously the idea of making a return while also doing good.

Here we explore the rapidly changing landscape for finance as sustainable finance slowly but surely moves toward the mainstream.

One of the biggest open questions arising from the Sustainable Development Goals (SDGs) is whether the goals are achievable within our current financial system. The SDGs are shaped around long-term challenges, many that have persisted in society even during times of broad prosperity. The reality is that our modern financial system generally rewards the opposite—short-term results.

This approach, of course, does have some benefits. Pushing for strong business results in the short term can result in increased investment from investors, which management can, in turn, invest into better services and products for consumers or improved conditions for its employees. In addition, reporting regularly on business performance can be an important motivator for and enabler of good governance and accountability.

It is clear, though, that to succeed in achieving a complete transformation from business-as-usual into a built-for-sustainability business—a significant task in and of itself—a long-term and more sustainability-led approach to finance is critical. Unfortunately, bringing about a fundamental shift in the philosophy and operational approach of financial markets is a gargantuan undertaking. While major global events and crises such as COVID-19 make the need for a long-term approach evident, there are numerous structural and cultural realities within the broader global financial system that slow the pace of change toward a more sustainable model. Here are just a few examples:

- A recent survey has shown that the average holding period on the New York Stock Exchange has declined continually over the decades, descending from a high of eight years in 1959 to just eight months in 2016.[1]
- Although there's a wide diversity of investing motivations, many investors still hold wildly unrealistic expectations in regard to returns. A recent study found that investors expect an average of 10.2 percent annual returns over the next five years.[2]
- Even the mere definition of what a "long-term stock holding" *is* can pose a big challenge. From the US Internal Revenue Service's perspective, any investment held for one year or more is considered a long-term investment.[3] This, however, is just one view. The definition of "long-term" can vary greatly—it's primarily a function of the investor's perspective on how long (or short) that period should be.
- Analysis by McKinsey and the non-profit organization (NPO) FCLT Global, whose mission is "focusing capital on the long-term", found that 87 percent of CEOs feel pressure to demonstrate strong financial performance within two years, while 65 percent state that short-term pressure has increased "over the last five years" (as of 2016). On the other hand, their analysis also revealed that the long-term approach delivered $7 billion *more* in market capitalization per firm between 2001 and 2014 than short-term peers.[4]
- Finally, a study by Taekjin Shin and Jihae You of San Diego State and Louisiana State University (respectively) that appeared in the *Journal of Management Studies* found that CEOs are more strongly rewarded for stressing the importance of "shareholder value" in shareholder letters. This reward translated on average to approximately $116,000 in additional compensation.[5]

Still, there are signs that things are starting to change. Evidence is increasing that taking the long-term view as a business or an investor results in better outcomes for both, as the McKinsey and FCLT Global analysis above shows. Private equity and VC, which have become key enablers of growth in the "New Economy", are starting to consider more permanent-like funds that diverge from the current ten-year fund life approach.[6] This is an encouraging development, as private capital funding will be a critical source of support for the many innovative technologies that are playing a central role in making the SDGs achievable.

We know, as well, that the vast majority of investors—nearly two-thirds of institutional investors—believe ESG will become an industry standard within the next five years. This major shift is due to regulatory changes and increasing data showing that there is "alpha" (a firm's ability to beat the market) to be found in ESG.[7] While our view is that ESG falls more into the realm of risk management rather than opportunity identification, it is an important step in the evolution toward a sustainable business model. And there are signs that this trend is quickly picking up steam.

Most recently, as we mentioned in the last chapter, 181 CEOs from America's top corporations and members of the leading US business lobbying group Business Roundtable signed a statement promising to move away from a purely shareholder optimization model toward one that commits to valuing *all* of their stakeholders, who they've defined as customers, employees, and suppliers, and the communities in which they work.[8] While the context of the statement focused, first, on the United States, one would hope that, as global organizations, they would extend this pledge to all of the communities in which they operate.

It would be an understatement to say that many of these organizations have a significant amount of work to do to fully follow through on this pledge. However, it's a very encouraging step in the right direction.

Perhaps most importantly, there are clear signs that we're in the midst of a transformation in the perspectives and values of investors themselves. Younger generations, coupled with a sizable portion of like-minded older investors, are beginning to advocate for a more sustainable approach. Areas such as impact investing and sustainable investing are witnessing unprecedented interest, with new individual and institutional investors taking a serious look at the idea of making a return while also doing good.

This trend is even drawing in those who are approaching or squarely in middle age (aka "Gen X"). According to Bank of America, this cohort has shown the fastest growth in interest about ESG investments in recent years. So much so that 63 percent of high-net-worth Gen X investors reviewed their portfolios for ESG investments, a notable jump from 2013, when it sat at 36 percent (millennials still lead the way at 78 percent).[9] While the assumption has been that younger generations who are coming of age in an increasingly precarious world will have higher awareness of the downsides of corporate malfeasance on ESG factors, Gen X may, in fact, be the generation that finally tips the scales toward sustainable investing.

A investment model suited to tackling the challenges laid out by the 17 SDGs is going to require more than a modest increase in investor capital being diverted toward SDG-related efforts, though, whether directly or via businesses. The United Nations Conference on Trade and Development (UNCTAD) estimates that it will take between $5 trillion and $7 trillion to fully fund the SDGs,[10] while the World Economic Forum estimates that attaining the goals would require an investment of $2.5 trillion annually.[11]

With funding required to reach this level, achieving the goals will be a pipe dream without the involvement of financial markets and their participants.

Whether from banks directly or from investors themselves, finance will play an integral role in not only providing funds for the SDGs, but also rewarding businesses, both large and small, who invest to move their businesses toward sustainability. It is unclear what will be the catalyst that truly propels sustainable finance into the mainstream. The knowledge, resources, support, and infrastructure needed to support this new model, fortunately, are taking shape.

There are various terms associated with the idea of moving finance toward a model that is more "responsible", one that not only generates positive financial returns but also positive societal ones. Here let's focus on two key concepts: impact investing and sustainable investing.

Impact investing: the soul of sustainable finance

> Impact investments are investments made with the intention to generate positive, measurable social and environmental impact alongside a financial return.
> The Global Impact Investing Network (GIIN)[12]

If you want to understand how we've arrived at the point where the concept of shareholder value maximization as a company's sole objective is being challenged like never before, you need to start with a sector of finance that has long been overlooked—impact investing.

Impact investing aims to deploy capital to businesses that generate measurable environmental, social, and financial returns. Although the term "impact investing" wasn't coined until 2007,[13] the concept of sustainable business as "good business" developed many years earlier. One could even make the argument that this concept dates to the origins of the modern corporation, with examples such as the provision of lodging and healthcare by employers for their employees; the strong social contracts between companies and employees in countries such as France, Germany, and Japan; or the integration of corporate stewardship into many companies' missions.

As capitalism took hold as the accepted system around the globe, however, this concept has often fallen by the wayside. Twenty-five years ago, one big idea challenged all that. As we've mentioned several times, serial entrepreneur John Elkington coined and popularized the Triple Bottom Line (TBL) concept that puts the idea that companies should examine their social, environmental, and economic impacts when assessing their performance at the center of the conversation. Elkington presented this concept with a focus on "People, Planet and Profit" in the 1997 book *Cannibals with Forks: The Triple Bottom Line of 21st Century Business.*[14]

TBL was key in changing the way we think about sustainability in two fundamental ways. First, it introduced the idea that companies should focus on stakeholders rather than shareholders. In the modern business era, the objective of "maximizing shareholder value" had been considered, up until that point, as the gold standard of best practices in business. This concept, also known as the Friedman Doctrine, was famously popularized by renowned economist Milton Friedman in his pivotal New York Times Magazine article "The Social Responsibility of Business is to Increase its Profits".[15] Elkington sought to shift the focus away from pure value maximization for shareholders to understanding how value is created for all of a company's stakeholders (which include shareholders, of course). Next, TBL laid the foundation for a new kind of accounting, integrated reporting, materiality, impact measurement, and, of course, impact investing.

Although his pivotal work did move the conversation about sustainability and business up the agenda, it didn't fundamentally change how much of business works. At least it didn't immediately, for later a new generation of ambitious and socially conscious entrepreneurs came along who saw this realignment as an *opportunity*. Over the last two decades, swathes of social entrepreneurs stepped up to the challenge of building the "twenty-first-century company" as articulated by visionaries such as Elkington.

While the 2008 financial crisis was devastating in its effects, particularly in Western countries, one positive outcome has been the impressive rise in social enterprise creation. Here are few notable highlights:

- United Kingdom: There are approximately 100,000 social enterprises in the UK according to government statistics, contributing £60 billion to the economy and employing roughly two million people.[16]
- United States: An estimated 11 percent of the working population aged 18 to 64 state that they're involved with some of social entrepreneurial activity as a nascent or operational leader (versus an average of 3.2 percent for all countries surveyed).[17]
- Italy: Between 2008 and 2014, the number of employees in social cooperatives grew from 340,000 to 407,000 (a jump of 20.1 percent), while mainstream companies lost almost 500,000 employees.[18]
- India: The estimated market opportunity for social enterprises in India is anticipated to grow to $8 billion by 2025.[19]

The sector has grown by leaps and bounds since the dawn of the twenty-first century, evolving into a thriving, increasingly global ecosystem. Various initiatives and entities have sprouted up to support this growth in social entrepreneurship. This ecosystem now has a solid foundation upon which to build, one that spans from investor networks such as Toniic (a network of asset owners that commit a portion of their investable assets to impact investing), the European Venture Philanthropy Network (EVPN), the Asian Venture Philanthropy Network (AVPN), and Nexus (which focuses on family offices and individuals with net worth in excess of $100 million) to hybrid information platforms and networks such as the GIIN (a partner of

Toniic); from accelerator and incubator programs such as Ashoka and the Social Good Accelerator to community-building events such as SOCAP (Social Capital Markets); and, of course, to VC funds, who are allocating an increasing amount of capital to social innovation.

Despite a growing interest and the impressive leap in social entrepreneurial activity, two critical challenges continue to affect the sector: (1) How can we measure the social and environmental impact of investments? and (2) how do we ensure sufficient funding?

The impact measurement conundrum

Social entrepreneurs and investors quickly realized why established companies often shied away from incorporating social and environmental impact assessments into their business models—measuring financial performance is fairly standardized and straightforward, but measuring social and environmental impact, particularly as it relates to business performance, poses a significant challenge.

The burgeoning sector has required innovative, new frameworks and metrics to demonstrate the value of their ventures. Moving from qualitative to quantitative approaches for assessing value is critical to social enterprises' success, whether for raising capital and attracting partners, and even for recruiting and retaining employees. Fortunately, several key leaders in the social innovation space have taken on the challenge.

One of the most transformative thinkers to emerge on the topic is Jed Emerson, a previous leader in the non-profit space who evolved into an impact investor and advisor to numerous impact investment funds, family offices, and foundations. From Emerson's perspective, social enterprises and their investors should center their energies on value maximization in all aspects of the company or investment. In 2000, Emerson pioneered the Blended Value framework, which is rooted in the idea that organizations shouldn't be focusing on an "either/or" approach when thinking about value generation. Rather they should have "a unified, holistic understanding of value as 'both/and,' integrated and non-divisible".[20]

Blended Value isn't a toolkit for how to value a company, or for companies to demonstrate that said value; rather, it's a framing of the elements that should be considered when creating a more holistic perspective to determining business value. It also provides an important lexicon for articulating all of the different players, facets, and challenges in the impact space that serve the important purpose of bringing those involved in the burgeoning sector onto the same page.

Early work on Blended Value made clear the hard reality that purely-for-profit financial markets and investments have no mechanism for arriving at a financial return for value creation in a social impact context. And, worse, financial markets often apply a "Sinking Economic Return" to investments via traditional social funding vehicles such as grants and charitable gifts, which, in essence, results in a "profit penalty". (In other words, from a pure financial market perspective, there are few to no monetary returns from social investments such as grants and charitable gifts. And, worse, they could be viewed as a weight on capital.) To address this structural deficiency in traditional financial value assessment frameworks, Emerson advocated for determining a "Blended Value ROI" (return on investment) that would fully incorporate the Blended Value paradigm within every activity of an organization, whether that organization be a non-governmental organization (NGO), a TBL company, a mission-driven outfit, or a primarily profit-driven concern.

Emerson predicted that "The future will see the introduction of an increasing number of investment vehicles and strategies that pursue the Blended Value Proposition and report on investment performance on the basis of a Blended ROI", and that social information systems and technologies would underpin this new model of value.[21] Although we have not yet achieved globally-accepted Blended Value models, Emerson's work accelerated a movement to identify much-needed frameworks and tools to assess social impact.

Founded in 2009, the GIIN has had a key central role in furthering the establishment of standards for valuing and assessing the performance of social enterprises. To grow the impact investing sector, the GIIN recognized early on that reducing the multitude of barriers that this burgeoning industry was facing was, perhaps, its most important area of focus. As such, developing a set of tools and resources under the umbrella of the GIIN's Impact Measurement and Management (IMM) project emerged as critical to its mission.

The GIIN provides a range of tools and techniques to support impact measurement. While used by impact investors, social enterprises can also apply metrics outlined in the GIIN's IMM to assess and track their performance and illustrate their progress to current and potential investors. Most notable in IMM is the IRIS+ system, a comprehensive, easy-to-use tool that enables clear, comparable data that allows investors to make informed, evidence-based investment decisions. IRIS+ has even begun to integrate SDG measurements, recognizing the importance of the UN framework as a driver of growth in the impact sector.

These tools are free to use publicly, which has been fundamental to driving their uptake. The GIIN is also engaged with key cross-industry initiatives such as the Impact Management Project, which we discussed at length in Chapter 3. (We also discussed other pivotal work in Chapter 3 that is currently underway in the field, such as the Impact Management for Everyone framework developed by Karl Richter.)

Individually, private equity and VC impact funds are developing their own analytical tools and approaches to support their investment activities as well. The world's largest impact fund, TPG's Rise Fund, is an excellent example of this in action, (which we will explore in more detail later in this chapter).

Drawing on the work of the Impact Management Project and in conjunction with the Bridgespan Group, its social impact advisory firm partner, the Rise Fund team developed the *impact multiple of money* (IMM), a highly rigorous method that enables impact investors to evaluate the projected return on an opportunity.[22]

The work around developing this method and expanding its application beyond the Rise Fund's portfolio has been spun off into an independent organization called Y Analytics. Building on the potential of Y Analytics to extend this application to new companies and sectors, Maya Chorengel, Co-Managing Partner of the Rise Fund, said:

> I do think there's significant potential to apply the impact multiple of money more broadly. It is important to have tools in the market that enable a more robust understanding of impact, whether positive or negative. In fact, Y Analytics was developed and eventually spun out of the Rise Fund because we found that many of our peers were hungry for a rigorous, independent standard that could be used not just in the private equity sector, but beyond.

This type of promising approach illustrates that getting to metrics that will meet the high bar often demanded by the broader finance community will likely come from the impact space, where years of experience experimenting with how to quantify impact is proving to be a real asset.

Finally, alternative corporate structures have also helped to provide much-needed structure to assessing social enterprise value and social and environmental impact. The B Corporation (discussed earlier in this book in chapters 2 and 3), as well as government-authorized corporate structures such Benefit Corporations or Social Purpose Corporations (SPCs) in the United States, Community Contribution Companies in Canada, and Community Interest Companies (CICs) in the United Kingdom, are the most notable examples. In the case of B Corps, obtaining the B Corp certification requires an organization to go through a thorough process to achieve a passing Impact Score on the B Impact Assessment.

As this assessment and its supporting tools are open to all, any organization can use it to establish an approach to assessing its financial, social, and environmental impact. With over 3,000 certified B Corps in more than 70 countries, B Corp's assessment is probably as close as you can get to a standard, recognized, company-focused framework (versus an investor-oriented one) that both social and for-profit enterprises that are looking to integrate impact into their business models can use to provide a complete assessment of their social, environmental, and financial impact. Most importantly, the certification establishes how they can improve their performance.

The dangers of searching for the measurement silver bullet

Although there has been significant progress on metrics and approaches to measuring social and environmental as well as financial impact, there is a risk that a singular focus on quantifying impact may eventually pull focus away from the broader discussion of moving toward more balanced business models.

This issue has been underscored as of late by Emerson himself. Much to his chagrin, he believes that the impact investing and social entrepreneurship sectors have become too overly focused on the "how" of impact assessment rather than on understanding "why" we are investing in and building sustainable ventures in the first place. Emerson explores this premise from a historical and philosophical perspective in his most recent work, *The Purpose of Capital*:

> Each of us is the market just as we contribute to the creation of and give lifeblood to capital markets. We each have the possibility of embracing a new, deeper and more inclusive understanding of capital's place and purpose in our lives and in determining the future survival of this planet. That is why we should pause to reflect upon how we got here while reconsidering and refining our understanding of the purpose of capital and how capital should serve us all—human and non-human—over centuries to come.[23]

We should question whether the rush to quantify measures of social and environmental progress in a business perspective is actually simply masking a desire to make these elements "financial". Doing so could, in fact, lead us back to the status quo model for assessing value where social and environmental benefits that are more qualitative in nature are ignored. It is possible that we will never arrive at a simple, straightforward approach to measuring the kinds of very complex aspects that social enterprises tackle; or, if we do, it may take much longer than we would like.

Even the financial metrics that we now accept without question as the best tools for assessing financial performance took significant amounts of time to become generally accepted practice. Take the cash flow statement which first appeared in the 1860s but wasn't required as a part of GAAP (Generally Accepted Accounting Principles) until 1988.[24] Or how about EBITDA (earnings before interest taxes depreciation and amortization), a key metric for private equity, which wasn't popularized until the tech boom of the late 1990s?[25]

There will undoubtedly be some commonly accepted social enterprise metrics that emerge, but investors and founders alike will need to accept a more evolved yet complex business model which will, by nature, likely always have a certain level of subjectivity.

A broader view of value will also require, as mentioned earlier, that investors accept the reality of a much longer investment horizon and that social entrepreneurs accept that they will likely be in it for the long haul. Quick exits are difficult in many "profit-first" ventures. They're likely to be doubly so in those where social and environmental impact are at the core.

Bridging the funding gap

In addition to measurement, impact investing also faces the daunting challenge of underfunding.

The GIIN has produced the most rigorous assessment to date of the size of the impact investing market. It estimates that there are 1,340 organizations globally managing $502 billion in impact investing assets.[26] While all signs point to robust growth for the impact investing sector, it is swamped in comparison to, say, the private equity market, which currently stands at $3.06 trillion AUM (assets under management),[27] or even to the broader sustainable investing and Socially Responsible Investing market, which has grown leaps and bounds in recent years to a staggering $30.7 trillion AUM[28] (more on this later).

Regardless, impact investment funding entities are flourishing, with new entrants coming onto the scene. One of the early impact investing funds was Calvert Impact Capital. Its origins go back to the 1980s, and in 1995 it began raising retail investor capital to lend to community development financial institutions in the United States and to microfinance institutions globally.

Calvert Impact Capital has been a pioneer of bringing smaller, retail investors into impact investing. Its Community Investment Note was one of the first impact investment products offered via brokerage platforms. In addition, individuals can also invest directly on its website, another important initiative to bring small investors into the sector. Today, almost all of its investors are individual investors (more than 18,000 have invested since 1995).[29] Yet, as many invest very small amounts (the minimum investment required is $20), individual investors only comprise about 25 percent of the total capital invested with Calvert Impact Capital. The remainder comes from investment firms, family and community foundations, NGOs, and faith-based organizations, a community it has highlighted as being critical in driving the growth of the impact investing sector.

Having observed a notable jump in interest in impact investing since the launch of the SDGs, Calvert Impact Capital has been actively aligning its strategy and product offerings with the 17 goals, and today its portfolio contributes directly to most of them. One key challenge it sees for the industry, though, is that the number of other investment products addressing the funding gap challenge of the SDGs which are able to attract new funding is still fairly limited.

The rise of retail investors in the financial markets has largely been facilitated by significant innovations—first by visionaries such as Jack Bogle, who made investing for millions of individuals easy, with low-cost, low-maintenance index mutual funds, followed by the dawn of the internet and technology age, which has opened up financial markets to new digital entrants who service swaths of new, retail investors. The impact sector not only needs to build on the important work of the Calvert Impact Capitals of the world, but also must leverage proven financial innovations while finding its own catalyst for growth.

Following Calvert Impact Capital's lead, the 2000s saw a myriad of new impact funds emerging. Thanks in part to the tech booms of the late 1990s and 2000s, a new generation of "impact attuned" high-net-worth individuals began to recognize the opportunity in impact investing. While many of their peers continued to focus on the next great tech venture, a significant proportion of these newly minted millionaires (and in some cases billionaires) and other successful business professionals wanted to orient their skills and capital toward tackling the world's most "wicked" problems.

Some of the most notable emerging from this unique period in time are the Omidyar Network, which played a central role in blurring the lines between private equity or VC, and foundation structures, Acumen Ventures, Khosla Ventures, Ananda Ventures, and, more recently, Better Ventures. The rise of these funds, founded and led by highly successful professionals in their own right, helped bring much-needed visibility to the sector.

It quickly became apparent from this movement that solving the world's biggest challenges would require a more complex, much larger in scale, and, arguably, ambitious approach. Perhaps a collective approach, rather than more individualistic or traditional private equity one, could be the catalyst needed to accelerate the allocation of much-needed funding to the impact sector.

Bill Gates and Warren Buffett, of course, popularized this concept with their Giving Pledge, encouraging the wealthy to give a majority of their wealth to philanthropy. TPG, a global private equity firm with $108 billion AUM, made this concept concrete with the launch of its first $2 billion Rise Impact fund. Founded by Bill McGlashan, Jeff Skoll, and musician Bono of U2, the fund is supported by a founders board of numerous leaders in business and philanthropy, such as Reid Hoffman of LinkedIn, former Unilever CEO Paul Polman, Celtel founder Mo Ibrahim, former DreamWorks board chairwoman Mellody Hobson, and Emerson Collective founder Laurene Powell Jobs, bringing invaluable experience and connections to the fund and their portfolio companies.

The Rise Fund now leads the way as the largest impact fund in the world. If all goes to plan, the fund is set to more than double in size if the team is successful in its current efforts to raise a second fund.

Similar to other mainstream VC firms, the Rise Fund's investment approach is highly rigorous and centers around the strengths of the team and TPG's experience historically. It has opted to focus its investments on core sectors aligning with its strengths, namely financial services, health care, food and agriculture, and education. Unlike many other VCs, however, the Rise Fund team invests globally, having made numerous investments in India,

Africa, and China thanks to the knowledge that team members and partners have in those markets.

Underpinning their investment approach is the thorough approach to defining impact and understanding its return that we covered earlier in this chapter. "As there isn't a commonly accepted template for what impact means, we risk diluting the standard of impact, or worse, promoting greenwashing if we're not rigorous," says Maya Chorengel, Co-Managing Partner of the Rise Fund. "We want to ensure that there's a high standard of impact across our field and hope our peers are doing the same."

As the societal and environmental problems we face are increasingly global, this type of investment approach will gain in importance as solutions developed by social entrepreneurs have increasing applicability around the world. Even with the scale of the Rise Fund's size and global footprint, it's clear that we need several more similar funds of significant size, scope, and heft in order to make a real impact.

Impact investing is simply one piece of the broader sustainability and impact puzzle. However, it is a critical one in spurring the wave of social entrepreneurship and technological and business model innovations needed to tackle the world's most wicked problems.

Mainstreaming impact

Although impact investing continues to be a promising yet nascent part of the overall investment market, it has demonstrated its potential in recent years, building on an increasingly strong track record and rapidly improving rigor around structure and measurement. However, getting to, at least, the trillion-dollar milestone requires moving impact investing into the mainstream. Fortunately, there's significant momentum on this, with the GIIN and many of the other key players in the industry mentioned here leading the charge.

We believe that there are a few important actions that are critical to further mainstreaming their mission:

Showcasing of impact success stories and best practice

There is nothing more powerful than examples of how what we call "mission-driven companies" are not only achieving impressive levels of success but also starting to shake up the sectors in which they compete. Our mission-driven vignettes go into this in detail. Growing proof shows that these types of businesses are the future.

A recent study conducted by New York University's Stern Center for Sustainable Business found that between 2013 and 2018 50.1 percent of CPG-category (consumer packaged goods) growth was driven by sustainable brands, with those marketed as sustainable growing 5.6 times faster than products not marketed as such. In addition, these products posted a 4.45 percent CAGR (compound annual growth rate) over the period, versus only 0.80 percent for conventional CPG products.[30] This impressive trend illustrates a real shift in consumer buying preferences in a category that is anticipated to grow to $14 trillion by 2025 (a big leap from $8 trillion in 2014).[31]

This type of success story should excite funds and investors of all stripes.

Doubling down on tech solutions

The tech sector has been the global driver of entrepreneurial, VC, and innovation activity for the past two decades. Looking for ways to disrupt areas of society viewed by many as inefficient or unproductive has created a generation of ambitious entrepreneurs who've launched an untold number of innovations around the world, changing lifestyles in unforeseen ways and producing significant financial spoils for investors and society alike.

Yet there are signs that the tech sector's value-generation machine is starting to slow.[32] Even worse, there's a growing perception that some businesses or segments of the tech sector are actually doing more harm than good to society.

In response to these trends, the tech community is starting to redirect its talents toward more daunting problems than connecting with friends or finding a taxi at 2 am. The environment, education, health care, food, and agriculture—all of these contain wicked problems that new technologies can play a significant role in tackling. Thanks to technologies such as AI and blockchain, we may have the tools to deliver solutions to those in need, irrespective of where they're located.

In addition, technological solutions get the attention of investors and tend to bring more visibility to the broader problem they're attempting to solve. Leveraging technology to address global challenges will not only help draw more investors to impact investing but also attract a greater number of entrepreneurs to the impact sector.

Better data, better analytics, better tracking

Technology will also need to play a central role in addressing the impact sector's data, analytics, and measurement challenges. We saw earlier how metrics such as the *impact multiple of money* is poised to be a game-changer in enabling better and more systematic impact investing decisions. Technology can make systematizing this metric and expanding its use to impact investments in the sector and beyond a reality.

Technologies such as blockchain will hopefully enable us to make significant gains in gathering, tracking, and analyzing the often myriad of data points that are needed to assess impact. There are numerous start-ups working on this challenge.

One that has deployed a particularly interesting approach is iXO, which aims to enable impact entrepreneurs to track and measure the impact of their project via a core protocol platform. Users can engage in a range of activities to generate and understand their project or business's impact, including collecting, processing, and storing data; tracking results; integrating verified, publicly available data sources; and tapping into powerful measurement, verification, and reporting tools. Of course, the platform it has developed is just the beginning. Services such as these will eventually form the analytics, tracking, and measurement backbone moving to the mainstream will require.

Innovation in financing mechanisms

As mentioned earlier, a step change in financial product innovation would be an important catalyst for bringing new investors, both institutional and retail, into the impact space. This is particularly pertinent as traditional VCs struggle with accepting the potentially longer exit period or understanding the nascent approaches to assessing value.

Blended equity and debt models, such as deal collaboration between venture funds and corporations that may in the coming years be looking to redeploy their Corporate Social Responsibility (CSR) budgets to more direct investments (as many have done in recent years in the digital space) could be a way forward. Creating more exchange-traded funds (ETFs) or other mutual funds composed solely of mission-driven businesses could be another. Start-up bond issuances, green bonds for environmental start-ups, microloans, crowdfunding, and platforms that enable retail investors to invest directly in mission-driven start-ups could have as much success in the impact sector as they have in the mainstream start-up space.

Of course, in addition to bringing much-needed funding to social entrepreneurs, these financing options also have the added benefit of expanding the impact investor pie, ultimately reinforcing the fundamental principle of impact investing—we don't need to sacrifice societal returns for financial ones. Both are achievable.

The future of finance will be sustainable

> Sustainable investing: A discipline that considers Environmental, Social, and Governance (ESG) criteria seeking to generate a positive societal impact within an investment framework.
>
> Fidelity Investments[33]

If impact investing is the foundation of sustainable finance, then sustainable investing—and, more precisely, ESG—is its accelerator. Few sustainability-oriented concepts have held as much sway over investors as ESG has. If we want the sustainable business model of the future to become a reality, moving investors' mindsets toward a more long-term, sustainable perception of growth and value has to be priority No. 1.

This is principally because it is impossible to overstate the importance of investors and financiers as catalysts of change. The Forum for Sustainable and Responsible Investment found in 2016 that there were 1,820 institutional investors, money managers, and community investment institutions in the United States alone that applied various ESG criteria in their investment analysis and portfolio selection, representing $8.10 trillion in US-based assets. Following 2016, "socially responsible investing" continued to exceed expectations, growing at 38 percent year-on-year since and now accounting for one out of four dollars of total US AUM.[34]

In Europe, this prioritization of ESG among the investment community is even starker. Morningstar's recent European Sustainable Funds Landscape highlighted the fact that the concepts of ESG and socially responsible investing are becoming so entrenched in Europe that the lines are, in fact, starting to blur between sustainable and traditional funds. The exclusion of many types of products and companies from European funds, such as tobacco and thermal coal, has accelerated this blurring trend.

One of the most promising financial product categories in the space has been passive sustainable funds, with one-fourth of new flows coming into ESG index funds and ETFs during the first half of 2019. They now make up approximately 18 percent of the European Sustainable fund market, up from just 10 percent five years ago. And within ten years, the launch of new sustainable funds has leapt from 95 in 2009 to 305 in 2018, resulting in a total of 2,322 funds that could be considered as "sustainable".[35]

In a market where the investment culture is limited compared to a market such as the United States, the growth of these funds is a positive sign that, perhaps, Europeans' higher level of engagement around sustainability-related issues may also be delivering the added benefit of attracting new retail investors to the market. In fact, an impressive 30 percent of socially responsible investments in Europe were held by retail investors in 2017, up from a mere 3.4 percent in 2013.[36]

Evidence is mounting that companies are now prioritizing ESG in response to investors' calls, and changing how they manage their companies accordingly. As we highlighted earlier in this book, ESG has mostly sat in the realm of risk management as companies have tried to head off potential business disruptors that arise from challenges such as climate change, poor governance practices and structures, or political turbulence. There are signs that we're moving beyond ESG reporting and risk management to the *integration* of ESG business strategies.

However, while companies may publicly state their vision or strategies around ESG and, more recently, sustainability or the SDGs, in most instances these strategies are just that—an intention to act, not action itself.

Investors, particularly institutional investors and asset managers, are taking a more proactive approach in ensuring that companies are acting on their ESG promises. Asset managers with whom we spoke are regularly monitoring companies that they invest in to assess their ESG progress. Their engagement takes the form of not only due diligence to evaluate how companies are performing in regard to ESG criteria, but also engaging companies in a constructive dialog to give them guidance on where and how to improve, including communicating tangible key performance indicators (KPIs) where they'd like to see more progress in the (near) future.

Thanks to the increasing number of success stories coming from companies that have moved toward a more sustainable approach, investors have wised up and are starting to demand more proof that companies are moving to execute these strategies and, accordingly, rewarding those that do. More recently, there is clearer evidence that sustainable funds and share prices from companies viewed as more sustainable are outperforming their traditional peers.

Even leading up to the latest period of ESG and sustainability fever, the strong performance of ESG and sustainability assets was becoming apparent. Case in point: Bank of America found that "Companies ranking highest in ESG criteria tended to have consistently lower future stock price volatility and higher average subsequent returns on total equity as compared to their lower-ranked counterparts."[37]

It is more widely accepted now by financial asset managers around the world that ESG-oriented investments are a good bet. Of course, it's also important to look not just at how ESG and sustainable assets perform when times are good—it's key to examine how they perform during challenging market periods. Do investors stick with these assets when times get tough?

In fact, this dynamic became more pronounced as the COVID-19 pandemic took hold at the start of 2020. Research by Blackrock showed better risk adjustment performance of sustainable indices versus their non-sustainable peers over the first financial quarter of 2020. This was a continuation of superior performance that Blackrock witnessed by these indices in 2015-2016 and in 2018. Bank of America observed a similar dynamic, particularly in Europe where ESG indices outperformed their benchmarks year-to-date.[38]

The benefits of ESG and sustainability strategies weren't always so apparent. One company best captures how far the business and investment communities have evolved on this topic: Today, when the business community and investors think of large corporations successfully flying the sustainability banner, more often than not Dutch-Anglo consumer-products giant Unilever springs to mind.

Just a decade ago, this wasn't the case. As world markets were in a tailspin during and just following the financial crisis, most companies also moved into crisis mode—cutting costs; focusing only on their core, base businesses; and putting any significant investments on hold. Unilever's new CEO Paul Polman, who decried the short-termism of companies and markets early on, took an alternative path.

Rather than follow his competitors and peers, he eschewed a short-term, cost-cutting approach and committed to a long-term, investment-focused one that put sustainability at the core, often working beyond Unilever to drive an industry-wide embrace of sustainability. His plan, known as Unilever's Sustainable Living Plan, was launched in 2010.

Unfortunately for Polman at the time, investors met this announcement with derision, and the company's share price dropped 8 percent.[39] In the years following the roll-out of his plan, it wasn't an easy road to success for the company, as it experienced various ups and downs. Polman stayed the course, often putting him in direct conflict with the investment community when he took steps such as refusing to publish profit updates in order to underline what he saw as the futility of a short-term approach.

Eventually, Polman proved the naysayers wrong as Unilever outpaced the FTSE index and competitors during his period as CEO.[40] Unfortunately, a shareholder revolt was brought on by his plan in 2018 to move from a dual London–Rotterdam headquarters structure to a single one based in Rotterdam. This unfortunate end to his tenure hasn't undermined the transformative mark that he made on his company, industry, and shareholders. Polman single-handedly proved that a long-term, sustainability-centered strategy can benefit both society and investors.

Sustainable investing as the gold standard

As with impact investing, there's still significant work to do to evolve sustainable investing from an alternative or niche investment strategy to the "gold standard" of finance and investing. There are many actions the industry can take, many of which are well underway, to accelerate this process.

Building sustainable finance capability among finance professionals

As leaders of financial institutions look for ways to incorporate sustainability into their investment approach, they've encountered various challenges along the way. One of the trickiest is the capability and knowledge gap about sustainable investing in the investment community.

The reality is that most financial service professionals have been trained by academic institutions, financial service firms they've been employed by, and even the financial and business media, to apply a fairly narrow approach to capital management—namely, generating short-term financial gains as the overriding objective. For several decades, this approach appeared to be the ideal one, as any downsides were perceived to be greatly outweighed by the financial upsides.

While there were doubts about this approach along the way, the overwhelmingly positive perception began to shift fundamentally when the 2008 financial crisis not only upended capital markets but the livelihoods of millions around the world. Now financial service professionals are increasingly being called on to incorporate ESG, impact, and other sustainability-oriented approaches to financial services activities such as portfolio management. The problem is that many don't know where to start.

We'll go into more depth later on about the role of academia and, particularly, the incorporation of sustainability into higher education and business programs. There is, however, an urgent need for practitioner-level education. Limited on time and working in a market that's increasingly fast-paced, financial service professionals need tools that enable them to get up to speed quickly on sustainability-oriented terminology, techniques, and financial products.

Fortunately, there are a growing range of resources available oriented toward tackling this problem. One of the organizations most active in this space is Intentional Media, a family of event, media, and now education brands working to enable the transition of our economy to what they refer to as a "blended finance" approach.

Intentional Media has many goals for its various businesses, but skilling-up financial service professionals' sustainable finance capability is a key area of focus. With the aim of "building capability one fund manager at a time", it is developing a Blended Finance Institute to develop the thought leadership and curriculum required to accelerate the flow of private capital toward the SDGs. At present, this initiative includes a series of convenings, workshops, and digital content to increase awareness and adoption of blended finance concepts. One particularly pertinent one is a Total Impact Portfolio series, targeted at financial advisors, now with nine sessions running annually.

Another important learning source is more forward-thinking actors already within the financial services industry. There are a growing number of online and offline tools available for financial professionals to get up to speed, several of which are offered by financial services firms. The PRI (Principles for Responsible Investment) Academy is, of course, a leading provider of practitioner training on ESG; ratings agency Fitch offers ESG training via its learning division; and leading sustainable finance investment firm Robeco SAM launched Robeco Sustainable Investing Essentials, delivered via an e-learning platform.

Sustainability and ESG: yes, it's your job

Even if fund managers increase their sustainability and ESG capabilities, it is also imperative that they take on the responsibility of integrating these principles into their investment strategies. There needs to be a broader realization that ESG isn't a concept that should just be a priority of the sustainability or CSR department. It should, rather, be present across the activities of the organization.

Leading global banking group BNP Paribas is taking a proactive approach to change the mindset and, as a result, investment approach of its portfolio managers. Mark Lewis, BNP Paribas' Global Head of Sustainability Research, elaborated on this at the 2019 TCFD (Task Force on Climate-related Financial Disclosures) Summit in Tokyo:

> The real challenge is to get the portfolio managers themselves to take over this role from ESG teams. By integrating ESG into your entire portfolio, that does put the onus on them. So what we are doing from next year is that every portfolio manager will be under two constraints that they've never been under before. This is the mainstream, not just the SRI [Socially Responsible Investing] funds, dedicated SRI funds that we run, but all portfolios across all asset class.
>
> Number one, every portfolio will have to have a better ESG score than the benchmark against which they're being measured. Now, clearly, that gives fund managers a great incentive to engage with companies where they like the company, but if we in the sustainability center give it a low score on ESG, that's going to impact their ability to hold that stock. So it's in their interest to engage with companies. I think integrating ESG is actually a very powerful way of putting the mainstream fund managers in that role. And then the second constraint they will be under is that every portfolio will have to have a lower carbon footprint than the benchmark they're being measured against. So that also gives them a very specific incentive to deal with the carbon footprint of companies that they would like to invest in [even though] that might be difficult for them at the moment.[41]

Financial product innovation

One issue that is often raised about ESG funds and other financial products is that their associated fees (paid by investors) are often higher than those of traditional investments. One could make an argument that identifying and screening the underlying assets within ESG funds, for example, requires a higher degree of research, due diligence, and analysis. Thus, higher fees would be justified. However, this creates yet another barrier for investors. ESG and other sustainable finance-related products ultimately need to be more competitive price-wise in order to draw in a larger pool of investors.

To tackle this problem, more financial innovation beyond a select set of funds and green bonds is sorely needed. A forward-looking fund manager that we met in Hong Kong told us that when it comes to globally-themed funds, it is hard to differentiate yourself from the bulk of other funds out there. The majority of such funds today play it safe by following index funds and market selection themes that track with large outfits such as BlackRock or Fidelity.

Today, that means that everyone is chasing ESG. In the Hong Kong manager's mind, the only thing to do as a stock picker that wants to take a unique approach to the market that can outperform competitors is to ignore all such indexes and themes, even around ESG, and instead personally design a social-impact-style open fund that is focused on solutions that advance the SDGs. Our interviews confirm that there is an evident demand for such focused funds, given the general consensus about the need for more financial product innovation.

In our view, SDG funds are the next, logical step in sustainable finance innovation. These types of investment products are still very much in their infancy, but are starting to pop up in the market. One example is London-based Hermes Fund Managers (now a part of US investment management firm Federated Investors). It launched the Federated Hermes SDG Engagement Equity Fund (ticker: FHESX), which includes investments in small and mid-cap companies whose activities are aligned to the SDGs. Another example is a recently launched ETF by Sustainalytics and Morningstar (ticker: SDGA) which includes publicly listed companies that have strong policies and practices regarding the SDGs and are actively engaged in the world's poorest countries.

Integration of sustainable finance principles in business education

We often like to say that business leaders didn't come out of the womb believing that a business's principal role is to maximize shareholder value. This was a concept that was learned, and really only since the early 1970s.

It was in fact, academia that has shaped how most business leaders think. And, more specifically, the MBA programs that grew in applications and enrollments in leaps and bounds throughout the second half of the twentieth century before slowing in recent years. Irrespective of whether business leaders are learning the concepts that form the foundation of modern business from an MBA program, as undergraduate students, or from a massive open online course (MOOC), the commonly accepted "rules of business" remain the same. If we want to encourage a change in how companies operate, we need to start with changing how we train young (and not-so-young) people to operate companies.

There is some evidence that academia is starting to wise up to the need to reorient business education toward sustainability concepts. This is perhaps most evident in subjects such as innovation or marketing, where responding to consumer needs and desires is a focal point. However, finance education needs a rehaul as well.

This is of course not limited to the classroom. Academia plays a fundamental role in developing the frameworks and methodologies that underpin business best practice. Fortunately, leading institutions around the world are starting to scale up their efforts on incorporating sustainability in their business programs and research efforts–NYU Stern, Cornell, Kellogg, INSEAD, Wharton, Stanford, and many others have launched sustainability or social innovation institutes; business sustainability courses have become much more commonplace in leading business masters programs—HEC Paris has a Master of Sustainability and Social Innovation and Bard College offers an MBA in Sustainability.

We'd like to see these institutions go even further, integrating sustainability as a core concept across all disciplines and, particularly, in finance, where more research is needed on the financial health of and market outcomes for companies adopting sustainable business models. There are now an abundance of alternatives in online courses and certificate programs that are widely available for those looking to learn, yet established academic institutions still need to do the intellectual heavy lifting to provide the much-needed research, frameworks, and methodologies that business leaders, investors, and others will use as organizations shift toward sustainable business models.

Putting sustainability front and center in annual reports

Most large companies now publish sustainability reports. In some markets producing this report was the result of an explicit decision of the management to do so, while in others it was as a result of regulation or government mandate. It is positive that this report has become such an important priority for companies. However, we'd argue that it isn't important enough.

The push for sustainability reports was incredibly important at a time when the topic of sustainability didn't figure on most companies' list of priorities, particularly during the pre-SDG period. However, now that it has risen to the top of the agenda for businesses of all shapes and sizes, the sustainability report itself shouldn't be viewed as a bonus for companies, but rather a minimum requirement.

We're entering a period where it is more important than ever for organizations to demonstrate substantive action on implementing sustainable business practices. Sustainability should, in essence, sit at the core of any organization's vision and strategy. Thus, it is in the annual report and quarterly reports where sustainability should be featured more prominently. These are the documents investors look at to get a sense of the health and priorities of a company. If sustainability is such an important topic for businesses, why wouldn't they take steps to ensure that it's front and center in their main vehicles for communicating to the investment community?

Move on from short-termism

This is where we started our discussion about finance. There is perhaps no single issue within our financial system that discourages adoption of sustainable business models than this.

As companies are pushed to prioritize ESG and integrate it into the way they do business, their investors also need to give them the time to do so. While governance topics are largely in company management's control, it is very challenging for them to align and adjust their activities and processes to act on, for example, the SDGs, with a short-term approach.

There are many working to move the needle on this, including the European Union, which continues to examine how to develop a sustainable finance system that takes a longer-term view, and the Natural Capital Finance Alliance, which helps financial institutions understand the role they play in transitioning toward sustainable economic growth. We are still in a period of great experimentation in regard to assessing the quantitative and qualitative impact on both corporate bottom lines and society of sustainability strategies.

Over time, businesses will get better at operating within this new paradigm, and the business case for sustainability will be undeniable. In fact, in our view the COVID-19 crisis is likely to accelerate the shift away from short-termism. Investors are going to need to stick with companies through this transitional period, and reward them accordingly.

Notes

1 Ned Davis Research (2016), NYSE Average Holding Periods, 1929–2016 Chart. Retrieved from https://topforeignstocks.com/2017/10/01/average-stock-holding-period-on-nyse-1929-to-2016/.
2 Conducted by Research Plus. Commissioned by Schroders (2017). Global Investor Study 2017: Investor behavior from priorities to expectations, 12. Retrieved from www.schroders.com/en/sysglobalassets/digital/insights/2017/pdf/global-investor-study-2017/theme2/schroders_report-2__eng_master.pdf.
3 US Internal Revenue Service (2020). Topic no. 409: Capital gains and losses. Retrieved from www.irs.gov/taxtopics/tc409.
4 Barton, D., Manyika, J., Palter, R., Godsall, J., and Zoffer, J. (2017). Measuring the economic impact of short-termism. *McKinsey Global Institute*, 2, 6. Retrieved from www.mckinsey.com/~/media/mckinsey/featured%20insights/Long%20term%20Capitalism/Where%20companies%20with%20a%20long%20term%20view%20outperform%20their%20peers/MGI-Measuring-the-economic-impact-of-short-termism.ashx.
5 Shin, T., and You, J. (2017). Pay for talk: How the use of shareholder-value language affects CEO compensation. *Journal of Management Studies*. Retrieved from www.wsj.com/articles/the-two-words-that-earn-ceos-a-pay-raise-1478622713.
6 Mittleman, M. (2018). Private equity wants you to feel good about investing. *Bloomberg*. Retrieved from www.bloomberg.com/news/articles/2018-04-10/private-equity-wants-you-to-feel-good-about-investing.
7 Conducted by CoreData Research. Commissioned by Natixis Investment Managers (2019). Report: Looking for the best of both worlds, investors turn to ESG to fulfill personal values and performance expectations. *Global Survey of Financial Professionals*, 1, 4. Retrieved from www.im.natixis.com/en-hk/resources/esg-investing-survey-2019.
8 Business Roundtable (2019). Business Roundtable redefines the purpose of a corporation to promote "an economy that serves all Americans". Press release. Retrieved from www.businessroundtable.org/business-roundtable-redefines-the-purpose-of-a-corporation-to-promote-an-economy-that-serves-all-americans.
9 Holger, D. (2019). What generation is leading the way in ESG investing? You'll be surprised. *Wall Street Journal*. Retrieved from www.wsj.com/articles/what-generation-is-leading-the-way-in-esg-investing-youll-be-surprised-11568167440.

10 Niculescu, M. (2017). Impact investment to close the SDG funding gap. UNDP Europe and Central Asia. Retrieved from www.undp.org/content/undp/en/home/blog/2017/7/13/What-kind-of-blender-do-we-need-to-finance-the-SDGs-.html.

11 Wilson, G.E.R. (2019). 4 key ways countries can finance their SDG ambitions. Global Future Council on Development Finance. Retrieved from www.weforum.org/agenda/2019/04/sdgs-sustainable-development-4-ways-countries-finance/.

12 GIIN (Global Impact Investing Network) (n.d.). What you need to know about impact investing. Retrieved from https://thegiin.org/impact-investing/need-to-know/#s7.

13 GIIN (2018). Sizing the impact investing market, 11. Retrieved from https://the giin.org/assets/Sizing%20the%20Impact%20Investing%20Market_webfile.pdf.

14 Elkington, J. (2018). 25 years ago I coined the phrase "Triple Bottom Line". Here's why it's time to rethink it. *Harvard Business Review*. Retrieved from https://hbr.org/2018/06/25-years-ago-i-coined-the-phrase-triple-bottom-line-heres-why-im-giving-up-on-it.

15 Friedman, M. (1970). The social responsibility of business is to increase its profits. *New York Times Magazine*. Retrieved from http://umich.edu/~thecore/doc/Friedman.pdf.

16 Social Enterprise UK, supported by Nationwide and Co-op Group (2018). The hidden revolution. Retrieved from www.socialenterprise.org.uk/policy-and-research-reports/the-hidden-revolution/.

17 Bosma, N., Schøtt, T., Terjesen, S., and Kew, P. (2016). Global Entrepreneurship Monitor: Special report on social entrepreneurship, 32. Retrieved from www.gemconsortium.org/report/gem-2015-report-on-social-entrepreneurship.

18 European Commission, Directorate-General for Employment, Social Affairs and Inclusion (2016). Mapping study on social enterprise eco-systems: Updated country report on Italy, 42. Retrieved from https://ec.europa.eu/social/BlobServlet?docId=16380&langId=en.

19 Ganesh, U., Menon, V., Kaushal, A., Kumar, K., and Bertelsmann Stiftung (2018). The Indian social enterprise landscape: Innovation for an inclusive future, 16. Retrieved from www.bertelsmann-stiftung.de/fileadmin/files/user_upload/201810_The_Indian_Social_Enterprise_Landscape_Study_EN.pdf.

20 Emerson, J. (2018). BV Framework. Blended Value. Retrieved from www.blendedvalue.org/framework/.

21 Emerson, J. (2000). The nature of returns: A social capital markets inquiry into elements of investment and the Blended Value proposition, 27, 38. Retrieved from www.blendedvalue.org/wp-content/uploads/2004/02/pdf-nature-of-returns.pdf.

22 Addy, C., Chorengel, M., Collins, M., and Etzel, M. (2019). Calculating the value of impact investing. *Harvard Business Review*, 102–109. Retrieved from https://hbr.org/2019/01/calculating-the-value-of-impact-investing.

23 Emerson, J. (2019). *The Purpose of Capital: Elements of Impact, Financial Flows, and Natural Being.* Blended Value Group Press, page 11.

24 MetaMark Learning (2015). Where do financial statements come from? Retrieved from www.metamarklearning.com/where-do-the-financial-statements-the-balance-sheet-the-income-statement-and-the-cash-flow-statement-come-from/.

25 Higson, C. (2013). The cult of EBITDA depreciation is probably the most misunderstood number in accounting. *London Business School Review*. Retrieved from www.london.edu/lbsr/the-cult-of-ebitda.

26 GIIN (2018). Sizing the impact investing market, 6. Retrieved from https://the giin.org/assets/Sizing%20the%20Impact%20Investing%20Market_webfile.pdf.

27 Comtois, J. (2019). Preqin: Private equity AUM grows 20 percent in 2017 to record $3.06 trillion. *Pensions & Investments*. Retrieved from www.pionline.com/article/20180724/ONLINE/180729930/preqin-private-equity-aum-grows-20-in-2017-to-record-3-06-trillion.
28 Chasan, E. (2019). Global sustainable investments rise 34 percent to $30.7 trillion. Bloomberg. Retrieved from www.bloomberg.com/professional/blog/global-sustainable-investments-rise-34-30-7-trillion/.
29 Calvert Impact Capital (2019). About us. Retrieved from www.calvertimpactcapital.org/about.
30 Kronthal-Sacco, R., and Whelan, T. (2019). Sustainable Share Index: Research on IRI purchasing data (2013–2018). NYU Stern Center for Sustainable Business. Retrieved from www.stern.nyu.edu/experience-stern/about/departments-centers-initiatives/centers-of-research/center-sustainable-business/research/internal-research/sustainable-share-index.
31 Hirose, R., Maia, R., Martinez, A., and Thiel, A. (2015). Three myths about growth in consumer packaged goods. *McKinsey & Company—Our Insights*. Retrieved from www.mckinsey.com/industries/consumer-packaged-goods/our-insights/three-myths-about-growth-in-consumer-packaged-goods.
32 Ali, A., Bamberger, S., Bock, W., Farag, H., Forth, P., Green, A., Kennedy, D., Lind, F., and Zuckerman, N. (2019). Value creation amid turbulence: The 2019 TMT Value Creators Report. *BCG*. Retrieved from www.bcg.com/publications/2019/value-creation-amid-uncertainty-in-tmt-sector.aspx.
33 Forum for Sustainable and Responsible Investment (n.d.). Sustainable investing basics. Retrieved from www.ussif.org/sribasics.
34 US SIF and US SIF Foundation (2018). Report on US sustainable, responsible and impact investing trends, 1. Retrieved from www.ussif.org/files/Trends/Trends%202018%20executive%20summary%20FINAL.pdf.
35 Bioy, H., Stuart, E., and Boyadzhiev, D. (2019). European sustainable funds landscape. Morningstar. Retrieved from www.morningstar.com/blog/2019/09/19/esg-funds-europe.html.
36 Eurosif (2018). European SRI study, 6. Retrieved from www.eurosif.org/wp-content/uploads/2018/11/European-SRI-2018-Study.pdf.
37 Bank of America (2016). Environmental, Social & Governance Report. Retrieved from https://about.bankofamerica.com/assets/pdf/Bank-of-America-2016-ESG-Summary-Report.pdf.
38 Katz, M. (2020). Research From BlackRock and Bank of America Shows ESG To Be Safe Haven in Market Storm. *Equity News*. Retrieved from https://www.equities.com/news/research-from-blackrock-and-bank-of-america-shows-esg-to-be-safe-haven-in-market-storm.
39 Riel, J., and Martin, R.L. (2017). Creating great choices: A leader's guide to integrative thinking. *Harvard Business Review Press*. Retrieved from www.iedp.com/articles/integrative-thinking-revisited/.
40 Skapinker, M. (2018). Unilever's Paul Polman was a standout CEO of the past decade. *Financial Times*. Retrieved from www.ft.com/content/e7040df4-fa19-11e8-8b7c-6fa24bd5409c.
41 Based on authors' notes taken while attending the summit.
42 *Fast Company* (2019). The world's most innovative companies by sector. Retrieved from www.fastcompany.com/most-innovative-companies/2019/sectors/middle-east; Allyson Kapin (2019, February 20). 50 women-led startups that are crushing tech. *Forbes*. Retrieved from www.forbes.com/sites/allysonkapin/2019/02/20/50-women-led-startups-who-are-crushing-tech/#40a7dbd752b3.

Mission-driven vignette 3

ECOncrete

Bringing life to concrete

It is commonly accepted that climate change, coupled with unsustainable activities such as commercial overfishing and poor waste disposal that pollutes coastlines, oceans, and seas, is having a profound impact on biodiversity around the world. It's also causing a stark rise in sea levels, putting many coastal communities and large urban areas at risk. Despite this worrying phenomenon, governments and businesses continue to build along coastlines, further degrading ocean and sea biodiversity.

As a marine biologist by training, Shimrit Perkol-Finkel of ECOncrete is acutely aware of the bleak future that lies ahead for ocean ecosystems if this problem isn't addressed. As coastline development looks set to continue into the foreseeable future, Perkol-Finkel and co-founder Ido Sella thought that a solution could be found in the building materials themselves, most notably in concrete.

A whopping 70 percent of coastal infrastructure is concrete-based, creating a significant sustainability challenge for the world's coastlines. Why is this such a problem? Concrete's surface composition can be toxic to various marine larvae, impairing their settlement of coastal areas and harming the biodiversity around marine infrastructure. Concrete also has a large carbon footprint due to the use of fossil fuels in its production process and the large quantities of carbon released during calcination (the conversion of limestone to CaO, one of the main components of concrete).

Concrete also gives most coastline infrastructure a drab, lifeless look and, with no ecosystem-enhancing substances in its composition, it is not well adapted to nurturing the growth of natural habitats. ECOncrete set out to change all this by enabling concrete to play a more active role in encouraging the health of ecosystems while maintaining its critical, robust structural properties as a building material.

Figure 4.1 ECOncrete is set to revolutionize the approach to building coastal infrastructure.
Source: ECOncrete.

ECOncrete focused on innovating around three material, texture, and design aspects:

- *Concrete composition:* The company created a bio-enhancing admix, which uses by-products and recycled materials to enhance the growth of marine plants and animals. The unique composition also boosts biological processes such as photosynthesis, a process which aids in CO_2 assimilations, and bio-calcification, a process of assimilating carbon into marine organisms, including oysters, coral, coralline algae, tube worms, and barnacles.
- *Surface texture and design:* It developed products such as Armoring Units, modular building blocks of marine infrastructure. These units provide solid coastal defense against hydrodynamic forces, while also delivering a design that creates marine habitats, increasing the growth of marine flora and species richness, and the reduction of invasive species.
- *3D design:* This approach was an integral part of ensuring its products fit seamlessly into the natural habitat. Its 3D design approach has been incorporated into several products in its portfolio, including the Marine Mattress, which promotes shoreline stabilization and erosion control while also elevating biodiversity; eco-friendly designed tide pools which mimic natural rock pools; the Armoring Units; and enhanced sea walls.

Step-change innovations often come to sectors that are brand new, as information and communications technology (ICT) was once upon a time, or where consumers or customers are clamoring for change, such as finance. Sectors that are very conservative and reluctant to change, such as construction, are notoriously innovation-shy. For a start-up to enter this sector and deliver products with the potential to transform how developers, construction companies, and local governments approach coastline development is quite remarkable.

ECOncrete's work has not gone unnoticed by other key stakeholders, having won numerous awards from around the world and, most recently, the WE Empower UN SDG Challenge award.

With an impressive product portfolio and very small 2 to 7 percent price premium over traditional products, Perkol-Finkel is quite bullish on prospects for growth. However, she stresses that when it comes to the types of large-scale projects that she typically aims for, sustainability is still not the top priority for many potential customers. For coastal development efforts, a clear and strong regulatory framework is still critical to ensuring sustainability.

Still, ECOncrete is growing its installations and presence around the world. It is currently in 30 locations across six oceans, including in four US states, the United Kingdom, the Netherlands, Germany, France, Monaco, Hong Kong, and, of course, its home country of Israel. The company has ambitions to expand its footprint in Asia, where rapid coastline development is particularly prevalent.

Perkol-Finkel says that, from a regulatory perspective, Asia is actually moving in a very positive direction. China has stipulated that at least 35 percent of its coastline must be ecological and enhance biodiversity, and the adoption of eco-shorelines figures prominently in Hong Kong's 2030 plan.

ECOncrete's breakthrough approach has not gone unnoticed, as it received a swath of awards and accolades in 2019, including ranking No. 10 among *Fast Company*'s most innovative companies in the Middle East and No. 13 on *Forbes*' "50 Women-Led Start-Ups That Are Crushing Tech" list.[42]

5 The road to sustainability

Best practices for building organizational capabilities and driving implementation

The Sustainable Development Goals (SDGs) are a rallying cry that is inspiring organizations, particularly large ones, to act. Businesses have taken many positive steps toward aligning their current activities with these 17 goals, including in both their operational activities and their Corporate Social Responsibility (CSR) and philanthropic endeavors.

Alignment, however, isn't action. So how can businesses that have already started with such an alignment further embed their sustainability- or SDG-rooted strategies within their organizations and drive execution? And how can ones that haven't done this yet—as is the case in many companies—get going?

Here are some important lessons we learned about the challenges and pitfalls that businesses are encountering, and how they are overcoming them.

The road to sustainability: a journey, albeit an accelerated one

The journey toward achieving a sustainability business model will never be the same for any two organizations.

We can draw on best practices from market leaders of various industries, but we need to be aware that each organization's journey is distinct, influenced heavily by its company culture, people, context, financial situation, geography, goals, and history. One thing that all organizations should do, however, is understand where they are along this journey.

As mentioned earlier, we've identified five principal steps that organizations tend to proceed through as they make the transition (see Figure 5.1).

While Step 1, a Base-level Understanding, may seem like a "lightweight" one, many organizations can get stuck here. This can be due to a lack of awareness—and perhaps even a lack of desire to understand—among senior management, or an inability to come to a consensus on what sustainability means in the context of their organization and where they should focus first.

Often the biggest stumbling block is the mindset of "Sustainability = CSR = philanthropy", which makes it an optional, non-strategic activity. While some organizations use *CSR* and *sustainability* interchangeably, we think that *sustainability* better captures what we believe will emerge as the twenty-first-century business model, that being one that puts profit and purpose on an

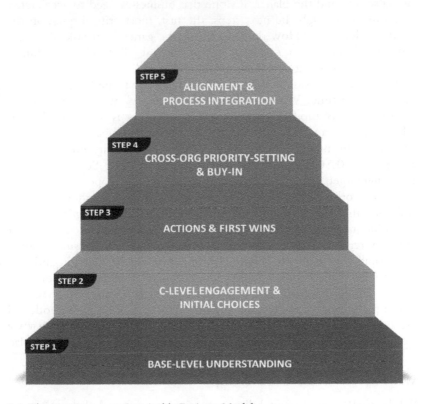

Figure 5.1 The Five Steps to a Sustainable Business Model.

equal footing. To drive organizational change, managers must see the challenges that sustainability addresses as *business critical* issues—not optional ones.

Outside of mission-driven organizations and sustainability "early adopter" multinational corporations or small or medium-sized enterprises (SMEs), most of the companies we spoke with in our research were at the second step we've identified. Many have aligned their current actions with the SDGs or other sustainability frameworks, diligently adhere to reporting requirements, and have set substantive business priorities regarding sustainability. They've also worked hard to get meaningful buy-in from senior leadership and other key stakeholders. Getting to Step 2 has required significant effort and dedication, particularly from those in sustainability roles.

However, this effort will likely pale in comparison to that for the company-wide change that will be required in steps 3 through 5 in order to truly make sustainability "business as usual" for organizations. Although we refer to this transformation as a journey, given the monumental challenges facing society and the planet, it's one that businesses need to accelerate.

To move through the next steps, the first, most critical question they will need to address is, "How do we manage the gargantuan task of transforming our organization into one that is capable—at all levels—of building and successfully managing a fully sustainable business?"

The concept of sustainability can be vague and is, perhaps, becoming even more so over time. While the term "sustainability" was almost never used in the early days of modern corporations, the concept is rooted in the notion of "doing good", and has evolved greatly over the years. What started out as corporate philanthropy evolved into CSR, then environmental, social, and governance (ESG), and now, arguably, the SDGs. So it's somewhat of a moving target, always evolving and broadening in scope.

Those working day in and day out in sustainability—often in departments and roles that are separate from other functions in the organization—are on a continuous learning curve. They may just "get" many elements intuitively, but they regularly have to figure out many others. The business discipline of sustainability is ever-evolving, and building out a breadth and depth of sustainability capability is a significant challenge for all organizations.

Still, though difficult, it's imperative to figure this out if we want to transform organizations toward sustainability-rooted business models. Before examining *how* to execute on the vision, we must understand what we need to do to build an organization that's capable of doing so in the first place.

Where it starts: bold leadership

While CSR and sustainability activities are often led by the best and brightest in the sustainability field, they are often too considered "important but non-business-critical". This positioning is beginning to shift, largely due to a significant change in the mindset of those at the senior most levels in organizations.

Champions of sustainable business models within the organization, such as CSR managers and heads of sustainability, have long been advocating for a fundamental transformation in how business operates. Today the significant challenges and risks facing society and, hence, all businesses, are finally starting to capture the C-suite's attention. As a result, their mindset is beginning to align with that of their sustainability champions.

Some CEOs have even viewed sustainability and the SDGs as non-negotiable realities for businesses. A powerful example is Yoshinori Yamashita, CEO of the imaging and electronics company Ricoh, who has boldly and repeatedly declared to customers, investors, and the company's own employees that:

It is in keeping with those tenets[1] and our embrace of the United Nations' Sustainable Development Goals ... that we are accelerating our drive to help materialize sustainability for societies around the world. I believe that helping to resolve social issues through business is vital to corporate prosperity. Companies that fail to help bring SDGs to fruition can never survive. We will accordingly endeavor to enhance our businesses and management from financial and from environmental, social, and governance perspectives.[2]

Isabelle Kocher, former CEO of Engie, struck a similar tone when she made her case for moving the leading French energy business toward a renewable energy model and extending her company's CSR ambitions throughout its supply chain. "Can a company ignore the overall impact of its activities and hide behind the pursuit of profit alone?" wrote Kocher in a recent article. "I believe that the fortress company model, deaf to the expectations of its wider environment, is doomed to disappear under the pressure exerted by four figures: the consumer, the employee, the regulator and the investor."[3]

Having strong support and active engagement from the C-suite is imperative if you want to see real change in adopting a sustainable business model. The SDGs are a very useful tool for heightening senior executives' awareness of the positive potential of adopting sustainable business models, and getting them to commit to concrete actions.

Not only have C-level (chief-officer-level) executives stepped up their commitment to sustainability internally, many have also engaged with advocacy groups to work together to change their industries. A key player in the fragrance and flavor industry offers us a strong example of this in action.

The leading fragrance and flavor company Givaudan rolled out a new approach to sustainability in 2017 called "A Sense of Tomorrow". Three main focus areas—Sourcing, Innovation, and Environment—address their most material topics, and contribute to the achievement of specific SDGs. To execute the strategy, and given the importance of Sourcing as part of its agenda, Givaudan decided to integrate procurement and sustainability under one Executive Committee member. This integration of sustainability within a core business function was still emerging in 2017, but is becoming more common now.

With strong support for its efforts from CEO Gilles Andrier, Givaudan sees strong stakeholder engagement as a key enabler of "A Sense of Tomorrow" and as a driver of change across the fragrance and flavor industry. It has stepped up engagement with various organizations, including the CEO-led World Business Council for Sustainable Development (WBCSD), which is galvanizing leaders across industries to take bold actions to transform their organizations.

In addition to the WBCSD, other high-profile stakeholders and industry associations are successfully leveraging the SDGs to engage senior executives.

Many sustainability executives we spoke with emphasized that a highly effective way to develop their CEO's and other C-suite leaders' thinking is to have their executives attend and become involved with United Nations (UN) or industry-led events and initiatives. Direct contact with peers that are pursuing these initiatives is the best way to create excitement around the concepts and opportunities, and make obvious the risks of not responding to changes in the market and their own industry. If organizations are looking to get started in their transition or move to the next stage, these types of C-level engagement opportunities are an important place to start.

Even if C-level leadership has laid out a clear vision with sustainability at the core, these leaders need to ensure the whole organization is engaged and committed to the strategy. This should ring true in good times as well as more challenging ones. For example, if the CEO has laid out a plan to transition to a sustainable business model, does the organization still put profits before purpose and abandon the plan if it has a difficult quarter?

Yui Isogai, a partner at PwC, says:

> We often say that sustainability is important, and this is our purpose, but on the other hand when purpose and profitability are in 'conflict' and management then says that profitability is more important, people get a different message on the ground.
>
> If management says sustainability is important but when they take actual decisions they prioritize profitability, the whole message collapses. This may happen because, often, senior management believes in this purpose and they, perhaps, haven't properly shared this vision with middle management, and middle management, in turn, chooses profitability. This ultimately discourage junior employees. Consistent messaging out from senior management to middle management to junior levels is extremely important.

Clear strategic choices: the enabler of success

We often think of the most successful organizations as those that build the best-designed products or bring new innovations to market that "change the world". But the businesses that "win" are usually the ones that do one thing particularly well: make clear, strategic choices. This is more easily said than done.

Being decisive requires leaders to make difficult choices, namely which activities or initiatives to stop, as well as which exciting ones to start. In the short term, such decisions can cause discomfort and anxiety within an organization. A good leader can effectively tackle this head-on and properly prepare his or her organization for the change to come. Though difficult, clear decisions are necessary, particularly when you are taking the organization in an ambitious new direction.

When transitioning toward a sustainable business model, decisiveness around strategic choices is imperative. Sustainability can feel vague to those outside of the field. Today, sustainability is integrated only marginally in key functions such as marketing, accounting, operations, finance, and human resources. Employees are often unsure of how actions focused on sustainability will impact their day-to-day jobs or how a sustainable business model could offer new opportunities for their organization.

Such uncertainty can deter organizations from pursuing a more progressive business path. Furthermore, while the SDGs have proven motivational for companies, there aren't just a couple of goals in a nice single-digit number; there are a full 17! Though it's not necessary that organizations act on all 17, at least in the short term, the sheer number of goals and ambition of the 2030 Agenda can seem overwhelming for many organizations. This is why it is important for leaders to break down their vision into a few concrete and coherent decisions that will inspire their employees and drive action.

Coca-Cola has been steadily moving in a more sustainable direction for some years. When one thinks of the world's best-known beverage maker, the red-label brand Coke is likely the first thing that pops into most people's minds. However, there's a significant shift underway in the evolution of the company's portfolio. From water and water technology to plant-based drinks including coffee and teas, Coca-Cola has been moving toward a more sustainable "total beverage portfolio" model as championed by CEO and Chairman James Quincey. This shift in its portfolio isn't only about offering consumers more options, it's also about addressing the rising health concerns faced by consumers around the world.

"We are a consumer-centric company, and it's the consumer that is changing consumer behavior," says Jennifer Ragland, Coca-Cola Senior Director for Government & Stakeholder Relations.

> There's a diversification underway, such as functional beverages and blends and all these different varieties that consumers are demanding. There's a lot of variability or kinds of variants when it comes to people's preferences, and there is also a desire to reduce sugar. So we're adapting to that.

As a result, Coca-Cola has made it a priority to address the sugar content in its brands and, more recently, took the positive step of supporting the World Health Organization's recommendation that people limit the consumption of added sugars to 10 percent of their daily caloric intake. To date, the company has reformulated more than 700 of its brands around the world and is using smaller bottle sizes and "mini and sleek cans" to support this strategy to support "portion control".

These moves are a great example of leadership communicating its purpose to the organization. Quincey, for example, explains the smaller size as being a return to the original idea of Coca-Cola being a "treat" for special moments. As a result, Coca-Cola employees can easily relate to and act on the decisive, understandable decisions by the company's leaders to diversify its portfolio and reformulate its beverages in direct response to changes in consumer needs and beverage choices.

In an even more striking move, Sekisui House, one of Japan's leading home builders, embarked on a fully sustainable business strategy years before many firms. Following the global financial crisis in 2008, which caused a sharp decline in the company's operating margins, Sekisui House's management decided to completely remove carbon from the housing lifecycle by 2050. The decision meant a shift away from the standard approach to building homes in Japan to an almost exclusive focus on building "green homes".

"We wanted to be preventative, not just responsive," said Dr. Kenichi Ishida, Sekisui House's Managing Officer of the environment promotion division at the Japan Climate Action Summit in October 2018.

> Our aim is to make our customers happy, namely end users— homeowners, by working to understand and respond to their needs. For our company, this means reducing carbon emissions and energy use and developing homes that can respond to the challenges of a 4 degree world.

Later, at the company's Tokyo branch office in Akasaka, Ishida explained that Sekisui's leadership believed there was such a significant consumer demand for green homes that it could sell them at the premium price required to recoup costs for the superior materials and design. Sekisui quickly started implementing its business new strategy in 2009 with a "Green First" model and, by 2018, 79 percent of newly built units were based on their Zero Energy Home (ZEH) concept.[4]

The choice, and the company's aggressive follow-through, have paid off big time for the firm. Sekisui consolidated its leadership position in Japan, expanded abroad in the United States and Australia, tripled its operating margins to 9 percent from 2009 to 2017, saw the rate of "very satisfied" customers grow by 10 percent, achieved a CO_2 emission rate reduction in newly built homes of 43 percent in 2009 and reaching 82 percent in 2018, and received a coveted spot in the highly regarded Dow Jones Sustainability Indices (DJSI) World Index, which designated it as the world's highest-rated company in the home building category.

Companies that decide to shift toward a sustainable business model need to be prepared to make tough choices. From what we've observed, organizations that view sustainability as an opportunity rather than something that should be relegated to risk management are best positioned for success. Leaders in these types of organizations understand that their future is inextricably linked to society's progress. For them, this makes making challenging decisions a non-negotiable necessity.

A systematic approach to building sustainability capability

Building capability around sustainability requires a systematic approach, as does any other business discipline. It would be unheard of for a marketing novice with no training or experience to design and execute a brand plan, or for an accounting intern to audit the finances of a major, long-standing client. The discipline of sustainability is the same in our view. If we're going to build capability, being systematic is absolutely necessary.

Organizational strategy expert Gilda Sala, who has worked with several organizations for whom sustainability plays a big role, underscores the systematic approach. Sala says that:

> If you really want to drive sustainability within organizations and for people to implement this, you need well-defined, understandable Key Performance Indicators (KPIs). You need to train people. It needs to be approached in a systematic way. The reality is, not many companies are actually doing this.

She also notes, though, that there actually is a fairly clear, systematic way that sustainability moves through organizations which we've illustrated here (Figure 5.2).

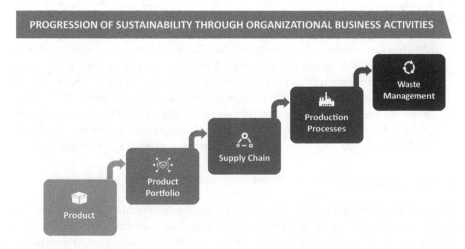

Figure 5.2 Progression of sustainability through organizational business activities.

Activities like CSR and philanthropy are almost always an organization's first foray into tackling societal challenges. If they are sincere in their intent, inevitably all of them realize that to succeed in their goals, they must integrate sustainability into their operations as well. Sala's framing of this evolution is helpful for making businesses recognize that they should tackle whatever they can manage first, that "limited set off their portfolios or business lines." For most companies, this translates to a first eco or sustainable product or group of products to test the waters before extending the approach to their broader portfolio of products or services.

As one moves up the diagram, the picture becomes more complex. In the step of "Supply Chain," there are often innumerable processes and, in the case of large organizations, suppliers. Adding to this complexity, every supplier providing any product inputs or other services to the business needs to be examined, not just principal or direct suppliers.

In our opinion, this can also be a useful way of thinking about where you can start first to prepare your organization for this transition. It gives us a way of honing in, for example, on which stakeholders should be involved, which business processes needed to be adjusted, what specific activities need to be started or sunsetted, or who needs to be trained and in what. There are innumerable processes and business activities that need to be adjusted to make this transformation a success. Understanding how an organization approaches this in terms of business activities makes it easier to plan properly and put in place a phased approach for building organizational capabilities.

While taking a systematic approach is key to embedding sustainability capability within organizations, "bringing everyone along" with the change is critically important. "When thinking about how to embed sustainability capability, it is important to take a structural approach—having the right KPIs, reporting lines, and governance systems," emphasizes PwC's Isogai.

> At the same time, these systems can be ineffective and empty if you don't sufficiently engage employees. You need to engage everyone, at all levels of the organization. However, many large companies have tens of thousands of employees, which can make this task very difficult. So, you need to create changemakers to cascade it down to different areas and, ultimately, individuals within the organization. Ensuring everyone understands and can convey the same vision and message is important.

Build an "A team"

Most of the companies we interviewed for this book readily admitted that one of the biggest challenges in moving their businesses toward sustainability is in skilling up their workforces to take on this significant challenge. As previously discussed, most large organizations have highly skilled CSR or sustainability departments. Sustainability-focused team members are highly knowledgeable about the field and well connected into the expanding professional community.

But we believe that those parts of the organization are generally too small and, often, detached from other functions within the business.

To drive success, businesses need to figure out how to generalize knowledge about sustainability across their organizations. Having champions that can encourage—and even inspire others to wholeheartedly join the effort—is essential to driving any change management program. But how do organizations find and build talent that will be able to execute the increasingly ambitious sustainable strategies championed by the C-suite?

When it comes to driving a sustainability program, a topic with which employees in businesses of all sizes are typically unfamiliar, you are unlikely to experience success by appointing someone to be the champion just "because it's their time", or for some other commonplace reason that companies give to assign roles. Because sustainability, a relatively new field, still has many vague elements, the best way forward is to let your potential employees come to you: Interest rather than extensive experience should be the priority for hiring these types of roles.

This is how Jeff Turner came to his role as Vice President of Sustainability at DSM, the Dutch-based multinational nutrition, health, and sustainable-living business that has sites in more than 40 countries. Roughly 10 years ago, the CEO of DSM, Feike Sijbesma, recognizing the need to change direction after a discussion with the humanitarian organization World Food Programme, directed senior leadership at the parent company to communicate to each business that it was required to appoint a head of sustainability.

Turner was Head of Strategy for one of DSM's business units when he heard the new directive. He says,

> I immediately put my hand up on the basis that I felt my role, my contribution to business, was to take care of all of the intangible value in the business. And I saw sustainability as a key contributor to this intangible value of the business.
>
> I recognized that your tangible contribution to society, contribution to the environment, could translate into huge intangible value in terms of what your brand stands for, what your organization is capable of.

Ten years on, Turner is Vice President of Sustainability for the organization, and DSM is seen as one of the leading large businesses on the topic of sustainability.

Finding talent: a wealth of sustainability-focused education

You will soon recognize that many of the people who will be tasked with building and managing the sustainable businesses of the future have yet to join your company. The good news is that many younger people, who desire to work for sustainable companies at much higher numbers than ever before, already have the mindset, motivation, and passion for sustainability to drive real value once they join businesses.

More, too, are being exposed to the concepts behind sustainability than ever before. Various initiatives are introducing sustainability as a fundamental value to youth around the world. For 15 years during the application of the Millennium Development Goals, UNESCO supported the incorporation of sustainability with its Education for Sustainable Development (ESD) program, which was implemented at all age levels in schools across every region internationally.

UNESCO promoted ESD to empower "learners to take informed decisions and responsible actions for environmental integrity, economic viability and a just society, for present and future generations, while respecting cultural diversity".[5] The goal was to raise a generation of citizens that would contribute to society from a position that fundamentally viewed all their actions from the perspective of sustainability.

In the United States, four career educators have launched TeachSDGs, a promising initiative designed to build awareness of the SDGs and sustainability via project-based learning that starts from an elementary-school level. The TeachSDGs team expressly encourages teachers to be active participants in the effort and empower their students to take action on the goals, in order to further expand knowledge of the SDGs.

Technology is a powerful tool for TeachSDGs to achieve the organization's goals, and the group explores technologies that can be catalysts for teachers and students to accelerate and succeed in their efforts. "We partner with a lot of educational technology companies, because they seem to be the groups that are highly motivated to find ways to bring the global goals to classrooms," says Jennifer Williams, co-founder of TeachSDGs. "At the elementary level, educators are seeking ways to use technology to support students to take action on the goals. So they'll have them create digital stories, or they'll use video conferencing."

One group that Williams is working with, Empatico, is a digital platform from the nonprofit arm of Kind Snacks, a healthy treats brand. The relationship is mutually beneficial, with one side offering technological know-how and receiving in exchange insights on sustainability. Williams explains,

> Empatico have a goal of connecting one million elementary students by the year 2020 through video conferencing, all around the topic of empathy. They have a growing number of lessons, and we're starting with 150 global educators, with a goal of getting 3,500 educators by 2020. And then they've taken the lessons, through working with members of TeachSDGs, and they've aligned them to the goals.

The topic of sustainability has also quickly moved up the agenda of the world's leading bachelor's- and master's-level degree programs. Recognizing that leaders of the future, whether they be in fields such as business, science, education, or healthcare, will need to grapple with the many challenges highlighted by the SDGs, universities around the world are offering more courses focused on sustainability in the business context, and some are even offering sustainability-focused business degrees at both the undergraduate and master's degree levels. To develop the frameworks and methodologies that business managers will inevitably need to incorporate sustainability into their strategy and operations, universities are investing in institutes and research centers to expand research in this important area. Some notable examples are Oxford University's Sustainable Finance program, New York University's Stern Center for Sustainable Business, Cornell University's Center for Global Sustainable Enterprise, and Stanford's Center for Sustainable Development & Global Competitiveness.

While we see many of the world's leading institutions building sustainability-oriented courses, programs, and research centers, organizations may want to consider looking beyond the usual suspects in higher education to other institutions that have sustainability deeply ingrained in their DNA from the start.

The Asian University for Women (AUW) is one such institution. AUW was opened just over ten years ago in Chittagong, Bangladesh to provide talented young women from developing countries with access to high-quality, university-level liberal arts education. The school also provides pre-college education programs, including a much-heralded Pathways to Promise program that is aimed at young women from difficult backgrounds who would otherwise not have had access to higher education, such as garment factory workers. (See the sidebar "Access to high-quality education is creating a generation of female leadership from emerging markets" for more on AUW's story.)

Access to high-quality education is creating a generation of female leadership from emerging markets

Currently led by Vice Chancellor Professor Nirmala Rao, OBE, FAcSS, the Asian University for Women (AUW) has emerged as a formidable institution. In the two years since joining the school, Professor Rao has overseen student enrollment as it has grown from 520 women scholars to 990, increased the range of subjects and degrees offered to include fields such as bioinformatics and finance, extended their outreach to more underserved communities such as the Rohingya refugees, and put in place a governance structure needed to ensure the university's long-term growth ambitions and delivery of top-notch education to students.

As a result, AUW continues to graduate increasingly impressive future leaders, with many going off to master's- and Ph.D.-level programs at world-renowned universities, including Oxford, Columbia, Stanford, and the University of London. And, perhaps most importantly, the knowledge and experiences many of the young women gain at AUW and abroad comes back to their home countries, cities, and towns, ultimately a win for both the women and their home communities.

Businesses see AUW as a key institution for future talent, with organizations such as Goldman Sachs, Abbott, IKEA Foundation, MetLife, Takeda Pharmaceuticals, Marriott, and Uniqlo providing scholarships and financial support, hosting internships, and beginning, as well, to offer full-time employment.

By looking at organizations such as AUW, companies can identify well-educated and highly capable talent that can become employees who bring the added life experience of tackling—first-hand, on a daily basis—the sustainability challenges that the SDGs aim to address. As AUW's Professor Rao says, "We strive to find and develop the talent and promise among young women from communities that are by-passed. AUW gives the wide access to education to women who otherwise wouldn't have any education at all."

With this background and support, graduates of AUW can offer companies valuable insights and real-world experience as they look to move to more sustainable business models.

Lifelong learning will also be a strong element of practicing sustainability. Companies, particularly multinationals, dedicate substantial resources every year to training and capability development programs for topics such as marketing, project management, strategy, leadership, and business planning. It is imperative that sustainability-related topics, including frameworks, case studies, and tools for measurement and application, be added to the mix. However, knowledge and best practices in the field are continuously evolving, and without many generally agreed standards and frameworks for success in the field yet, there's room for even more major changes to come. Companies will need to identify platforms that can offer their employees opportunities to regularly update their skills in this area and adapt their work as required.

Fortunately, there are a growing number of entities, including the UN Global Compact, the UN University, online learning platform edX, and many others, who are offering a regular stream of content and, in some cases, online tools to help employees hone their skills. Companies will want to find ways to repackage this content and pull in other learnings they've gained along the way to identify knowledge- and capability-building approaches that best suit their organization.

The secret sauce: a multi-stakeholder approach

As mentioned earlier in this book, if you haven't already moved to do a stakeholder-focused materiality assessment, we strongly recommend that you consider doing so. Not only does a materiality assessment help organizations to identify the sustainability-related business issues most germane to their business, performing one also requires organizations by definition to take a stakeholder approach, where they may not have before.

Companies do not operate in isolation. They are, rather, a part of much larger systems, with connections to and responsibilities for numerous stakeholders. Understanding how such stakeholders value sustainability-related business issues and, more precisely, how the value that they apply internally differs from your own organization's will be integral to the success of any sustainability strategy you opt to pursue. Once you understand this, you can hone in on areas where your values align or identify engagement strategies to bring your closest stakeholders around to support your vision. Performing your materiality assessment in this way may be challenging, but the success of any sustainability plan will hinge on your external partners almost to an equal degree as your internal ones.

Danish pharmaceutical giant Novo Nordisk has long taken a multi-stakeholder approach. Well known as an early adopter of a sustainability-driven business model, it is a best-in-class example of how clear vision and stakeholder collaboration can produce positive results across the internal and external business system.

Deeply incorporating sustainability in its business decisions and strategy, Novo Nordisk is acutely aware of the importance of partners in putting its strategy into action. Vice President of Corporate Sustainability Susanne Stormer emphasizes the value to her organization thus:

> When we make investment decisions, such as where to build a new factory, we do add in environmental and social concerns. We ask important questions such as 'Is there access to water? Can they reasonably expect to get renewable energy? Or health and safety? How will we contribute to the local economy?' We know that we cannot deal with these issues on our own. Wicked problems[6] require a systematic approach and skilled competencies that not one company would have on their own.

Novo Nordisk has not only succeeded in connecting with like-minded organizations to deliver impactful solutions for patients around the world, but it has also made it possible for organizations within its realm to evolve more quickly on their sustainability journey as well. In 2007 the company embarked on an ambitious partnership with the Danish energy supplier Ørsted—one of the first of its kind—to enable businesses to commit to energy savings and investments in clean energy. Both were key objectives of Novo Nordisk.

When it first entered into the partnership, Ørsted had a split of 85 percent to 15 percent between energy generated by fossil fuel and by renewable sources. Novo Nordisk's commitment to buying capacity from Ørsted's Horns Rev 2 offshore wind farm inspired the energy company to transition to producing electricity exclusively from renewable sources, aiming to be "carbon free" by 2020. Their collaboration not only inspired other Danish firms to change their own energy consumption, but has also resulted in impressive results for both companies, including:[7]

- Novo Nordisk's energy consumption at its Danish factories has decreased by more than 20 percent over the past ten years.
- The company has reduced its energy bill by DKK 270 million ($42.3 million).
- Energy efficiency measures put in place by the partnership have reduced carbon emissions by 200,000 metric tons of CO_2, an amount that is equivalent to the annual CO_2 emissions of 220,000 Danish households.

The Ørsted collaboration is just one example of many initiatives in which Novo Nordisk has engaged to deliver on the priorities and objectives that it set for itself. With the SDGs coming online, the company anticipates that stakeholder engagement and collaboration will become even more critical. Executing any business strategy that integrates sustainability requires involvement from a range of stakeholders, including those that may not seem relevant at first glance. A multi-stakeholder approach is, quite simply, the only one that positions companies for success.

Collective industry action, too, can have a significant impact. A successful example of this in action is the Higg Index from the Sustainable Apparel Coalition, a suite of tools that enables players in the apparel sector to accurately measure and score their sustainability performance. Initially championed by two unlikely allies, Walmart and Patagonia, it now has more than 200 members and has become a global standard for the integration of sustainability into the design, production, and retail processes.[8] (See Chapter 6 for more on the Higg Index.)

New alliances across industries are being formed all the time. Another is the Consumer Goods Forum, which brings together 400 business members from over 70 countries to address various issues affecting consumers and supply chains.[9] In recent years, sustainability has moved up their agenda in a significant way, bringing topics such as deforestation, food waste, plastic waste, and the climate impacts of refrigeration to the forefront.

Then there's the recently heralded example of the Fashion Industry Charter for Climate Action, which was launched in 2018 at COP24 (the UN

Climate Change Conference) and, among other goals, has set a target of 30 percent greenhouse gas (GHG) emission reductions by 2030. The charter a commitment to analyze and set a decarbonization pathway for the industry by drawing on methodologies from the Science-Based Targets Initiative. Initially championed by PUMA SE and H&M Group, the charter now has over 50 signatories.[10]

"If we want to see changes in supply chains and in the approach to energy and policy around the world," says Hendrik Alpen, Sustainability Engagement Manager and Team Lead at H&M Group, "then we need to work collaboratively."

There are a seemingly endless number of collaborative industry initiatives now, meaning that businesses do not have to pioneer through this transition on their own. They have advocates, information, potential partners, and other resources that they can and should tap into along their journey. We'll cover this trend and the opportunities it creates for improvement across markets more in the next chapter.

Flexibility in translating global to "local"

Regions, countries, and group companies

One of the biggest challenges that was raised by international organizations with whom we spoke was how to extend global sustainability strategy, which is usually set centrally, to its affiliates around the world. Those who lead sustainability efforts within their companies pointed out that the importance placed on the topic of sustainability varies greatly around the world.

These leaders said that they found that concerns about the environment, or societal issues such as gender equality, quality of life, or economic fairness, were just starting to be recognized as relevant in Asian countries and emerging markets in Africa or the Middle East. In some such countries, they saw that such issues were simply conceived of in a completely different way. European countries, on the other hand, tend to have a higher level of staff awareness, understanding, and concern about these issues, and, thus, these countries would like to see their organizations go even further in their sustainability ambitions.

It can be difficult given these varying perspectives to align the organization around an ambitious vision or get execution of key initiatives across all regions.

For organizations that operate in a more limited number of markets, the challenge might not feel as relevant. This, however, isn't the case. Although a company may not have a *physical* presence in multiple markets, it still could have suppliers or customers abroad with whom it will need to align to drive its sustainability efforts. As well, those customers in foreign markets may themselves be more integrated into global networks than the business itself and thus push such a supplier from the outside to do more.

In our research, we found that some companies are skeptical of the SDGs, particularly those that already have been integrating sustainability into what they do for quite some time. Yet, from our perspective, the SDGs can be quite helpful, especially when rolling out sustainability efforts to local or new markets. All of us can identify with some aspect of the SDGs, with their universal themes that resonate in all countries to some degree. They give us a common framework to build bridges across different cultures and contexts.

Sony deals with the challenge of working across multiple heterogeneous markets daily. Achieving engagement and alignment in such a complex business is an immense predicament when you are dealing with operations in roughly 150 countries and some 117,000 staff working across segments as diverse as movies, music, video games, financial services, and a range of electronic products and services.

Sony has put in place a global strategy called "Road to Zero" to address the complexity. Road to Zero is more than a sustainability strategy; rather, it is a broad-reaching and ambitious program to achieve by 2050 a Zero Environmental Footprint (ZEF) throughout the lifecycle of Sony products and business activities. It's a far-reaching plan which focuses on two main areas:[11]

1. *Environmental action:* Moving to zero emissions products, conserving resources via the elimination of virgin materials in their products, controlling chemical substances to avoid those posing environmental risks, and promoting biodiversity
2. *Lifecycle:* Achieving zero environmental impact by 2050 across all stages of its value chain, namely innovation, product/service planning and design, operations, raw materials and components procurement, logistics, and "Take Back" and recycling

With such a sprawling organization touching myriad geographies and industries, rolling out such an initiative and securing commitments to it outside of Sony's corporate hub in Tokyo would seem to be quite daunting. But Sony has taken two vital steps to engage group companies and regions on the topic and get their input and buy-in.

As previously mentioned, strong leadership is first and foremost essential to success. Shortly following his appointment as CEO, Kenichiro Yoshida addressed sustainability in his first internal blog post to reaffirm the organization's strong commitment to the subject. Yoshida drove alignment on the topic across the organization, signing Sony up to the RE100 commitment to sourcing 100 percent renewable power and frequently speaking—internally and publicly—to stress the importance of social value as a core aspect of sustainability.

Then, Sony focused on local management engagement as another key approach. The process starts with a backcasting approach to simulate what operational changes are needed to hit overall goals, setting a successful outcome at a future date and then working backward to determine what needs to be done to achieve that outcome. From there, more detailed, five-year group company targets are set.

The backcasting process isn't top-down; instead, global management should be seeking the input of regional and group company managers about what actions and detailed targets are feasible. These inputs then, when taken all together, make it possible for management to successfully develop a global plan.

Local strategy and actions need to contribute to global objectives and align with an organization's broader strategy and values, of course. When sustainability-driven strategies are implemented across locations, in order to succeed they also need to be adapted to local environments and situations in the same way as other aspects of business, such as brand-portfolio strategy, finance, or operations. Ivory-tower approaches rarely work and are particularly risky when it comes to sustainability and the SDGs, where the societal challenges often start locally.

"When we are putting together our global initiatives and targets, we want to have a regional perspective based on inputs into the design of the target by our local offices and stakeholders," says Keiko Yokoyama, Director of Corporate Environment, Safety and Health at Sony Electronics in the United States. "And, when it comes to sustainability, we tend to proceed with what works in the region while supporting global objectives and targets."

Act, assess, and adjust

Taking a company in a new direction is always challenging. Even more so if the new direction profoundly changes the way the organization approaches its business. As they gear up to embark on a transition to a sustainable business model, organizations must spend time understanding best practices from other companies that are further advanced in their journey, learn about the tools and techniques at their disposal to make the process more robust, and make connections with stakeholders inside and outside their industry who can provide guidance and serve as potential partners.

Most of the companies that we spoke with for this book spend time aligning their current activities to the SDGs or laying out and communicating their sustainability-aligned strategy. Doing so is highly important. Too much time spent on strategizing and planning, however, can also inhibit organizations from taking action and heighten their risk aversion, causing inertia to take hold. Quite simply, putting their plans into action is critical for organizations. Remember what Rebecca Self, HSBC's CFO of Sustainable Finance told us in Chapter 3: "Don't wait for perfection. Don't get caught up in which framework is the best one for measurement of what you do. There will always be a bit of trial and error in this."

Some of the most successful actions that organizations take are often not the most dramatic or flashy ones—simple, straightforward actions often have the most impact. Ricoh, which enjoys such strong advocacy from its CEO on the importance of the SDGs to business, has been pushing to deepen its own staff's understanding of the SDGs and sustainability by tying it directly to their daily roles and responsibilities.

Sergio Kato, the previous Corporate Vice President of Ricoh's Sustainability Management Division (currently Senior Vice President, Commercial Printing), launched a sales campaign recently that integrated the SDGs in sales proposals, one of the most interesting initiatives we learned about in our research. All Ricoh sales staff were required to add the SDGs to the front page of their proposals and pitch their customers not only on products and promotions, but also to explain, as necessary, the SDGs.

Many customers, who were not as aware of the UN 2030 Agenda, quickly zoomed in on this new concept that Ricoh included, wanting to know what it was all about. This gave Ricoh's sales team a lead into discussions about Ricoh's commitment to the SDGs, the aligning of its business strategy with them, and how that related to the products and services they were presenting to the customer. Rather than simply selling a product, now sales staff were conveying a company position that radically differentiated them from the competition.

When we first met Kato and he explained the campaign, he mentioned that the sales team had responded in the first week to his request with more than 4,900 proposals that included the SDGs in their documentation. Less than a week later, Kato reported back to us that Ricoh had sent out more than 30,000 proposals that integrated the SDGs.

A month later we met him at Ricoh's headquarters just outside central Tokyo's Ohta Ward. Kato was ecstatic about the continuing success of the effort: "57,585 proposals were sent out by our sales team in one month. Sixteen per person!" he reported, even happier with what he saw as the real impact of the campaign: "Now people take Ricoh seriously when we discuss our sustainability programs and the SDGs."

Ricoh is in the process of assessing the success of this campaign in terms of conversion rates. But that is not the only worthy metric to grade it by—it was also highly successful in that it quickly disseminated knowledge of the SDGs through the organization. To succeed, sales staff themselves had to study and understand the SDGs and their importance to Ricoh, creating knowledgeable workforce who could become champions of the company's sustainability efforts throughout the company and externally to customers.

When taking action, such as Ricoh's campaign, organizations must make sure that they have a system or technique in place to effectively assess the success of such efforts. Incorporating KPIs, metrics, competitive benchmarking where possible, and scorecards, bundled into periodic business reviews, is essential, as with other business functions.

To track its progress in achieving a fully sustainable business model, Sinyi Realty, one of Taiwan's biggest real estate brokerages and developers, has a robust assessment model that is the responsibility of its business planning department, which reports to the CEO. Keeping the assessment responsibility within business planning enables Sinyi Realty to have better access to the necessary data and reporting. The company has opted to use the Global Reporting Initiative (GRI) Sustainability Reporting Standards and follow the lead of Unilever, a standout on sustainability efforts, on which measurement approaches to use.

"Unlike many companies in Taiwan that hire consultants to do their reporting, we do it in-house by referring to the GRI guidelines and using leading European and American sustainable companies as a template," says Nico Chen, Sustainability Department Manager at Sinyi Realty in Taipei. "Based on this guidance, we track progress on our carbon footprint, employee turnover rate, the ratio of female managers, and other such metrics to check our progress."

The assessment stage can be another difficult one for companies. It is vital not to get bogged down in endless assessments and analyses—the assessment stage should never precipitate inaction.

Managers need to be able to quickly adjust initiatives, or identify new ones, or lobby for the resources to do both. This is even more imperative when companies have a highly ambitious sustainability-aligned strategy and operational-change programs, such as many of those with whom we spoke. Organizations that succeed in making sustainability a fundamental part of what they do strategically will proceed through this Act–Assess–Adjust cycle much more quickly than others, ultimately rising as leaders in their sectors and seeing positive results to their bottom line.

Educating customers is part of the job

Even when a company doesn't ever come face-to-face with a retail end customer, all businesses are in some way connected to those that are on the front lines of dealing with a more and more demanding public, such the fast-moving consusmer goods (FMCG), apparel, and retail banking sectors. As well, they will also be somewhere along the line of contact with increasingly activist investors. Whether your company is B2B (business-to-business), B2C (business-to-consumer), or B2B2C (business-to-business-to-consumer), you will need to understand the role your organization plays in responding to a more complex business environment where sustainability is rapidly becoming a priority.

The launch of the SDGs has caused the urgency around this topic to heighten even further than before.

Be aware, though, that not every consumer is "all in" for sustainability. While consumers state they want more sustainable products and services in many places around the world, how they make trade-offs in their purchasing decisions on these same products or services isn't yet obvious to most companies. Customers may be willing to pay more, but how much? Ten percent? Fifty percent? One hundred percent?

Most consumers in developed markets have gotten used to a lifestyle structured around the concept of convenience—convenient packaging; food year-round rather than when it's in season; buying clothing that is inexpensive, trendy, and easily available (aka "fast fashion"). Are consumers willing to break from these habits to move to a consumption model that's better for society and the planet?

Consumers still appear conflicted on these questions and may not fully grasp yet how their actions, even seemingly small ones, may have a major impact on the environment and society. One frequently cited example is that of the effects of fast fashion, where consumers' desire for the latest styles and low prices has grown to such an extent that there are now an estimated 20 new garments purchased per person each year,[12] 60 percent of which are produced in two countries, India and China, that rely heavily on coal-fueled power plants.[13] The reality is that companies on the journey toward sustainability will need to lead their consumers and customers, just as they do with stakeholders, rather than follow their lead.

The Italian consumer products leader Bolton Group has very visibly stepped up to this challenge. Bolton Group is a family-owned company that is quickly becoming a FMCG powerhouse, with a presence in 126 countries and a diverse portfolio of brands in food, household and laundry care, adhesives, personal care and well-being, and cosmetics.

Bolton Food, Bolton Group's company operating in the canned fish and meat sector, has the longest legacy. The company has built up a leading position both in Europe and, increasingly, beyond. In addition to a robust acquisition strategy, the organization's leading position has also been reinforced by the transition of its brands to a sustainable model, an effort headed up by Bolton Food's Sustainable Development Director Luciano Pirovano.

The company's approach to this transition has been extensive, touching every aspect of its strategy, supply chain, and go-to-market activities. Although the principal sales markets are largely in Europe, Bolton Food's supply chain is worldwide. Taking a sustainable approach required the company to make ambitious commitments, such as achieving 100 percent sustainable fishing by 2024, from today's 50 percent. For this reason, Bolton Food has been encouraging transitions to sustainable sourcing in its suppliers, one of the most important being Tri Marine, fully acquired by Bolton Group in 2019.

This wholesale approach to transforming its operations has been highly successful, and has led to the establishment of a best-in-class sustainable fishing operation in Tri Marine's production facility in the Solomon Islands, which employs 1,000 people, significantly changing lives for the better for many families within the local community.

Please note that Bolton Food first embarked on this journey ten years ago. Retail customers then had brought to the company's attention that some consumers were interested in more environmentally friendly products. Although this wasn't true for all consumers, Bolton Food's management recognized that moving to a sustainable model was the best long-term strategy for its brands.

"Sustainability is a long-term result—we're in the middle of a long trek. Being a family business helps, and it's been very important that the family understands the value of this (transition)," says Pirovano, pointing out that despite the company's significant progress since embarking on a sustainable path, it's an ongoing journey. "But one needs to be patient. It takes time before seeing results. This patience has given us time to work on this in the right way."

Fish stocks are increasingly under threat, and there is a growing belief in the industry that operating from within a sustainable fishing model is the only possible outcome in the future. Consumers, while aware that overfishing is an issue, may not yet automatically search on the shelf for sustainable canned fish.

"Consumers are aware that fish are overfished and the oceans are under pressure. It's difficult to understand though how important this is in their 'moment of truth'," says Pirovano, describing the moment a customer is at the shelf making a purchase decision.

> Pricing and other factors come into play. There's a lot of curiosity about sustainability, particularly [among] younger consumers, thanks to smartphones, digital technology. So we know that the attention of consumers is growing, but on the other side you need to educate them.

In response to the current reality, Bolton Food stepped up its activities to build awareness of sustainable fishing among the public. The company took three key actions to grow consumer awareness. First, it worked to obtain the highly rigorous certification from the Marine Stewardship Council (MSC), the non-governmental organization (NGO) that sets standards for sustainable fishing. Then in 2016, the company partnered with the World Wildlife Fund (WWF) to improve sustainability across the industry, and committed in 2018 to going 50 percent FAD-free by 2020 (namely reducing the amount of fishing using fishing aggregating devices, or FADs). These three actions have been highly important moves to "walk the talk", which consumers are increasingly demanding of companies.

Based on Bolton Food's experience, Pirovano believes that "a great brand can explain (to consumers) what is meant by sustainable fishing, what certified fisheries are".

Bolton Food became a credible voice in its campaign to heighten awareness of the issue of overfishing among consumers and benefitted from this by being able to positively differentiate its brands from the competition.

The power of communication

One great strength of the 17 SDGs is their presentation. Colorfully designed and framed in simple, relatable terms, they have emerged as a framework that has proved to be extremely helpful for businesses in communicating very complex topics. So much so that we found in our recent study of how leading companies are integrating SDGs into their business communications that 80 percent of the companies we surveyed made mention of the SDGs in either their sustainability or annual reports (see Figure 2.4 in Chapter 2).

This is an encouraging sign of company engagement on sustainability, but we also realized in our research that there is still much work to do in improving communications, particularly internally. You cannot depend on the SDGs alone to successfully build knowledge about topics within your organization. And, as mentioned earlier, while the CEO's voice is a critical in building alignment around transitioning the organization to sustainability, there must be even more communication tools in place besides just having the CEO express the importance of sustainability strategies.

A coordinated campaign within the company is required to communicate regularly and systematically about what the organization is doing in regard to sustainability, with emphasis on where the company is today and where it aims to be in the future. At the moment, though, often the knowledge and capability largely sit with the sustainability or CSR officers and teams in most businesses. This must change if the company wants to encourage action.

Leaders of non-listed companies have often stood out as models to follow in regard to making decisive decisions to move their businesses in a more sustainable direction. Lars Lindén, the CEO of family-owned waste management company Ragn-Sells, has fully committed his organization to the Circular Economy. Ragn-Sells recognizes that, while waste management and recycling has traditionally been an important but not core activity within the industrial supply chain, this will fundamentally change in a circular world. Waste management companies will soon emerge as key partners for most organizations.

"If you think about it, waste flows will disappear," says Lindén.

> Today, what we are, in the waste management and recycling industry, is in essence a middleman. But in the future, we will be embedded in these new flows in society. Someone has to identify these new value chains. Someone has to promote these changes that are circular rather than linear. That's the role we're taking in our strategy, in our ways of working, and in our mission and vision.

Lindén's vision for the future of Ragn-Sells and the industry is backed up by an internal campaign touting the group's core values that was designed by Pär Larshans, the company's Chief Sustainability, Corporate Responsibility and Public Affairs Officer. A long-time sustainability practitioner, Larshans developed a "Victory Formula" (Figure 5.3) that defines and helps disseminate an organization's core values by situating them in the intersection of changes in society, the environment, and public transparency.

"The victory formula is about creating winners, but it starts with understanding the challenges in society how the world is developing," says Larshans, who was inspired by Winston Churchill's "V for Victory" sign to imagine how disparate factors are funneled down to a collective meeting point. Larshans takes a high-level, holistic view to the issue of corporate messaging, starting from the outside to understand the need for proper messaging both externally and internally. "It's all about communication," he says. "When society becomes more transparent it creates challenges for companies because you don't have the time to prepare for crises anymore. You need to do the right thing from the start."

The Victory Formula

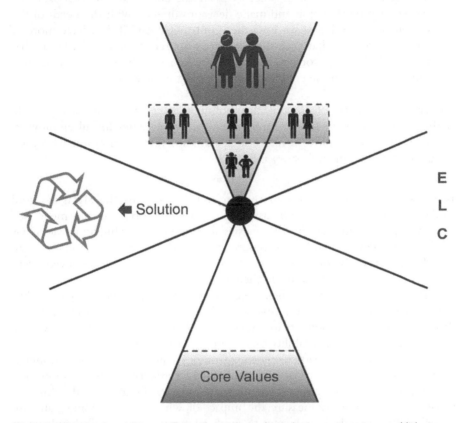

Figure 5.3 Pär Larshans' Victory Formula proposes that when a corporation establishes core
values and spreads them through the organization and society via education,
lobbying and communication (or ELC), then it will produce proper solutions that
benefit the population as a whole.

Source: Courtesy of Pär Larshans.

The first points of contact for Larshans are not only customers, but
potentially employees as well. He brings up the recent problems that
Volkswagen experienced in a diesel emissions scandal as an example. "The
biggest problem they have today is about 'How can we get young kids to
want to work for us?' The brightest minds that should have been the future
of Volkswagen, they don't want to work there," he points out, "because they
don't rely on the company. So you see there that increased transparency in
society is forcing companies to do the right thing directly."

The place to start to adapt to the new transparency in society is within organizations, he says:

> It starts with education, we need to educate the organization and make the line managers to hear it in order to create the core values, so that each co-worker can do their job and make decisions directly with the needs of the customer in mind, and see how they contribute. And if they have more of a connection like that with their job, they appreciate and understand what they contribute to society, they may be more willing to do work five minutes extra, sell the company a little bit better or whatever.

Similar to the story of Ricoh, this holistic vision of the company's role within society helps to develop understandable core values for all employees, and to turn those employees into ambassadors for the organization who then want to tell the company's story themselves.

*****

Returning to how companies, more than ever, are utilizing the SDGs as a tool to demonstrate their actions on sustainability in public-oriented documents, it's important to reiterate that these businesses are more often highlighting the SDGs in their standalone sustainability reports rather than their annual reports. We found approximately only 30 percent of the companies we surveyed were discussing the SDGs *meaningfully* in their annual reports.

Sustainability in the more general sense is obviously mentioned frequently, but there is still much room to improve here. The UN Global Compact has found that 55 percent of respondents to a recent member survey stated that they have not yet incorporated sustainability metrics in their financial reports.[14]

Financial reports, and particularly annual ones, are perhaps the most prominent external communication tools of organizations, particularly public companies. This gap may be because many companies haven't yet figured out the "metrics piece" yet—i.e. how to measure the impact of what they are doing—and are therefore, understandably, reluctant to speak on certain topics until they have an agreed, established approach for measurement. Company reports are just one set of external communication tools that companies can leverage, of course. But these findings, coupled with the points earlier about internal communications, demonstrate that there is still a lot more work for companies to do on the external communications front when it comes to sustainability.

The answer may not come from within

As we have discussed, consumers' interest in products and services that they consider sustainable has risen significantly in recent years. Consumers increasingly state that they want to "buy from brands they trust", with products that are natural and environmentally friendly or have health, wellness, or organic benefits.[15] There's increasing evidence that they're even willing to pay more for more sustainable products and services. This sentiment is evident across various demographic segments, but the biggest driver of this shift in values comes from millennials.

A full 73 percent of millennials state that they are willing to pay more for sustainable products, versus an average of 66 percent in other adult demographics.[16]

The growing interest in sustainability is also shaking up the world of investing, where new and older generations of investors are uniting to bring societal issues back to the realm of finance, as also mentioned earlier in this book.

Finally, associations, NGOs, and even governments have been working hard to increase the public's awareness of sustainability topics. As of September 2018, for example, 72,227 products in Europe have been certified for the EU Ecolabel, which was established in 1992 and encompasses 26 different product categories.[17] While successful in some countries, though, there is room for improvement for the initiative in others: Awareness of the label across Europe is highly variable, standing at 66 percent in France versus 16 percent in the Czech Republic.[18] Ecolabel is just one of many certifications around the world that consumers are increasingly looking to for guidance on product sustainability.

A proliferation of new, innovative, and sustainable products and services around the world is one consequence of the fast-growing interest in sustainable products and services and of the growing awareness of societal and environmental challenges. A plethora of new brands that have built businesses around such consumer awareness are outpacing the growth of existing brands, particularly in the FMCG and apparel sectors.

Although established companies have seen these upstarts as a threat, more recently they have come to recognize them as an opportunity as well, resulting in an uptick in acquisitions and collaborations between established and new brands. Unilever's purchase of Seventh Generation, a home and beauty personal care company, in 2016; SC Johnson's of Method, another rising leader in home and personal care, in 2018; and Pepsi's of Naked Juice in 2006 are just a few examples.

General Mills, Pepsi, L'Oréal, and other such companies have also been integrating sustainable products into their portfolios for quite some time. Unilever may be the champion of this approach, having acquired several sustainable brands and emerged over the years as a corporation-of-reference in regard to sustainability. The reality for many established companies is that they often lack the credibility, flexibility, and know-how to build a highly successful sustainable brand. Bringing these brands into the fold through acquisitions not only gives them promising new revenue streams but also the opportunity to gain valuable learnings from smaller, nimbler companies that can then be extended to other brands and key functions within their business.

This approach is just as valid on the B2B side, although it may mean integrating or taking financial positions in supply-chain partners that bring sustainability capabilities or connections to new customer segments that value a more sustainable approach.

Of course, there are risks to this approach. From loss of credibility for the acquired brand to culture clashes, operational differences, or the short-sightedness of a heavy-handed acquirer, there are many aspects of acquisitions that can cause them to fail. Companies must execute their acquisition plans thoughtfully in order to be successful, with a clear, well-structured process to create an operational model that benefits both companies.

In the next chapter we'll explore specific industries that we believe could be "Hotbeds of Sustainable Innovation", those that have the power to spark a broader shift to sustainable business by acting together. But first, to review the learnings from this chapter, here are the ten takeaways you can act on to accelerate the transition within your organization to sustainability.

Achieving sustainability: how to get there

1. Engage leadership first and get buy-in

Ambitious organizational transformation efforts always require strong, committed senior leadership to drive success, and transitioning to sustainability is no different. If your senior leaders are not yet fully engaged, look for opportunities to increase their involvement at the industry level, which will offer them a higher-level view into how their peers, partners, and competitors are evolving on sustainability.

2. Make clear strategic choices

Companies that move to sustainable business models will need to be prepared to make tough choices. The understanding of sustainability is generally confined to domain experts within most organizations, so it is crucial to make clear, decisive choices to clarify the direction to staff, customers, and other stakeholders.

3. Take a systematic approach to building capability

Most companies do not have an organization-wide understanding of sustainability and how it applies to their business. As with other organizational change initiatives, this capability must be built using a systematic approach. Allocate sufficient time to determine which stakeholders should be involved before you look to roll out your plan, the business processes that needed to be adjusted, which KPIs are needed, which specific activities need to be started or sunsetted, and what training is needed. And, vitally, make sure you designate champions within your organization to ensure the vision and key messages are fully cascaded and understood across the organization.

---

4. Build an "A team"

Running organizations with sustainability at the core will require skills that most business managers and their direct reports do not possess today. Younger generations, though, and talent from different types of institutions, networks, and educational experiences are entering the workforce better prepared and with a skillset more adapted to sustainable business models.

When you search within your organization to identify who can lead this transition, look to those who have an interest in sustainability and are willing to skill-up to lead your business through the transition. Often, they will self-select for the task, and a merit-based talent management approach—rather than an "it's your time" one—is optimal in positioning yourself for success. And ensure that your organization adequately invests in the staff you already have.

5. Pursue a multi-stakeholder approach

Companies are part of much larger systems, with connections to and responsibilities for numerous stakeholders. Not only is understanding your organization's perspective on materiality vital, but also knowing who your stakeholders are and what is important to them. When you understand your stakeholders' perspectives, you can hone in on areas where your values align or identify engagement strategies to bring around your closest stakeholders to support your vision. Finding areas of mutual benefit and identifying opportunities for collaboration will help drive the success of whatever strategy you opt to pursue.

6. Stay flexible when rolling a global strategy out locally

Aligning an organization around an ambitious vision or the execution of key initiatives across all regions is challenging when dealing with varying cultures, experiences, market dynamics, and perspectives. As with other aspects of business such as brand-portfolio strategy, finance, or operations, sustainability-driven strategies need to be adapted to local environments and situations in order to work. Leaders can increase engagement from colleagues in locations far from headquarters by leveraging the SDGs, which offer a universal and understandable framing of sustainability challenges (more on this later).

7. Act–Assess–Adjust

If you're looking to start or expand your efforts, dedicate time to understanding the best practices in your industry and beyond; learn about the tools and techniques to make the process more robust and make connections with stakeholders who can serve as potential partners. But don't let analysis and outreach become an impediment to action. You must master the Act–Assess–Adjust cycle: Identify some actions you believe will drive impact, put in place tools and frameworks that you will use to comprehensively assess the effectiveness of your actions, and adjust your strategy as needed. Your success in moving to a sustainability model will depend greatly on your ability to master this cycle.

8. Educating customers is part of the job

Although consumers' and customers' knowledge of sustainability issues has increased significantly, they still are conflicted about how to incorporate this awareness in their product-decision processes and may not yet fully grasp how their actions, even seemingly small ones, can have a major impact on the environment and society. Educating your customers, and consumers in a B2C context, on the increased value you deliver through more sustainable products and services should be a core activity.

9. Leverage SDGs to drive alignment

The SDGs are universal goals, presented in a colorful way with relatable terms and concepts. However, there are a total of 17! Use the readymade framework of the SDGs by first isolating several of the goals that are most material to your business, put them at the core of your plan, and communicate about your progress frequently and clearly to your organization and external stakeholders.

Ensure the communication is two-way, offering your colleagues, employees, and other stakeholders the opportunity to contribute ideas and offer feedback. Regularly assess whether these messages are resonating, and revise them as needed to enable understanding and action. As you look to extend your engagement to other SDGs, expand your communication efforts accordingly.

10. Consider looking externally to accelerate your transition

High-quality, sustainable products and services have proliferated in the market due to the increased interest from consumers in sustainability. Consider partnering with the companies that produce them or even bring them into the fold, rather than looking at the new competition as a risk. They can provide promising new revenue streams, as well as valuable know-how about running a sustainability-led operation that can be extended to products, services, and key functions within your existing business. If you do decide to go down this route, though, be sure to put a clear, well-structured process in place to guarantee a win-win operational model that benefits both companies.

Notes

1 Ricoh founder Kiyoshi Ichimura's founding principles: The Spirit of Three Loves—a dedication to people, one's country, and a passion for work.
2 Ricoh company website (2018). Ricoh CEO message for sustainability. Retrieved from www.ricoh.com/sustainability/message/.
3 Kocher, I. (2018). The age of responsibility. LinkedIn. Retrieved from www.linkedin.com/pulse/age-responsibility-isabelle-kocher/.
4 Sekisui figures in this chapter are based on an interview conducted by the authors.
5 UNESCO (2019). What is education for sustainable development? Retrieved from https://en.unesco.org/themes/education-sustainable-development/what-is-esd.
6 A wicked problem is a problem that is difficult or impossible to solve because of incomplete, contradictory, and changing requirements that are often difficult to recognize. The use of the term "wicked" here has come to denote resistance to resolution, rather than evil. Australian Public Service Commission (2007). Tackling wicked problems: A public policy perspective. Retrieved from www.apsc.gov.au/tackling-wicked-problems-public-policy-perspective.
7 Ørsted (2017). Historical partnership saves the climate from 200,000 tonnes of CO_2. Press release, November 5. Retrieved from https://orsted.com/en/Media/Newsroom/News/2017/05/Historical-partnership-saves-the-climate-from-200000-tonnes-of-CO_2.
8 Sustainable Apparel Coalition (2019). The Higg Index. Retrieved from https://apparelcoalition.org/the-higg-index/.
9 Consumer Goods Forum (2019). Home page. Retrieved from www.theconsumergoodsforum.com/.
10 UNFCCC (2018). About the Fashion Industry Charter for Climate Action. Retrieved from https://unfccc.int/climate-action/sectoral-engagement/global-climate-action-in-fashion/about-the-fashion-industry-charter-for-climate-action.
11 Sony (2010). Sony Global Road to Zero plan. CSR/Environment webpage. Retrieved from www.sony.net/SonyInfo/News/Press/201004/10-0407E/.
12 Drew, D., and Yehounme, G. (2017). The apparel industry's environmental impact in 6 graphics. World Resources Institute. Retrieved from www.wri.org/blog/2017/07/apparel-industrys-environmental-impact-6-graphics.
13 Editorial (2018). The price of fast fashion. *Nature Climate Change*, 8, 1.
14 UN Global Compact (2018). United Nations Global Compact Progress Report. Retrieved from www.unglobalcompact.org/library/5637.
15 Nielsen (2015). Consumer brands that demonstrate a commitment to sustainability outperform those who don't. 2015 Nielsen Global Corporate Sustainability Report. Retrieved from www.nielsen.com/us/en/press-releases/2015/consumer-goods-brands-that-demonstrate-commitment-to-sustainability-outperform/.
16 Ibid.
17 European Commission Environment (2018). Facts and figures. Retrieved from https://ec.europa.eu/environment/ecolabel/facts-and-figures.html.
18 Goyens, M. (2017). EU report confirms Ecolabel must keep benefiting consumers and the environment. EEB.org. Retrieved from https://eeb.org/eu-report-confirms-ecolabel-must-keep-benefiting-consumers-and-the-environment/.

Mission-driven vignette 4

TBM Co., Ltd.'s LIMEX

Reimagining paper and plastic

How does a company look backward and forward at the same time? This was the question that underpinned the mission of TBM Co., Ltd. (Times Bridge Management) at its founding as a start-up—how to make a bridge between the past, present, and future.

TBM Co., Ltd. was launched to develop new products that would benefit society in the long term, by drawing on both modern technology and knowledge from the past. In his search for innovative technologies that could fit this objective, serial entrepreneur and founder Nobuyoshi Yamasaki learned about the existence of a Taiwanese technology of producing a paper substitute out of stone.

Yamasaki identified limestone as an ideal material to work with as it is abundant, affordable, and greatly reduces the negative impact on water and forestry resources in contrast with paper. Still, Yamasaki's first efforts to sell in Japan the innovative product that he had uncovered in Taiwan fell short. The product at that stage didn't meet the high quality standards demanded by the Japanese market, so Yamasaki decided to draw on the support of Japanese researchers to develop a new manufacturing and design approach to enhance the product.

The texture of the "sheet" produced from limestone—thicker, glossier, and durable—made it an ideal alternative to glossier, heavier stock paper. He found as well that pricing for this type of "paper", which he dubbed "LIMEX", was in line with that of higher-quality traditional paper. This made LIMEX a perfect alternative for items such as menus, brochures, sales leaflets, maps, and business cards.

LIMEX is fairly easy to recycle and upcycle, so any discarded or unused product could be returned to TBM Co., Ltd. to be repurposed. Finally, Yamasaki developed a production and distribution model that helped drive steady growth.

Figure 5.1 Assorted products made from TBM Co., Ltd.'s LIMEX.
Source: TBM Co., Ltd.

He discovered eventually that LIMEX could be used as a plastic replacement, reducing the amount of plastic used for various products and making the paper substitute even more attractive. LIMEX is particularly useful for producing non-plastic forms of heavily used items such as coffee lids, utensils, or trays and containers used for readymade meals.

While developing LIMEX as a paper alternative has been the focus of its product development, TBM Co., Ltd. believes that the plastic-alternative route offers a host of opportunities for the company, enabling it to extend into numerous new sectors and use cases.

Over the course of eight years, Yamasaki has built one of the leading companies globally in this technology. As the business's reputation has grown, so has its customer base. TBM Co., Ltd. now has 4,500 companies in Japan that use its products and has been tapped by international clients, such as CSR Europe's SDG Summit in Brussels and carbon disclosure leader CDP.

To continue its international growth outside of Japan, TBM Co., Ltd. is establishing a network of partners which has already borne fruit, with 500 active international leads. The company is looking to public–private partnerships as a key part of its capacity development and international expansion.

For example, TBM Co., Ltd. has entered into a partnership with the National Industrial Cluster Development Program of Saudi Arabia to construct a LIMEX plant, and is expanding its collaborations to other regions of the world, most recently with a collaborative initiative (i.e. feasibility study, test marketing) with the Mongolian government.

The company has big ambitions for LIMEX, with a goal of ultimately shifting the paper industry toward more environmentally sound solutions. A big shift in how paper is made, used, and disposed of requires a fundamental change in systems as well.

It's critical that the sustainability case for moving to alternative substances such as limestone be made. To to achieve this, TBM Co., Ltd. conducts a lifecycle assessment of its products, examining how manufacturing and procurement impacts the environment and adjusting its processes to reduce impact as necessary. It also works with its suppliers on how to make their product processes more sustainable.

What happens to LIMEX products once they're in the marketplace is a considerable challenge however. Most recycling systems in the world have equipment and operational processes that have taken years to develop and are well known by the public and municipalities. They are accustomed to working with certain substances and formats, and have equipment and processes to accommodate those.

Limestone-based products aren't one of those substances that are, currently, easy to accommodate. In the absence of an optimal solution TBM Co., Ltd. currently advises customers to follow local disposal rules, and engages local governments to encourage them to identify new ways to accommodate the innovative new material.

Bringing in new substances will require a revised approach that ushers in the need for new training, systems, and processes. One of TBM Co., Ltd.'s biggest ambitions is to create a closed loop ecosystem that will address this problem by partnering with municipalities. The company has partnered with the Kanagawa Prefecture in Japan to launch the Kanagawa Upcycle Consortium, a unique public–private initiative promoting the use, collection, and upcycling of LIMEX in the area. These types of initiatives will play a central role in removing the barriers that may exist around introducing new papers or plastics as well as further reducing their environmental impact.

Finally, TBM Co., Ltd. aims to reduce the environmental impact of its products even further by shifting to biomass-based or biodegradable sub-raw material. This has already been achieved on products such as bags, where biomass-based materials can be used.

TBM Co., Ltd.'s vision is ambitious and its geographic reach is expanding by the day, making it well positioned to reimagine how we make both paper and plastic.

6   What's next

Industries as hotbeds of sustainable innovation

Although we can celebrate when one company decides to make the transition to a sustainable business model, shifting the paradigm requires an industry-wide transformation. History has demonstrated many times that even the most dubious of practices can be dramatically minimized or eliminated through intra- and inter-industry collaboration.

While the push to become sustainable is impacting all business sectors, there are a handful that are in a prime position to embrace sustainability and impact both their own industries and other sectors that they connect with. If these industries get it right, this will be a powerful enabler in the broader transition toward sustainability—or, in the event of a failure to do so, a powerful hindrance to making it happen.

We will explore here how five industries—insurance, tourism, real estate, fashion and apparel, and health and wellness—have the power to bring sustainable products and operational and social innovation to business, transfiguring the way we live and setting society on a more sustainable path.

We've spoken extensively about how reimagining finance will change the game for everyone. There's strong proof that investors are seeing not only the risks posed by unsustainable business practices, but also the opportunities that sustainable products and services will offer companies for the foreseeable future. The age of sustainable consumption is upon us, driven by changing consumer tastes and values, shifts in disposable income levels in both developing and developed markets, increasingly dramatic consequences of climate change, and nearly continuous, real-time information on the impact of *unsustainable* practices and behavior.

Companies must change how they operate in order to shore up the sustainability of their supply chains, and retool their product portfolios as a result. Yet businesses making the shift individually will not be enough to make the required difference—what's needed are industry-wide transformations.

Child labor, for example, which has dogged society for millennia, has shown dramatic improvement over time. It has become nearly non-existent in developed markets[1] thanks to the industrialization of Europe and North America in the early twentieth century, agreements such as the 1973 Minimum Age Convention by the International Labor Organization (ILO), and other efforts such as the rise of Corporate Social Responsibility (CSR) and the Fair Trade movement.

While the number of victims of child labor is still too high in places, according to the ILO's report "Global estimates of child labor: Results and trends, 2012–2016",[2] the progress that continues to be made in emerging markets as well is undebatable. Today, most companies and industries around the world take a strong position against child labor, putting in place relevant policies and taking concerted actions to curtail it.

It's important to remember, however, that today's reality wasn't always the case. To move opinion and business practices on this issue, whole industries have had to come together to tackle such destructive labor practices head-on. Industry-wide transformation is rarely achieved by one or even a few organizations. It takes an entire industry to change the game.

Let's take a look at five industries that we believe will be significant enablers—or derailers in the event of failure—of the broader transition to sustainable business and achievement of the SDGs.

Insurance

The industry that has perhaps the most to gain or lose from the success or failure of efforts to move business toward sustainability is the insurance sector. Every Sustainable Development Goal (SDG) poses a challenge and opportunity for the sector.

Let's take as an example the goal that has the most obvious, direct impact on the sector, SDG 13, Climate Action. If the world fails to tackle climate change, and we continue to see an acceleration in weather-related disasters, insurance companies will naturally see insurance claims increase and payouts rise as a result.

The industry is trying to quickly address the issue by turning to predictive weather modeling and other analytical or technical approaches to properly integrate climate risk into their pricing and business models. Insurers rely on the reinsurance market to pay out claims, which helps manage the problem in the short term. But as climate change wreaks an increasing amount of havoc on property, infrastructure, health, and welfare around the world, this backstop will eventually fall short.

One could come to the inevitable conclusion that the logical way for the industry to buffer against this growing payout risk would be to transfer these costs to businesses and consumers through higher insurance premiums or more stringent claim payout policies. But this is not a feasible solution, as doing so would put all kinds of insurance out of the reach of many current customers.

On the other hand, if, societies manage to successfully combat climate change, then a completely different picture of the sector's future appears. Insurance would continue to be important, but a more financially sustainable model for the sector would quickly emerge. Instead of needing to prioritize topics such as resilience or scoping strategies to minimize payouts, the industry could, instead, focus on expanding to new, previously underserved customers and delivering better value to customers through product and service innovation, enabling a more prosperous and secure society to better manage life's natural (and unnatural) transitions.

Some insurance giants are waking up to the need to adjust their model to deliver a better approach. Allianz SE is one industry leader which is building a strong reputation in regard to sustainability. It appears in many of the top sustainability rankings, most notably the Dow Jones Sustainability Index,[3] and as the top-performing insurance company in Robeco SAM's Corporate Sustainability Assessment.[4] But Allianz's goal is more profound than topping these rankings.

The German insurance company has developed a multi-pronged, robust approach to sustainability, embedding it squarely in the core of its strategy and actively implementing it in its business critical activities. This includes expanding services focused on the underserved in emerging markets, assessing its insurance transactions for environmental, social, and governance (ESG) risk, ramping up its sustainable investments, investing in social entrepreneurs via its Social Innovation Fund,[5] and, importantly, integrating key sustainability elements into its remuneration structure, to just name a few activities.

As illustrated by the Allianz example, tackling the sustainability of its own operating model must be a top priority for the sector. This is not the first time that the industry has been compelled to undertake a massive transformation in its approach—the biggest disruption in the modern era has come from digitalization.

An industry once defined by local offices and reams and reams of paperwork is quickly embracing digital technology. Much has been made about the cost savings and efficiencies gained by insurers that embrace digital models, making this type of transition a "no brainer". But digital is also a key piece in the sustainability puzzle that will help insurers as they aim to move to sustainable business models.

Reducing paper use is an obvious benefit (although companies also need to carefully manage and offset their digital carbon footprint). Another is the insurance industry's ability to extend new insurance products and services to underserved populations. Insurtech start-ups that offer promising new solutions for serving these consumers, are often natural partners for larger, more established organizations that may find it difficult to quickly respond to this opportunity.

Finally, the industry can also play a big role in hastening the transition toward more sustainable models for business and society. With vast resources at its disposal, the insurance sector is also a key investor, placing capital in various types of asset classes in the markets. In recent years, there's been a growing movement in the sector to move toward sustainable investment models.

One of the sector leaders in this area is the world's No. 1 insurer, AXA Group. It has been a pioneer in Responsible Investing and aims to focus its investment strategies on companies or assets that address sustainability concerns and align their CSR activities with their core operations. Dating back to at least 2014, when its AXA Investment Managers group (AXA IM) launched the Impact Investment Initiative,[6] AXA has recognized its power to not only transform how it deploys its capital, but to also move the investment community as a whole toward a model that seeks financial *and* societal returns.

AXA's Responsible Investment Committee has set out a comprehensive policy in this direction, identifying five "sensitive sectors" for more rigorous analysis and enabling systematic integration of ESG criteria in their asset management. As AXA IM also manages other investors' assets, this approach offers significant opportunities for its business. With increasing investor demand for more ESG and, soon, SDG-related asset classes, investors will eventually gravitate toward asset managers who align themselves with this new model. Matt Christensen, Global Head of Responsible Investment, is seeing this in action today.

"We're looking at SDGs across multiple asset classes, equities that are conviction-oriented, fixed-income, and such," says Christensen.

> You're going to see a huge number of SDG-oriented funds come across in the coming years, and not just here in Europe. I think it's going to be a major push in the market over the next two years in particular.

While companies in the sector can take many actions to transform their business model, we believe that in fact it's the approach that it takes to its investment activities that can yield the biggest impact.

Tourism

Undoubtedly one of the fastest-growing industries in the modern age, at least until the COVID-19 crisis, has been tourism. International arrivals, the most frequently cited metric for gauging the growth of the sector, more than doubled over 20 years, hitting 1.245 billion in 2016.[7]

Citing tourism as one of the key drivers of economic growth, countries around the world have relaxed entry restrictions for tourists, offered financial incentives to companies and other innovators in the sector, invested in improved infrastructure and services for tourists, and launched flashy ad campaigns in an effort to lure tourists (and their money). At the same time, a rapidly growing middle class in markets like China and India, the increased affordability of air travel, and innovations that transformed the sector, such as online travel aggregators and Airbnb, have turbocharged sector growth in developed and emerging markets alike.

Tourism now stands at 10.4 percent of the world's global GDP and accounts for 313 million jobs around the world.[8] While this breakneck growth has been a big positive for the industry, countries, and tourists, it hasn't been without its drawbacks.

Exploding housing prices in many urban areas, increasing complaints from residents, general wear and tear, and occasional vandalism arising from overtourism have been daunting for the sector. It's clear, however, that the nature of the industry makes it well positioned to offer real solutions to the world's ongoing economic uncertainty and to its many social challenges.

The industry is, arguably, one of the few where its impact, both positive and negative, on all 17 SDGs is apparent. Although highly global, it is an industry that is shaped by what happens locally. Thus, it can directly impact communities around the world, bringing progress on SDGs that many other industries struggle to act on, such as SDG 1, No Poverty, and SDG 15, Life on Land.

It is also an industry that has many facets, including aviation, lodging, food service, entertainment, and other transportation, all of which need to work collectively to bring about meaningful and valuable experiences for tourists. This dynamic makes it one of the best positioned to demonstrate how Partnership for the Goals, SDG 17, offers substantial opportunities for both business and society.

There are many transformative initiatives underway that are paving the way for a new, more sustainable model for the industry. For example, certifications and standards, such as those championed by the Global Sustainable Tourism Council (GSTC), are becoming a particularly helpful tool in the industry to get both companies and tourist themselves engaged on sustainability. Travelers are accustomed to looking for ratings, certifications, and the like as a gauge of quality when making decisions about their travel. As such, we'd advocate that players in the industry examine the requirements around these and the support they can bring in enabling more sustainable business models.

If tourism-related companies with extensive global reach were to make the transition toward sustainability, our progress on the SDGs would be greatly accelerated. Even before the COVID-19 crisis, aviation was one segment of the sector that had quickly recognized the challenge that the rising consciousness around sustainability could pose to its business model. Although fuel cost volatility was the principal impetus that encouraged carriers, manufacturers, and suppliers early on, a preoccupation with fuel efficiency has had the unintended consequence of moving the industry toward more sustainable solutions.

With fuel accounting for nearly a quarter of total expenditures,[9] airlines were clamoring for fuel-efficient solutions. This is just part of the story, though. Airlines are acutely aware of the importance of reducing their substantial carbon footprint, and these dynamics have opened up an exciting innovation opportunity that won't go away once the effects of COVID-19 dissipate.

Boeing has set rigorous and ambitious targets around carbon and is taking substantial steps to improve its sustainability across numerous facets of its value chain and manufacturing operations. Its new UK-based manufacturing site is on course to receive an "excellent" BREEAM (Building Research Establishment Environmental Assessment Method) rating, the highest rating from the world's leading infrastructure and building sustainability assessment.[10]

The sustainability story isn't possible without innovation. This is perhaps even more so the case in aviation, where new technologies such as electric, hydrogen-powered, and hybrid aircraft exist but are still far off from becoming commonplace. There are certainly other solutions that we haven't even imagined yet that are possible in the sector.

With an evident link to all 17 SDGs, the hotel sector is better positioned to have a wider impact. Global hotel chain pioneer Hilton, a long-time champion of sustainable solutions, aims to lead the sector rather than follow by significantly stepping up its actions in the coming years.

More than ten years ago, Hilton took two noteworthy steps toward sustainability. First, it launched its "LightStay" program, which has grown into an energy-, waste-, and water-management program that requires that all of its 500-plus properties around the world to set and hit targets on sustainability. It has also set Science-Based Targets for carbon reductions—an industry first—and is actively engaged in making this approach an industry standard.

These were simply first steps. The SDGs deepened its commitment, becoming an imperative for its business. Daniella Foster, Hilton's previous Senior Director of Global Corporate Responsibility, told us that "The message we want to convey is that this is strategic and core to business. This is our (the industry's) future customer. This is the future of the industry."

In addition to aligning its current activities to the SDGs and identifying those it wants to "double down" on, Hilton also set an ambitious 2030 agenda, with the challenge of cutting its environmental impact in half and doubling its social impact investment by 2030. Achieving the plan will hinge on generalizing sustainability knowledge across the organization, investing in innovations that will enable sustainability, and scaling up in new, previously underserved parts of the world.

That last strategy is perhaps the boldest part of its plan, involving the opening of 50 Hilton properties across sub-Saharan Africa in the coming five years, which will help enable its laudable goal of creating jobs and training for one million young people.

This is but one company. There are many across the industry that are also set to bring about the biggest changes in the industry since the Internet transformed travel 20 years ago. Many positive examples can be found on the United Nations (UN) World Tourism Organization's "Tourism for the SDGs" platform, which is a good resource for discovering new ideas and initiatives, particularly around Decent Work and Economic Growth (SDG 8), Responsible Consumption and Production (12), and Life below Water (14), which the UN has challenged the industry to deliver on.[11] Furthermore, the COVID-19 crisis is likely to bring about even more fundamental changes to tourism. It is undeniable that the crisis has wreaked havoc on the industry, disrupting the tourism business model as we know it. However, there is a silver lining here. Industry leaders now have an obligation to rebuild their industry. They should view this as the opportunity to double down on the efforts we've mentioned in this section, and finally build a better, sustainable, and more resilient industry for the long term.

Real estate development

More than a decade ago, global pollution forced people to become more aware of our basic needs: food, water, and clean air. Today, our concerns have expanded to the space we center our life around. The reliability, the comfort level, and the price of the built environment have a direct impact on our everyday life. In the development of sustainable living, the real estate sector plays a critical role.

This sector, especially construction, has taken a toll on the environment. A report published by the World Economic Forum in 2017 estimated that buildings are the largest consumers of energy in the world as well as being the most significant contributors of CO_2 emissions. What's more, the built environment is accountable for 30 percent of raw material consumption and 25–40 percent of solid waste generation.[12] Without a doubt, there is an urgent need for green real estate that meets sustainability criteria.

The result of this pressing demand for improvement is a dizzying array of reporting standards, programs, and indexes. Companies today are confused by an alphabet soup of options about to whom they should report. Is it the BOMA 360 by the Building Owners and Managers Association International? The Global Real Estate Sustainability Benchmark (GRESB)? Sustainability Accounting Standards Board (SASB), GRI, CDP, or DJSI? Or building programs such as BREEAM, Green Star, or LEED (Leadership in Energy and Environmental Design)?

The burden to report has pushed some companies to file a few different documents each year to meet investors' requirements, while other companies wait on the sidelines for a more standardized system to appear.

The abundance of measuring and reporting methods are not the only hurdles in the development of sustainable real estate. There has been a common perception that building a green property comes with a high cost in construction and certification. Many studies, though, have shown that "there is no significant difference in average cost for green building as compared to non-green buildings".[13] Building and investing in properties that conform to sustainability guidelines can reduce costs due to energy efficiency, and attract buyers, tenants, and investors.

The most recent GRESB assessment shows that sustainability performance for buildings has increased across the world, with Oceania performing strongly across various key metrics.[14] Some governments have acted through regulations and incentives to encourage the green-building movement in their local markets, such as the European Union's GreenBuilding program aimed at non-residential buildings, while evidence is growing that client demands are equally important growth drivers.

The US Green Building Council's World Green Building Trends 2018 SmartMarket Report noted that the top three triggers for green-building activity were client demands at 34 percent, environmental regulations at 33 percent, and healthier buildings at 27 percent.[15] It's critical that governments help create the conditions for the industry to move toward green-building, and encouraging that demand from customers for this new approach to designing and constructing buildings is on the rise.

The acceleration of innovations in all elements of the building process, from materials used to the process of retrofitting existing buildings, is also fueling green-building's rise, and will ultimately drive its expansion. As it moves into the mainstream, the existing perception that it's cost-prohibitive should be eliminated.

In Asia, where real estate plays a central role in many countries' economies, the sector's sustainability performance, although still trailing some markets and sectors, has made sharp improvements in the recent years. The leading real estate companies in Asia, having impressive portfolios that comprise integrated developments and services, are often advocates of sustainable building development in their own countries.

In Taiwan, where most businesses still focus on CSR, Sinyi Realty is pioneering sustainable development by incorporating the SDGs into its business planning. Sinyi Realty has been a trusted name in brokerage and agent sale services for decades, and more recently has extended its activities into property development and construction. In the broader Asian market, it has created a comprehensive business system that revolutionizes its service model, making stakeholders its top priority while also successfully managing its carbon footprint.

Although Sinyi aims to make even greater advancements in regard to its environmental commitments, its approach has already resulted in a host of positive outcomes for the company, from increased customer and stakeholder trust to stronger talent recruitment and retention, and higher levels of employee engagement. Sinyi's success has encouraged other businesses in Taiwan to follow suit, launching a movement that has compelled the government to take more decisive actions on policy.

As Sinyi's market grows from Taiwan to China, Japan, and Malaysia, it is sharing its experiences and know-how to the local real estate businesses, bringing much-needed change to the industry at a regional level.

Sekisui House Group, Japan's largest home-builder, is another example of a sustainable real estate player in Asia—and now a global leader. As discussed in the previous chapter, Sekisui House actively contributes to global decarbonization and drives the industry toward sustainability.

Regardless of in which countries or under what reporting systems such businesses operate, the actions of the real estate sector are vital in achieving SDG 11's directive to "Make cities inclusive, safe, resilience, and sustainable". Its actions to advance on SDG 11 will have additional impacts by contributing to the other goals that are interconnected to 11, such as 7, 13, and 15.

In the face of climate change, energy price surge this sector will have an increasing responsibility for more lives in the future. By 2050 2.5 billion more people are projected to be living in urban areas.[16] Given its tremendous impact on the world's economy, environment, and society, the industry is expected to continue growing, and, at the same time, to turn from being the greatest hazard to the environment to becoming a champion in defending it.

Fashion and apparel

There are few sectors that have been under as much scrutiny when it comes to sustainable business models as the fashion and apparel industry. The rise of "Consumer Culture" in the latter half of the twentieth century was both a boon for the sector and a curse. The rise of celebrated brands, the birth of high streets and shopping malls, and the emergence of the middle class around the world all converged to create an ideal market environment for retailers and the global fashion and apparel groups that were becoming increasingly consolidated.

The quick runway to retail and fast-fashion models, pioneered by the likes of Top Shop and Zara, further fueled consumers' desire for the latest and greatest fashion, ramping up the volume of apparel produced and shipped around the world. Success in the sector became predicated on who could build the most efficient and cost-effective supply chains, accelerating the move to rapid prototyping, quick materials sourcing, fast production, and seamless and swift distribution through retail outlets to consumers.

The downside has been an increasing burden on the environment, society, and communities in emerging markets. As globalization took hold and demand has ticked up, production moved eastward toward Japan and Taiwan first, China next, and then Bangladesh, Vietnam, and Indonesia. Contract manufacturing became the norm across the sector.

This shift was hastened by a World Trade Organization (WTO) policy that had unintended consequences. In 1973, the United States and several other countries signed up to a WTO quota system that limited the textile and apparel imports from certain emerging markets. Although the aim of the policy was to protect domestic production and employment in the sector in the United States and other developed markets, it drove up wages, becoming an impetus for businesses to move production to contract manufacturers in lower-wage markets.

When the quota system was rolled back in 2005, the trend accelerated, establishing contract manufacturing as the operational norm.[17] Predictably this supply chain transformation has resulted in many challenges for the sector.

The most famous scandal, perhaps, was the one at Nike, which injected the word "sweatshop" into the public consciousness. The 1990s became Nike's "decade *horribilis*," with an onslaught of labor and environmental scandals at its Asia-based contract manufacturers. One Ernst and Young study found that a whopping 77 percent of workers at one supplier factory had respiratory problems and were exposed to dangerous carcinogens, 177 times above the legal level.[18]

Nike has made a dramatic turnaround from those days and is now seen as an industry model for how to embrace sustainability, but it took years to undo the damage, and for the industry as a whole to follow its lead and right the ship.

Spurred by bold sustainable fashion innovators and an evolving consumer mindset about sustainability issues in fashion and apparel, the industry is entering a period of reflection and reinvention. As we've seen in the information technology sector, innovation rarely emerges from incumbents. Instead, it comes from small and disruptive innovators who see the problems the sector faces as opportunities to drive innovation and reimagine how the system works.

Innovation in fashion and apparel looks to be following a similar trajectory. At every stage of the value chain, innovation has taken hold. Seeing opportunities in innovations enabling sustainability, global fashion and apparel groups are embracing and beginning to invest in fashion tech start-ups and innovations.

One company that has a leg up on its peers is H&M Group. Since the early 2010s, H&M Group has been rolling out various initiatives to orient every step of its value chain toward sustainability. As the first retailer to make its supplier list public, it embraced transparency as its journey.[19]

Its next big push was tackling fair wages through its effort to encourage its manufacturing partners in emerging markets to implement wage management systems. It has found that these systems are an important first step in enabling better wages and empowering workers to engage in collective bargaining and wage negotiations.

H&M Group hasn't yet made a "living wage" the operational standard for doing business with suppliers, but it has developed systems to isolate and remove wage costs from any price negotiations, so that costs for paying the applicable wage level would be guaranteed to be covered with any order made. It is encouraging to see that as a result 67 percent of H&M Group's product volume is now produced in factories that are implementing improved wage management systems, well exceeding its initial 50 percent target. This translates to 500 factories and 635,000 workers, a significant step forward in just five years' time.[20]

These are just the first steps that H&M Group is taking in this important area. Its larger goal is to change wage setting systems for the whole industry and, ultimately, entire countries.

"Together with about 20 other brands and the Global Union Federation IndustriALL, we've joined the industry initiative ACT (action, collaboration, transformation)," Hendrik Alpen, Sustainability Engagement Manager and Team Lead at H&M Group, tells us.

> This initiative aims to establish collective bargaining systems in which suppliers and local trade unions can negotiate wages and working conditions fairly. This includes, for example, commitments to financial support and to stay with suppliers in these markets *even when wages increase* [our emphasis]. Importantly, this initiative is also supported by a unique commitment from brands to "responsible purchasing practices".

The next big push for H&M Group is to move to full circularity in its production and operations, certainly a difficult task for a fast fashion business.

Intuitively, fast fashion and circularity are two concepts that are difficult to reconcile. Yet H&M Group is committed to find a responsible way to do so. Really, it has to—in addition to the negative impact of a non-circular model on the environment, Alpen says that it also understands that the extensive supply disruptions that would arise in a world upended by the effects of climate change could, effectively, put it out of business.

So how does it plan to get there? One important enabler will be technology. Nowhere is technology's central role more apparent than in its global Garment Collection Program, an industry first that has been running for more than five years. There has been growing criticism around the true circularity of collection programs as a result of the vast amount of collected apparel that still ends up in landfills or incinerators, but H&M Group has largely been bucking this trend.

It has achieved this via its "recycle–reuse–rewear" approach, which includes a "0 percent" landfill commitment. Somewhere between 40 to 60 percent of reclaimed materials are reused or reworn or "upcycled", and the remainder is "downcycled"; that is, used in other applications such as making housing and car insulation, with a very small percentage going to incineration. Downcycle applications are, of course, better than landfilling or incineration.

The holy grail of fashion is reusing textiles to make new garments. The technology on this is nascent, but there are strong signs of positive progress. H&M Group is particularly excited about new, emerging innovations in the space, and is actively investing in or collaborating with companies and other stakeholders to support their development. Two such companies are Worn Again Technologies, a polymer recycling start-up, and HKRITA (the Hong Kong Research Institute of Textiles and Apparel), whose full-loop hydrothermal method for recycling cotton and polyester blends is able to maintain the structural quality of the materials, a difficult feat to achieve.

While it's critical that "Big Fashion" take a leadership role in reconsidering and evolving their business models toward ones that put sustainability at the core of their strategy—as we saw with the rise of digital technology—the heart and soul of the sustainable fashion movement are the many small innovators and like-minded investors.

The Brands

Although we are still in the early stages of what's likely to be a significant industry shift, there are a swath of new, innovative, sustainable fashion brands and supporting platforms popping up around the world. Coming on the heels of pioneers like Eileen Fisher, Stella McCartney, Patagonia, and brands such as KEEN and Toad & Co that we have profiled in this book, the next generation of sustainable fashion innovators are embedding this thinking more squarely in mainstream markets.

Ricci Everyday, a Japan-based family-owned brand, strives to make fashion more human-centered. Led by President Chizuru Nakamoto, Ricci Everyday produces bags and other accessories made from vibrant African prints. But what is truly unique about Ricci Everyday is its production model. Rather than sourcing fabric in Africa and producing it at a contract manufacturer thousands of kilometers away, it has opted to produce all of its products by hand with artisans at its facility in Uganda.

Not only has it decided to produce locally, all of the artisans it employs are single mothers or former child soldiers who receive training, incomes significantly higher than the national average, and benefits such as pensions, transportation costs, and more. With two flagship stores in Uganda, distribution in various department stores in Japan, and a new Tokyo flagship store, its model, which is rare for the industry, is working.

The Platforms

It is undeniable that e-commerce and the platform concept have transformed fashion over the last 20 years. The challenge of finding what fashions suit you from a style or price point online has been made significantly easier through high-end online fashion platforms such as the Net-a-Porter websites, online brand shops from companies such as Zara, and well-known e-commerce platforms such as Amazon.

However, these sites do very little to help sustainability-minded shoppers find "conscious fashion" brands. A myriad of innovators are picking up the slack by working to create transparency around the actual sustainability of brand offerings and helping consumers to find ones they may not have been aware of. Some notable examples include:

*   *Goshopia:* Founded by Araceli Gallego, a former project manager and fashion blogger based in Dubai, the Goshopia platform features products that embrace at least one of what it defines as the 3S's—Slow Fashion (not mass-produced items), Sustainability, and Social Responsibility.
*   *Wearwell:* Philadelphia-based and founded in 2015 by Emily Kenney and Erin Houston, Wearwell is a fashion subscription service that selects outfits for subscribers according to their style preferences and budget, from conscious brands from around the world.
*   *Goodonyou:* Established by non-profit organization Ethical Consumers Australia, Goodonyou consolidates data on fashion brands based on reporting from industry certification programs and non-governmental organization (NGO) investigations, and uses it to deliver sustainability ratings of brands to shoppers via an app and on its website.

The Funders

While the brands and platforms mentioned above are critical to educating consumers and bringing sustainability transparency to fashion, they are just the tip of the iceberg in regard to the type of innovation and new technologies the industry needs to truly undergo a revolution in its operational practices.

Many of the technologies the industry needs require significant investment to develop, improve, and scale across their industry and globally. Many in the industry are excited by the possibility of breaking down fabric into its original fibers so that donated and discarded clothing can be used again. Not only would this keep such clothes out of incinerators and landfills, it would offer the significant benefit of helping companies to reduce their raw materials costs.

Like H&M Group, global fashion market leaders such as LVMH, Kering, and others are investing directly in small and medium-sized enterprises and start-ups with these types of breakthrough technologies. They're also serving as limited partners in new funds aligned around sustainable fashion or sustainability in general.

One such fund is Alante Capital, which was launched by experienced investors Karla Mora and Leslie Harwell and backed by sustainable fashion pioneer Eileen Fisher. Alante Capital invests in innovation across the value chain, but is particularly interested in innovations that tackle challenges in production, distribution, and circular recovery. To find these breakthrough innovations, it taps into a system of ecosystem partners from across the industry.

Funds in this space are increasing in number, and include fashion specialists such as the Good Fashion Fund, launched in September 2019 and based in Amsterdam, and funds with a broader remit, such as Paris- and New York City-based consumer start-up fund Eutopia, and Closed Loop Partners and social innovation fund Collaborative Fund, who are also both in New York City.

There are numerous encouraging changes in mindset and innovations that are poised to propel the world of fashion and apparel into a more sustainable future. Enabling this future won't be possible without bold new operational approaches, a cross-industry willingness to collaborate to drive change, and significant resources to scale and embed these products and solutions globally.

Health and wellness

You may wonder why we've highlighted health and wellness as a single sector. Generally, one would separate them into their component parts; for example, pharmaceuticals, over-the-counter healthcare, medical devices, packaged foods, dairy goods, and other. We believe that the future will see a much greater blurring of these sectors.

One thing that our modern lifestyles have taught us as a society is that managing one's health requires a comprehensive approach. While it will always be critical to deploy resources toward developing treatments to fight deadly diseases, we also know lifestyle—in particular diet and physical activity—and, increasingly, genetic predisposition, must be understood to prevent the onset of the disease in the first place.

What this means is that all of the aforementioned sectors, in addition to many others, will be called upon to work in tandem to bring about the next step change in health and wellness management. In essence, to achieve the 2030 Agenda goals around hunger and health, SDG 17, the Partnership for the Goals, will reign supreme.

We anticipate that three significant current challenges in regard to health and wellness will accelerate and drive the interconnected future of healthcare:

1   *The aging of society:* Much has been made about the impact rapid aging has on a society. As societies around the world rapidly become older, economic predictions have become increasingly dire, ranging from slight concern to dramatic, near-doomsday scenarios. With the long-term trends of increasing life expectancy and declining birth rates, we are on a path to living in societies where, unlike the past, there are fewer young people to care for a growing elderly population.

2   *A rapid growth in lifestyle diseases:* While a rising middle class in emerging markets is a welcome development, negative health outcomes is a key adverse effect that arises from increasing wealth. While risk of death from poverty-driven diseases has fallen significantly over time, the incidence of chronic, lifestyle-related diseases and conditions, such as obesity, Type 2 diabetes, certain cancers, and cardiovascular diseases, has exploded. Lifestyle or non-communicable diseases now account for 71 percent of deaths globally, ranging from 37 percent in low-income countries to 88 percent in high-income countries.[21] But this high/low income disparity won't continue for long, as Africa and the Middle East are expected to post the biggest increases in lifestyle disease prevalence in the lead up to 2030.[22]

3   *Continued strain on health systems (both public and private):* Most developed countries have opted for some type of national health care system despite the existence of various models for managing healthcare. Such systems may vary in their structure, ranging from single-payer to social insurance models,[23] but they all rely on some form of government participation to fund elements of the system. Driven by the dynamics around aging and the increase in lifestyle diseases, plus rising health care delivery costs, governments are exploring ways to minimize costs or off-load some costs to private insurers or even patients themselves. Where private insurance plays a critical role in the financing of care, the insurance industry will need to consider new models to enable health care access for its customers.

So there are immense challenges for society, but also great opportunities for organizations, both public and private, to deliver real impact. To be feasible, governmental and commercial organizations will have to tear down the silos that currently separate them and work collaboratively. There are promising signs that such silos are starting to fall.

For many years, pharmaceutical, food, and ingredients companies have operated public health divisions to help address the health needs of impoverished communities around the world. Addressing deadly afflictions such as malaria and malnutrition, these public health units frequently offered aid, including funding and free or reduced-price medicine, or other assistance such as health care services to these communities, either directly or via NGOs.

Recently, a shift in approach has appeared in some organizations. As extreme poverty has declined and rising incomes have brought about new health challenges such as diabetes and certain cancers, companies are beginning to take a more *strategic*—rather than *benevolent*—perspective on their engagement with developing countries. For these companies, the NGO is no longer solely an entity for aid delivery, but rather a true partner in addressing the health and wellness needs around the world.

A consortium that includes DSM, the Dutch development bank FMO, the DFID Impact Acceleration Facility managed by CDC Group, and International Finance Corporation (IFC) launched Africa Improved Foods, a public–private partnership with the government of Rwanda in 2017. The focus of this initiative is to deliver nutrient-rich cereals to the segment of society that no longer relies on food aid but still lacks access to basic, daily nutrition.

Novo Nordisk is following a similar path in one of its principal therapeutic areas, diabetes. In collaboration with the Red Cross, it provides reduced-price access to diabetes medication for people affected by humanitarian crises. As Novo Nordisk sees it, these patients are a critical but often underserved group, whose precarious situation limits their access to vital medicines. The Red Cross can provide the direct access to groups such as these with which Novo Nordisk lacks an inroad.

Undoubtedly, food will also play an even greater role in health and wellness than it does today. With organic,[24] non-GMO (genetically modified organisms), and local food movements[25] taking hold around the world, there's ascertainable change underway in consumers' relationship with food.

We may continue to eat things that can, if consumed regularly, put our health at risk, but there is an increasing awareness that diet is a significant driver of our overall health and wellness. Consumers are demanding more from their food, a trend that companies in the industry are responding to with acquisitions of health-oriented upstarts[26] and investments in foodtech innovations such as nutraceuticals. The nutraceuticals segment is projected to grow 8 percent per year from 2018 to 2023, with much of that growth coming from Asia-Pacific.[27]

These changing dynamics aren't only an opportunity for food companies, but also for retail. The United States and Europe have seen their fair share of retail innovations over the last 20 years, with the rise of Whole Foods and Natural Grocers in the United States, Naturalia in France, Planet Organic in the United Kingdom, and Denn's in Germany. This innovation naturally didn't stay confined to specialized food markets. Most large retailers in developed markets now carry many more organic and all-natural options than they did in the past, with several dedicating whole sections of their stores to these products.

In Japan, leading retailer Aeon's focus on sustainability has expanded from more environmental-focused initiatives, such as its long-standing tree planting program that boasts 11 million trees planted to date, to marked growth in "better for you" options offered to consumers. Aeon now offers its own brands that are natural, "free from"[28] ingredients such as gluten, or certified organic, and anticipates its growth to continue for the foreseeable future.

Actions such as these are merely a first step though. As consumers become more knowledgeable about food ingredients, there's an opportunity for retailers to offer facilities where consumers can, for example, create and blend their own foods. Or, instead of following category trends as they usually do, retailers could *set them* by partnering with players like DSM and Givaudan, who've recently expanded into nutraceuticals,[29] to integrate innovative new food ingredients into their own brands before the likes of P&G, Nestlé, and Unilever corner the market for those types of products. And, finally, partnering with vertical farming start-ups could let them bring fresh produce much closer to consumers.

It goes without saying that there are many more innovations that will revolutionize how we manage our health. Most healthcare systems today are not yet designed for the collaborative, partnership-driven approach that these solutions necessitate. But this will and must change as governments, businesses, and civil society come to realize that collaboration is the only viable path to better health outcomes.

Industry collaboration is the secret sauce

These are but a few examples of industries that we believe have the power to not only deliver sustainable innovations that will transform life as we know it, but also spark a wider revolution in how business operates. To realize this vision, there's one element that must be present: industry collaboration.

Many argue, with good reason, that SDG 17, Partnership for the Goals, is the most important of them all. Practically, you can't achieve system-wide change if only one actor adjusts their behavior. All—or, at worst, nearly all—need to move together in a better direction.

This is difficult for companies. Many are used to thinking of their competitors as their nemeses. They are reluctant, often with justifiable reasons, to work together or share even rudimentary levels of information.

Yet the type of change that is required to move industries toward better, more sustainable models undoubtedly requires a different paradigm. Inter- and intra-industry collaboration, including parties from government and civil society, will form the foundation of this new approach.

Notes

1 Ortiz-Ospina, E., and Roser, M. (2016). Child labor. Our World in Data. Retrieved from https://ourworldindata.org/child-labor.
2 ILO (2017). Global estimates of child labor: Results and trends, 2012–2016. Retrieved fronm www.ilo.org/wcmsp5/groups/public/—dgreports/—dcomm/documents/publication/wcms_575499.pdf.

3 Allianz SE (2018). Dow Jones Sustainability Index. Press release. Retrieved from www.allianz.com/en/press/news/commitment/community/180913-allianz-tops-dow-jones-sustainability-index-2018.html.

4 RobecoSAM (2019). Industry Leaders List. RobecoSAM Corporate Sustainability Assessment. Retrieved from www.robecosam.com/csa/csa-resources/industry-leaders.html.

5 Allianz Group (2018). Sustainability report: Shaping our sustainable future, 5. Retrieved from www.allianz.com/en/sustainability/strategy-governance/sustainability-report.html.

6 Duncan, H. (2014). Axa builds "fund of funds" for socially responsible investing. *The Guardian*. Retrieved from www.theguardian.com/sustainable-business/axa-fund-socially-responsible-investment.

7 World Tourism Organization (1995–2017). International tourism, number of arrivals. Yearbook of Tourism Statistics, Compendium of Tourism Statistics and Data Files. Retrieved from https://data.worldbank.org/indicator/st.int.arvl.

8 Travel and Tourism Council (2019). *Travel & Tourism Economic Impact World 2018*, 3.

9 Mazareneau, E. (2019). Share of fuel costs in the aviation industry 2011–2019. Statista. Retrieved from www.statista.com/statistics/591285/aviation-industry-fuel-cost/.

10 Boeing (2019). Boeing global environmental report. Retrieved from www.boeing.com/principles/environment/report/index.page.

11 UN World Travel Organization (2019). Tourism for the SDGs platform. Retrieved from http://tourism4sdgs.org/tourism-for-sdgs/tourism-and-sdgs/.

12 World Economic Forum (2016). Environmental sustainability principles for the real estate industry, 6. Retrieved from www3.weforum.org/docs/GAC16/CRE_Sustainability.pdf.

13 Mathiessen, L.F., and Morris, P. (2007), The cost of green revisited: Reexamining the feasibility and cost impact of sustainable design in the light of increased market adoption, 3. Davis Langdon. Retrieved from https://global.ctbuh.org/resources/papers/download/1242-cost-of-green revisited-reexamining-the-feasability-and-cost-impact-of-sustainable-design-in-the-light-of-increased-market-adoption.pdf.

14 GRESB. 2018 GRESB Real Estate Results. Retrieved from https://gresb.com/2018-real-estate-results/.

15 Benjamin, H. (2018). World green building trends in 2018: Green keeps growing. USGBC. Retrieved from www.usgbc.org/articles/world-green-building-trends-2018-green-keeps-growing.

16 United Nations. (2017). World population prospect revision. Retrieved from www.un.org/development/desa/publications/world-population-prospects-the-2017-revision.html.

17 Gonzalez, N. (2015). A brief history of sustainable fashion. Triple Pundit. Retrieved from www.triplepundit.com/story/2015/brief-history-sustainable-fashion/58046.

18 Abnett, K. (2016). Just fix it: How Nike learned to embrace sustainability. Business of Fashion. Retrieved from www.businessoffashion.com/articles/people/just-fix-it-hannah-jones-nike.

19 Dienel, E. (2014). Two questions for H&M CEO Karl-Johan Persson: How do you promote transparency and transformation? BSR.org Blog. Retrieved from www.bsr.org/en/our-insights/blog-view/two-questions-for-hm-ceo-karl-johan-persson-how-do-you-promote-transparency.

20 H&M (2018). Fair Living Wage Strategy: Key impacts and learnings. Retrieved from https://hmgroup.com/content/hmgroup/groupsite/sv/sustainability/sustainable-fashion/wages/key-impacts-and-learnings2.html.

21 World Health Organization (2018). The top 10 causes of death. Retrieved from www.who.int/news-room/fact-sheets/detail/the-top-10-causes-of-death.

22 Al-Maskari, F. (2010). Lifestyle diseases: An economic burden on the health services. *UN Chronicle*, Vol. XLVII No. 2. Retrieved from https://unchronicle.un.org/article/lifestyle-diseases-economic-burden-health-services.

23 Cheung, M. (2017). Health care reform: Learning from other major health care systems. Retrieved from https://pphr.princeton.edu/2017/12/02/unhealthy-health-care-a-cursory-overview-of-major-health-care-systems/.

24 MarketWatch (2018). Organic food & beverages market projected to grow at CAGR of 14.8 percent during 2018 to 2022. Retrieved from www.marketwatch.com/press-release/organic-food-beverages-market-projected-to-grow-at-cagr-of-148-during-2018-to-2022-available-in-new-report-2018-08-31.

25 Rushing, J., and Ruehle, J. (2013). *Buying into the Local Food Movement*. AT Kearney.

26 Laurence, E. (2018). Megacompanies are investing in small, healthy food brands: Are your indie favs selling out? Well and Good. Retrieved from www.wellandgood.com/good-food/healthy-food-investments-future-of-food/.

27 Technavio Research (2019). Global nutraceuticals market 2019–2023: Industry developments to augment growth. MarketWatch. Retrieved from www.marketwatch.com/press-release/global-nutraceuticals-market-2019-2023-industry-developments-to-augment-growth-technavio-2019-01-10.

28 "Free from" products that give consideration to additives, ingredients, and components that customers are concerned about.

29 Givaudan (2017). Givaudan to acquire Nutrition Division of Centroflora Group: Strengthens global offering of natural extracts. Press release. Retrieved from www.givaudan.com/media/media-releases/2017/givaudan-to-acquire-centroflora-nutra.

Mission-driven vignette 5

KEEN

"We are not just here to make shoes"

KEEN has focused on the notion of "care" since its founding. Founders Rory Fuerst and Martin Keen, an avid sailor, saw a big gap in the footwear space as few designs delivered the comfort and safety that sailing requires. Together, they teamed up to design the first KEEN shoe. The result of their collaboration, the Newport Sandal, became a runaway success, bringing an innovative new look to outdoor shoe design.[1]

In 2004, this notion of "care" was significantly expanded. Fresh off its successful launch, KEEN's management was preparing for its first $1 million ad campaign when the Indian Ocean earthquake and tsunami struck in December that year. Reacting quickly, KEEN's founders made a decision that forged the path for the future of their company.

"They allocated the entire advertising budget to helping out with the disaster," Chris Enlow, Corporate Responsibility Director and Head of KEEN Effect Team, told us.

> The first $500,000 went to tsunami relief via Americare. The second $500,000 set in motion the company's giving program, which I was brought in to formalize, putting in place partnerships with organizations such as American Whitewater, Leave No Trace, and the Conservation Alliance. This was really the moment in time that really solidified the values of the company.

From that point on, KEEN, as a company and as a brand, became synonymous with relief aid, conservation support, and political advocacy, which it delivers via its KEEN Effect Team.

During a time when many US companies were shying away from overt political action in the workplace, KEEN has taken a very different path, believing that everyone has a responsibility to make a better world. This notion is powerfully illustrated in its "Better Takes Action" campaign. One

Figure 6.1 KEEN, an innovator in shoe design, is also synonymous with relief aid, conservation support, and political advocacy.
Source: KEEN.

impressive example of the campaign is its in-house Call to Action Phone Booth, which provides information and instructions on how to contact your congressional representatives and senators.

Having witnessed the power of this concept, it is now taking the phone booth on the road to trade shows across the United States and providing instructions online on the best strategies and approaches for engaging lawmakers in Washington DC.

KEEN's sustainability-rooted values are a thread that runs through all of its business activities. In contrast to many businesses, the KEEN Effect Team also has the responsibility of reducing negative impact activities within its production processes and supply chain. Key actions include:

- *Durability = Sustainability:* KEEN has eschewed the "smart retailing" model. Durability is central to its design, and the company even supports consumers by repairing their shoes over time. From the company's perspective, it's not only core to its brand identity to make a shoe that is built to last, but also what its values require it to do.
- *Operationalizing sustainability:* To fully "walk their talk", sustainability needs to be at the root of its operational model. To achieve this, KEEN focuses on initiatives such as ensuring all of its factories and those of its contract manufacturers are certified with the Sustainable Apparel

Coalition's Higg Index for supply chain sustainability, putting in place key performance indicators such as supply chain detoxification (getting to 100 percent perfluorinated chemicals [PFC] free), and going beyond what is industry standard in providing chemical and product specs for all its shoes.

- *Sustainability as an innovation driver:* Though it may sometimes come at a (slightly) higher initial cost and have a longer development cycle, it has opted for an in-house innovation model. This enables it to ensure innovations align with their values. For example, KEEN developed a probiotic based technology to naturally remove footbed odor rather than relying on a chemical-based solution.

Although KEEN's values have put the company at the forefront of the footwear industry, it aims to do even more. Pushing for greater change across the industry in regard to sustainability, enabling broader political action, tapping into technological solutions to further minimize environmental impact such as virtual reality, going even deeper on its impact measurement, and more; KEEN is aiming even higher in its ambitions to transform its industry and the world for the better.

Fifteen years have passed since its founding, but for KEEN, it's only the beginning of its story.

Note

1 Heath, T. (2015). Keen footwear founder works way up the body, tackling evils of bad posture. *Washington Post*. Retrieved from www.washingtonpost.com/business/economy/keen-footwear-founder-works-way-up-the-body-tackling-evils-of-bad-posture/2015/02/20/0caa09ae-b785-11e4-aa05-1ce812b3fdd2_story.html.

7 Achieving the breakthrough
Sustainability becomes business-as-usual

Sustainable business = business as usual?

We believe that a fundamental paradigm shift is underway in how businesses think about their purpose and their responsibilities to their stakeholders. We have witnessed impressive progress and evolution recently—even just over the course of writing this book—and we believe the rate of that change is accelerating.

But is that enough to create the fundamental transformation we need to make our businesses sustainable?

Let's conclude with some final thoughts on how businesses can accelerate this process to ensure that in 2030 "sustainable business" equals "business as usual".

This book provides an extensive overview of how sustainability in business has evolved, the current state of play, how organizations can implement sustainable business models, and areas or industries where these innovations can shift business fundamentally.

We've also shown how companies can overcome the biggest obstacles in becoming sustainable, delving into practical actions to do so with our ten recommendations in Chapter 5. As we say there, the sustainability journey starts with bold leadership.

But how do you set the wheels in motion across your organization and keep them going? We can leave you with three concrete suggestions out of the many we provided in this book—prioritize them to sustain momentum, motivate your teams, and start moving your business forward:

1. Leverage the SDGs with a plan

Recognize the Sustainable Development Goals' (SDGs') power to help and guide the organization and your teams. Make sure that they are being applied across all functions and business activities, and not just used by Corporate Social Responsibility (CSR) teams for updated messaging about the company. Then, continually apply an "iterative" (or "repeated and progressive") process for decision-making and strategy development, execution, and assessment to advance adoption of a sustainable business model that is aligned with the

SDGs. The SDG Action Cycle introduced below provides a clear way to do this (Figure 7.1).

2. Bridge the knowledge gap

Create and provide your teams with as many opportunities as possible to establish the strategic sustainability knowledge base within your organization that is necessary to make sustainability-driven business decisions. Do it in the beginning to kick-start your journey and build an A team, and continue to reach out and train teams as you proceed to achieve total alignment across the organization and throughout your processes.

3. Be systematic

Be consistent and rigorous about integrating sustainability into your business. The SDG Action Cycle is useful here as well, as it tells you what to do at which stage and has questions that expand on what to do and how to approach each action. Take a systematic approach at every stage—gaining visibility on your competitors, deciding on your scope of activities, setting key performance indicators (KPIs), assessing impact, and more—to make sure that along the way you utilize the approach laid out in the cycle.

Here's the plan, and a system

In our opinion, few models are better at structuring the challenges and opportunities of sustainability than the SDGs. Although not initially developed with businesses primarily in mind, they have evolved to the point where companies are successfully leveraging them to drive significant, positive action at both the organization and industry level. In essence, they provide something for everyone, and give everyone the confidence to take a step—or, ideally, several— in the right direction. We believe that they are a highly constructive framework for incorporating sustainability in your organization's strategy and operations.

Regardless, working with the goals day-to-day can be challenging. Making the SDGs work for you demands a systematic approach to embedding them in your operations.

We believe there are six "iterative" stages for aligning your business planning and operations with sustainability principles and achieving a sustainable business model. These six stages make up the SDG Action Cycle (Figure 7.1).

For context, the Five Steps to a Sustainable Business Model that was discussed in chapters 2 and 5 represents the common organizational evolution of a company that sets off on its journey to integrate sustainability into its processes and align itself with the SDGs. It's a macro view of how the business changes over time. The SDG Action Cycle, in contrast, is the regular internal process that companies must apply in their development of sustainability strategies if they are to succeed in aligning their operations with the SDGs [or any sustainability-driven model].

THE SDG ACTION CYCLE

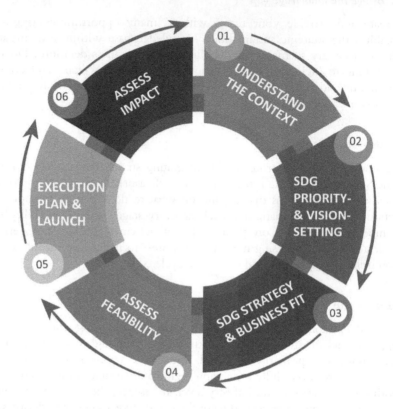

Figure 7.1 The SDG Action Cycle is made up of six "iterative" stages that align your business planning and operations with sustainability principles and help you to achieve a sustainable business model.

Source: Image courtesy of Read the Air (www.readtheair.jp).

Businesses will regularly return to and proceed through the stages of the SDG Action Cycle to create and maintain that alignment with the SDGs or other sustainable practices. If you are visually inclined, you can imagine the Five Steps to a Sustainable Business Model as a line extending straight up, with the SDG Action Cycle then ascending in a spiral that circles continuously through its six stages every rotation around the straight line of the Five Steps.

Fundamental questions must be addressed at each stage when taking an SDG-oriented approach (see the sidebar "Fundamental questions for navigating the SDG Action Cycle").

Fundamental questions for navigating the SDG Action Cycle

Stage 1: Understand the context

1   Are you ready for a 1.5- to 4-degree world?
2   Do you have visibility on how your competitors are addressing the SDGs and sustainability?
3   Have you identified how your company can benefit from the SDG framework or a core sustainability strategy?

Stage 2: SDG priority- and vision-setting

1   What is the sustainability vision for your business?
2   What do you want to achieve?
3   Which SDGs will you prioritize?
4   Have you incorporated sustainability-oriented criteria in how you identify and prioritize key elements of your strategy?

Stage 3: SDG strategy and business fit

1   What will you do differently?
2   Do your business activities align with your sustainability choices? If they don't, how will you modify them?
3   What will be the scope of your activities? What will you prioritize?
4   What will you start doing?
5   What will you stop doing?

Stage 4: Assess feasibility

1   Is your strategy actionable, achievable, and measurable?
2   What do you need to change to implement your vision and strategy?
3   What are the barriers and enablers within your business?

Stage 5: Execution plan and launch

1   What actions will you take to prepare your organization to execute your strategy and vision?
2   Which internal and external stakeholders do you need to engage?
3   What KPIs will you use, at both the business levels (e.g. financial, market-oriented) and societal levels (e.g. as per your priority SDGs— planetary resources, education, etc.)?

Stage 6: Assess impact

1   How will you measure impact for your business and on society? Which criteria will you use?
2   What information do you need to track and assess performance?
3   Have you integrated both business- and societal-level KPIs within your employee review and compensation model?

These six stages are equally applicable to any sustainability-guided evolution, whether you are pursuing an SDG-aligned model or another one. We describe this as iterative, as we believe that it should be done at regular intervals to push your progress further along the journey to sustainability—no organization can implement a sustainable business model in one fell swoop, or maintain one as conditions on the ground change, society's ambitions for what can be achieved rise, and our understanding of what it means to be sustainable evolves.

One requirement to succeed in using the SDG Action Cycle is to take a systematic approach. When a company systematically and continuously progresses through the six stages—whether it be annually, project-driven, or some other timeframe—it can expect to come continually closer to its unique vision of sustainability. Processes will become aligned with the SDGs and sustainability will be operationalized. Embracing SDG integration guarantees that you'll always be adopting the highest standard that stakeholders expect from a business.

In meeting with clients and interviewing businesses for this book, we've seen that many leading businesses have reached the SDG priority- and vision-setting stage (2), but the majority are struggling to move to the next step of determining their SDG strategy and business fit. Even the few companies that have made it through all six, continue to learn and improve as the cycle repeats.

Teach them well

The key to advancing through the SDG Action Cycle (and the Five Steps to a Sustainable Business Model) is in spreading sustainability knowledge within the organization. Without a basic understanding—at a minimum—of sustainability concepts, it is near-impossible for teams to make progress in moving through the stages of the SDG Action Cycle.

Without that progress, a business will not ascend the Five Steps to a Sustainable Business Model. In particular, it will have difficulty at the start in the fundamental requirement of establishing a base-level understanding, and then in leveraging that understanding to build A teams, set high-level objectives, and make initial choices around sustainability. Companies must make it possible for the required knowledge to grow within the organization in order to take these very first steps. Once things are moving, they should continue to engage in capability-building for and disseminate sustainability thinking to all functional roles across the organization via leadership development and training. Only when a business does this can it achieve the cross-organization buy-in that is required to fully assume a robust new sustainability stance.

The greatest obstacle that we have observed in companies that are trying to move past the vision-setting stage of the SDG Action Cycle to the creation of a real business strategy was a lack of this knowledge among functional teams.

The largest sustainability team that we heard of was 25 people—and that was in a company of 100,000 employees. There are not enough specialized sustainability practitioners today to meet the demand for knowledge about this subject (though the number is growing). Businesses therefore need to find smart ways to disseminate the necessary expertise to the rest of their organizations.

Many of the recommendations discussed in Chapter 5 offer ways to convey this knowledge, such as bold leadership from senior executives, clear internal communications, meaningful publicly declared commitments, and the creation of A teams. Another important way to share practical knowledge is the establishment of initial training programs on what sustainability means, generally, to the company, and the individual's role in the company.

Providing individuals and teams with training helps them to understand the reasons for and embrace the onset of an organizational realignment with more socially and environmentally friendly ways of operating. And it helps them to acquire a set of core sustainability competencies that will empower the decision-making they are responsible for in their functional roles, which in turn accelerates the transformation of the business.

The goal is to ultimately have an organization where teams, departments, and divisions are no longer leaning on a single sustainability officer or a small team of experts, or, if that doesn't exist, then even CSR professionals who represent a different kind of skill set and orientation within the business. Instead, the goal is to have, across your business, a legion of sustainability champions and change agents that function simultaneously within their functional roles and as sustainability practitioners.

Then, like the future executive in our Prologue who muses that no one even talks about sustainability anymore, the practices and principles of this way of thinking will be so ingrained that there will no longer be a point of notice—they'll be a natural part of the fabric of the enterprise.

IKEA brand owner INGKA Group has jump started this development by having 30 of its country retail managers take on the additional roles of being these local operations' Chief Sustainability Officer (CSO).[1] This is a highly effective way of asserting the importance of the subject to employees throughout the organization in the country. Such hybrid country regional manager-CSOs will inevitably develop sustainability strategies that will require their teams to build their capabilities in order to contribute to the implementation of such strategies with practical programs. Thus, IKEA is creating a whole environment through which it can outpace the industry in its business operations and sustainability leadership.

A choice such as this should ensure that bold leadership around sustainability is embedded in an organization. But we still can't stress this enough—leadership development and training is essential for individuals and teams that have not needed to make decisions based on sustainable business principles before.

The training that they received before they entered the workforce and what they've been exposed to since has helped them advance to where they are today in their organizations. Yet that training, almost certainly, has been delivered in the context of a singular focus on driving shareholder value or maximizing profits. As companies pivot towards sustainability, employees with this background will be ill-equipped to adapt accordingly without sufficient training and development. A proper grounding in sustainability will enable them to drive the company forward in this new landscape and continue to advance their own careers within the organization.

Sustainable business *is* smart business

To tie it all off, let's return to "Why?"—why *you*, why any business, should embark on the journey to sustainability today.

The argument supporting sustainability is becoming more apparent daily, making it an extremely risky proposition for businesses to ignore the issues that the SDGs so eloquently describe. Yet the opportunities that sustainability offers both businesses and society are an even more exciting motivation. Whether it be driving innovation, responding to the needs and wants of a rapidly evolving and enlightened consumer base, or outpacing your competitors, aligning purpose and profit is better business (see Figure 7.2).

Sustainable business today *is* smart business. It may soon be the only kind of business.

For many years, the case for sustainable business models was elusive. This is no longer the case. The evidence that organizations that embrace sustainable business models are better positioned for success is increasing in leaps and bounds. If nothing else, the COVID-19 crisis should make this abundantly apparent.

The next ten years, and likely more, will be guided by the spirit of the 2030 Agenda—the SDGs. This future is being formed by an international consensus that all stakeholders should be heard. It is being shaped by voices from all levels of society, and shepherded by the civil society organizations that represent them. And it is backed by enlightened managers of capital.

With the SDGs, the world has a plan, and business is part of it too. When companies treat that plan as a gift that reveals what society wants from business, then the SDGs become a powerful way for them to move forward in alignment with their stakeholders, for the betterment of both.

As we progress through the twenty-first century, businesses that don't embrace sustainable business models will likely not be around to see the dawn of the twenty-second. Those that do will enjoy the rewards that they all should seek: a sense of purpose in their actions, a profit as a result, and the opportunity to continue to deliver on both.

Note

1 IKEA (n.d.). Ingka Group takes the next step in putting sustainability at the core of its business. Retrieved from www.ikea.com/us/en/this-is-ikea/newsroom/ingka-group-takes-the-next-step-in-putting-sustainability-at-the-core-of-its-business-pub3273fb11.

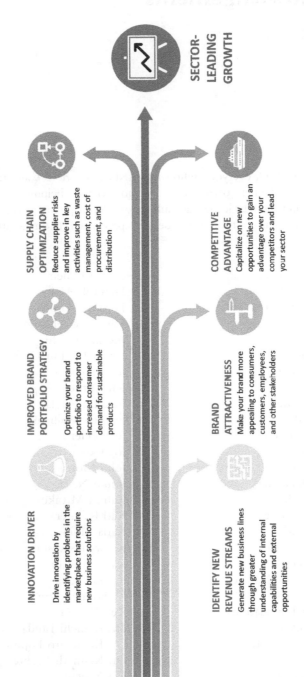

SUSTAINABLE BUSINESS IS BETTER BUSINESS

INNOVATION DRIVER

Drive innovation by identifying problems in the marketplace that require new business solutions

IMPROVED BRAND PORTFOLIO STRATEGY

Optimize your brand portfolio to respond to increased consumer demand for sustainable products

SUPPLY CHAIN OPTIMIZATION

Reduce supplier risks and improve in key activities such as waste management, cost of procurement, and distribution

IDENTIFY NEW REVENUE STREAMS

Generate new business lines through greater understanding of internal capabilities and external opportunities

BRAND ATTRACTIVENESS

Make your brand more appealing to consumers, customers, employees, and other stakeholders

COMPETITIVE ADVANTAGE

Capitalize on new opportunities to gain an advantage over your competitors and lead your sector

SECTOR-LEADING GROWTH

Figure 7.2 The opportunities that sustainability offers businesses are just as great a motivator for updating your business model as any of the risks you incur from ignoring these trends in society and the market.

Source: Image courtesy of Read the Air (www.readtheair.jp).

Acknowledgements

We'd like to thank everyone who supported us in various ways in writing *Leading Sustainably*. Whether participating in interviews, helping us connect with businesses and thought leaders around the world, or giving us much-needed input or feedback, your contribution is deeply appreciated. Most notably, we'd like to thank:

Amanda Feldman
Amy Jadesimi
Anastasia Milovidova
Araceli Gallego
Asako Nagai
Bruce Roch
Caitlin Rosser
Cameron Cross
Caven Mitchell
Cherie Sim
Chizu Nakamoto
Chris Enlow
Daniella Foster
Darren Menabney
Emi Onozuka
Emilie McGlone
Eric Nietsch
Erik Christianto
Erin Houston
Dr. Florian Kolbacher
Frank Thomas
Future-Fit Foundation
Geoff Kendall
Geraldine O'Grady
Gilda Sala
Gordon Seabury

Hein Oomen
Hendrik Alpin
Hiromi Masuda
Hiromitsu Hatano
Ingrid Bianchi
Dr. Jackie Pin-Chih Wang
Jed Emerson
Jeff Turner
Jennifer Raglan
Jennifer Williams
Jo Fackler
Joe Colistro
John Morris
Junko Nagao
Kahori Miyake
Karl Richter
Karla Mora
Kathryn Savasuk
Kathy Matsui
Katsuki Sakai
Keiko Yokoyama
Ken Kosugi
Dr. Kenichi Ishida
Dr. Kenichiro Fujimoto
Dr. Kenneth Pechter
Kes Shotam

Kiyoshi Hashimoto
Kumiko Akabori
Kylie Legge
Lars Lindén
Laura Heuston
Lila Karbassi
Lissa Glasgo
Luciano Pirovano
Maho Uehara
Dr. Mark Milstein
Matt Christensen
Maya Chorengel
Michelle Arnau
Michiko Araki Kelly
Miki Kanoh
Misa Yasukawa
Nazila Vali
Nichapat Nathalang
Nicholas Turner
Nico Chen
Prof. Nirmala Rao
Pär Larshans
Dr. Philip Vaughter
Rachel Bass
Rachel Gerrol
Rakesh Mani
Rebecca Self
Rene Corstens
Ryan Williams
Sergio Kato

Shailesh Rao
Shantanu Bhagwat
Shaun Conway
Shimrit Perkol-Finkel
Shinji Onoda
Sue Gannon
Sunhee Suk
Susanne Stormer
Tami Kesselman
The GIIN
Tinia Pina
Temple University, Japan Campus
Tokuro Hatori
Tony Mo
Toshio isohara
UN Global Compact
Valerie Unger
Valerie Smith
Dr. Venkata Ramana Putti
Viknesh Srirekam
Vinod Kesava
WBCSD (Taiwan)
William Shaffer
William Stephens
William (Swint) Swinton
Yuki Isogai
Yukiko Araki
Yuko Miyahara

A very special thanks to our research assistants whose diligence and enthusiasm this project and the topic of sustainability was inspiring:

Hsiao-Hsuan Chu
Maria Qazi Azmi
Rehnuma Salsavil
Solène Schuster
Chung-Hao Chen
Y. Vivian Huang

And extra special thanks to those who guided and assisted us through the cover design, Katerina Grabo and Michael Rollins at Netwise (circular solutions), Jason Scuderi at Lasergun Factory (champion of depth), Rob Todd (instantaneous conception), and Sébastien-Philippe Fortin (clean design guru and final tweaker).

Trista

Last but certainly not least, I'd like to extend a huge thanks to my friends and family. Their unwavering support and encouragement throughout my career and in the process of writing this book have been invaluable. It's been a long road to completing my first "magnum opus", and you've been with me every step of the way.

I'd most like to thank:

My "two boys": Miles and Mark
My biggest supporters: my parents Mary and Albert Bridges
My best friends: my sisters Jarita and Jenica Bridges
My aunties: Aunt Jean and Aunt Valerie
The Bivens Clan: Karin, Rodger, Mike, Grace, Keira, and Faith Bivens
My lifeline in Japan: Mika Kobayashi
My adopted sisters: Carol Henry, Pam Estwick, and Dionne Marsh
My co-author and friend: Donald Eubank

Donald

Dedicated to ARME, who never talked much about business, or "sustainability" for that matter, but loved words and wanted everyone to be nice to each other.

Thank you to Elisa, Ivy, Maelle, and Zozo for your patience, your impatience, and your inspiration. Thank you to Huston and Eliza for first showing me how it's done. To Sam and the Godfather for your passion for what's right, and being vocal about it. To Tatsuo for being the salt of the earth and keeping things practical. To Perry and Linda for your creativity. To Vinod for pointing me to the way in and bringing me along. To all of you who aren't listed here, I am thinking of you. To the Tokyo Metropolitan Central Library in Arisugawa for being awesome. To Trista for suggesting that we set off to tell this story in the first place—thanks for starting this adventure.

Thanks to Rebecca and Sophie at Routledge for taking us on, and Andrew of I Can Edit That, Aoife at Taylor and Francis, and Tamsin at Swales and Willis, for all helping us to navigate the book publishing process.

And finally, thanks to any readers who take the time to dive in and think about how these ideas apply to the work they are doing today and what they want to do tomorrow.

Index